Roads of Destiny

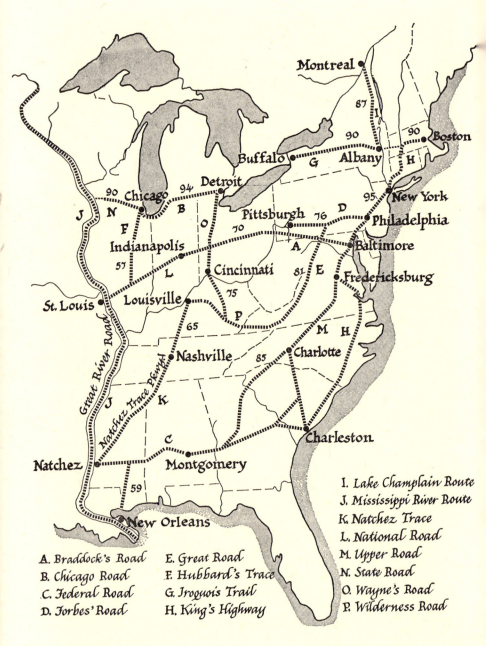

I. Lake Champlain Route
J. Mississippi River Route
K. Natchez Trace
L. National Road
M. Upper Road
N. State Road
O. Wayne's Road
P. Wilderness Road

A. Braddock's Road
B. Chicago Road
C. Federal Road
D. Forbes' Road
E. Great Road
F. Hubbard's Trace
G. Iroquois Trail
H. King's Highway

The Old "Roads of Destiny" and the Modern Expressways

Douglas Waitley

ROADS of DESTINY

the trails that
shaped a nation

ROBERT B. LUCE, INC.

WASHINGTON—NEW YORK

To

Mary and Jeff

my co-voyageurs into the past

Preface

Old roads have held a fascination for me ever since I was nine years old and took a trip with my mother and father to the Rocky Mountain area. As we wound up the switchbacks, I caught frequent glimpses of the narrow, incredibly steep, curved, and bumpy trails that packhorses—and the first autos, too—had taken up these same slopes. I could picture the Indians filing over the original path, feathers slanting over their bent heads and sweat coursing down their windburned cheeks. Then came the bearded fur traders, their horses staggering under loads of beaver pelts. Gradually the Indians and the fur men vanished, to be replaced by determined pioneers, whose prairie schooners creaked and rocked toward the long-dreamed-of land of homesteads and Herefords.

As I grew older, I read and reread the ample books on the Western trails. But when I dove deeper into history with my first book *Portrait of the Midwest,* I found to my surprise that in civilized times the Western trails were active for only about fifty years—until the advent of the transcontinental railroads. During two hundred and fifty earlier years (from the days when the first Puritans pushed out on the Old Connecticut Path to when migrants on the famed National Road broke out of the forest and into the awesome prairies of Illinois) the Eastern third of the United States was being crisscrossed by scores of roads, many of which played far more important roles in the survival and development of America as a nation than the short-lived Western trails.

Therefore, I was astonished that so little had been written

about the old eastern, midwestern, and southern roads. Indeed, although a few of the twenty-two paths, trails, and waterways which I subsequently included in *Roads of Destiny* had been discussed by modern authors, the most recent comprehensive study was published in 1901—nearly three quarters of a century ago; and even this work, by A. B. Hulbert, did not include such essential routes as the King's Highway, the Great Road, the Iroquois Trail, or the French river roads—to mention just a few.

Realizing there was need for a new study, I personally traveled the old roads: to see them in their modern setting as a comparison to reports of the wayfarers who took them in their heyday. In the course of my journeys I took with me the diaries and journals of travelers long dead, but who lived again as I retraced their arduous trips and viewed the locales of their ofttimes perilous adventures. Over fifty of these journalists became my friends; and it is with true regret that I now terminate my all-too-brief comradeship with them.

I must mention the aid given me by my wife, Mary, who helped with the driving, note-taking, and baby-tending; also my son Jeff, age four, who took charge of map-crumbling and book-losing. If there is enthusiasm and sparkle in the text, it is due to this delectable duo—companions on much of the ten thousand miles of investigation, wonder, and missed lunches.

Table of Contents

ery, Memphis. The vicious Natchez War. Competition
from Charlestonians using trails skirting Birmingham
and Montgomery.

Part II. The King's Highway, 1636–1774

The Old Connecticut Path. Establishment of the Boston Post Road to New York. Early travelers describe
Cambridge, Hartford, New Haven, New York, etc.

Young Ben Franklin's ordeal crossing New Jersey from
New York to Philadelphia. The pleasant trips of John
Adams and other later travelers. Picturesque towns on
the route: New Brunswick, Princeton, Trenton. The
glory of Colonial Philadelphia.

Muddy Baltimore. Alexandria, a major shipping center. Dusty Williamsburg. Tom Jefferson has an adventure.

Crossing the dreary swamps of North Carolina. Splendor at New Bern. A brush with danger near Wilmington, N.C. Charleston: fair metropolis of the South.

Part III. The French and Indian War, 1755–63

British traders on Ohio Indian trails. Washington's
hairbreadth escape on the Venango Road. Braddock's
Road and his crushing defeat in 1755.

The French River Roads, 1535–1750

1.   Scalps to Hang Like a Precious Chain

Burly sailors lined the rails of the three ships. They had been many weeks at sea; and although there had been the usual amount of bickering among them, there was none of it now. Their eyes opened wide as they stared in silent disbelief. The huge fruit trees, the abundance of wild grapes, the flocks of ducks, geese, and other game birds—could this be paradise?

The calm water of the broad-flowing St. Lawrence hissed along the barnacle-encrusted hulls. There was a thrill and there was an awe among these rough men who had thought they had seen everything from the dens of Marseille to the wondrous fjords of Norway. This was all new; never before had Europeans sailed this great water highway that led them ever deeper into this unknown continent. Even Jacques Cartier, their captain, who had viewed the mouth of the St. Lawrence in 1534, one year earlier, could not repress the thrill of the passage into the mysterious interior.

On westward the little fleet sailed, reaching at last the land known as Canada, which in Iroquoian meant a collection of huts. The chief area of habitation was along a narrowing of the river called the Quebec. The natives had evidently been observing their slow progress up the river. Now, eager for the white mens' goods, they flocked out of their village to greet them:

> One of the Lords of that village, Stadagona, [wrote Cartier] came to us accompanied by many men, women, and

13

children, who after the fashion of their country, in signs of mirth and joy, began to call us. The women, singing, danced up to their knees in the water. Our Captain [Cartier], knowing their good will and kindness toward us, permitted the boat they were in to come to him and gave them certain trifles such as knives and beads of glass, whereat they were overjoyed . . .[1]

Cartier, feeling that such obvious desire for trade goods promised the success of any settlement among the Indians, was anxious to explore the possibilities farther up the river. But the Stadagona tribesmen, both hungering for ever more goods and resenting the willingness of Cartier to give such items (particularly knives and muskets) to their enemies upriver, were reluctant to permit him to go on. At last the French captain ordered twelve of his cannons fired. The roar of the guns terrified the Indians, "for they thought heaven had fallen upon them." Amid their howling and shrieking, Cartier hoisted sail and continued toward the next village, known as Hochelaga, one hundred and seventy-five miles away.

Cartier was delighted with the natural highway on which he was traveling. The banks were festooned with garlands of grape vines: the fruit sweet, the juice savory. Cranes, swans, geese, and ducks thronged along calm bays, honking as the three strange ships moved past. And in the hovering forest he saw spotted deer bounding past trees where nightingales sang. It was "as goodly and pleasant a country as possibly can be wished for," Cartier noted, his thoughts on French colonization.

As for the Indians, it was Quebec all over again. A thousand hurried out of palisaded Hochelaga, the men dancing on one side of them and the women on the other. Such was their joyous awe that they even brought their babies to have Cartier and his men touch them, hoping, perhaps, that some of the white mens' magic would rub off on the tots. That night the Indians built great fires to light the ships, which rested majestically in the scarlet water. Then they danced and hooted in Cartier's honor until dawn.

Early the next morning Cartier climbed the rugged hill (which he named Mount Royal) overlooking the town. To his dismay, he saw a short distance west the wild Lachine Rapids which still make the St. Lawrence treacherous at this point. Gone was his fond expectation of a smooth-flowing strait to the Pacific. Yet, since the St. Lawrence penetrated fully six hundred miles into the interior before it met the rapids, surely the Pacific could not be far off—at least such was Cartier's hope.

Returning to France, Cartier convinced Francis I that a settlement in Canada was highly desirable and six years later, with ten shiploads of soldiers and colonists, he was back in the vicinity of Quebec. But a harsh winter brought such famine and disease that the settlement was nearly wiped out and the venture was abandoned. Yet Cartier had shown the way. The St. Lawrence was made known, along with the Indians' wealth in beaver pelts and their consuming desire for manufactured goods.

For the next sixty-seven years France, rocked by religious warfare, was unable to take advantage of Cartier's explorations. Nevertheless, his report was not forgotten and in 1608 Samuel de Champlain, a spirited soul for whom the New World was something of an obsession, put out from France in a small ship bound for the St. Lawrence. Champlain was no stranger to the Western Hemisphere. As a young man he had visited fabulous Mexico City where the Spaniards were still stripping the Aztec empire of its gold and silver. Later he had gazed in wonder at the gathering of the treasure galleons off Panama. He had returned from the Caribbean just in time to join a newly-formed company bent on exploiting the St. Lawrence, North America's greatest natural highway. When Champlain arrived on the river, it soon became evident that a tremendous number of pelts were available, for the Indians were as hungry for goods as Cartier had indicated.

Champlain, hunting for a townsite, approached Cartier's Stadagona, now deserted. He noted the promontory which dominated the St. Lawrence and realized that it was the ideal location for a fortress. "I could not find any more convenient or

better situated place than the point called Quebec by the savages," he wrote. Soon he and his twenty-eight followers were
constructing their drafty quarters, including a warehouse
jammed with trade goods. The heart of the minute colony was
called the Place Royale, today the center of the Lower Town.

Whereas the colonies that the British had planted (Jamestown in 1607) and were soon to plant (Plymouth in 1620) would
be based on agriculture (and thus roads could be left to develop
at slow, rather indifferent rates), the French effort, depending on
trade, required the rapid extension of a thorough transportation
network. In addition, it required safe, marauder-free routes. This
brought Champlain and his tiny band of colonists, reduced to
eight by scurvy, squarely up against the mighty Iroquois nation.

The Iroquois were a most exceptional group of tribes. Instead of the rude, turtle-shaped, bark wigwams of the St. Lawrence Algonquins, the Iroquois lived in substantial log houses
fifteen feet wide and as long as a modern football field. Their
towns were surrounded by upright timbers sharpened to dagger
points at the top. And each Iroquois brave was indoctrinated
with a code of valor, a contempt for physical pain, and an
obediance to his chiefs that was not to be found among the
Algonquins. "Iro!" each warrior would add imperiously at the
end of a sentence: "I have spoken!" For this reason the other
Indians called them Iroquois.

Originally they had been a group of weak, disorganized
tribes living around Quebec and Montreal—where Cartier found
them. Driven out by the more populous Algonquins, the Iroquois
fled up the St. Lawrence to Oswego on Lake Ontario. There they
grew both in numbers and ferocity. At the end of the sixteenth
century, there appeared among them a most unusual man. This
Hiawatha formed the five squabbling tribes into so strong a
federation that even when the site at Oswego could no longer
support their numbers and they migrated into the interior, the
Five Nations continued to hold regular meetings in what was
the most unusual and progressive political organization ever perfected by North American Indians.

The Iroquois homeland was tied together by a trail that

gave each tribe excellent communication with the others. In the west were the Senecas whose villages extended as far as the Genesee River, but whose main center was around the modern city of Geneva on Seneca Lake. To reach their neighbors the Cayugas, the Senecas took the trail which ran along what is now Highway 5 to Cayuga Lake, where the Cayugas had a string of villages along the eastern shore all the way down to Ithaca.

The next tribe was the Onondagas, largest in the Iroquois federation. To reach the Onondagas, red warriors and diplomats continued east on Highway 5 to the placid shores of Onondaga Lake (where plaques in an extensive lakefront park in Syracuse indicate the location of this, the Iroquoian capital.)

The Oneida tribe had a town on the site of the modern city of the same name, as well as one at Utica—both of which communicated with the capital by way of the trail that was almost identical with the New York Thruway. From there the Mohawk River provided easy access to the Mohawk tribe, most eastern of the Iroquois, whose towns dotted the beautiful valley as far as Schenectady.

While the Iroquois were not primarily canoe Indians, they did make use of the natural waterway that ran through their forested domain when Dutch, and later English, traders established contact with them from Albany. Then the crude Iroquois canoes filled with heavy packets of beaver pelts began using the Seneca-Mohawk river system. Possibly the best description of this waterway (now utilized by the famous Erie Canal) was given by a white man traveling with traders some years later:

Our bateau lay in the outlet about three miles north of the north end of Canandaigua Lake, to which point there was water sufficient for bateau navigation. From this point, having loaded the bateau with peltries, conveyed in wagons from the Indian village, we proceeded slowly down the narrow, winding outlet; sometimes being obliged to stop and cut away trees that had fallen across it, and sometimes to get out and drag our flat-bottomed boat over the ripples. In this way we proceeded for nearly four days; passing the several outlets of the Seneca and Cayuga, the Owasco and other lakes; the stream gradually became larger, and its obstructions fewer. On the fourth day we arrived at the mouth of the Oneida outlet, here called Three River Points, distant from Canandaigua, by land about sixty miles, but at least one hundred by water. Ascending the outlet, we crossed the Oneida Lake, about thirty miles in length, to the mouth of Wood Creek, up which small, crooked stream we with much difficulty forced our bateau to within a mile of the Mohawk, whence, transporting it across the ground where Rome now stands, but where then, on the Mohawk, stood but a solitary house, we proceeded down that river to Schenectady.[2]

The Iroquois, who were angered by the French trading with their Algonquin enemies, posed a threat to Champlain's everlengthening trade route along the St. Lawrence. So when local Algonquin chiefs proposed that the Frenchmen aid them in an expedition against the Five Nations, Champlain agreed. Yet it was a rash promise. For Champlain with only two fellow Frenchmen and a motley army of fear-riddled Algonquins was venturing into the kingdom of ten thousand Iroquois warriors, the most vicious fighters in North America!

Sailing the St. Lawrence in a small wooden boat, Champlain, with his Indian allies, eventually reached the mouth of the Richelieu River. Then they began ascending the river which was the major military route between the Iroquois to the south and the Algonquins to the north. Soon they were skirting the cliffs of Beloeil and then entered the Chambly Basin, surrounded by pleasant meadows, where Champlain was surprised to find "no savages settled on account of the wars." Emptying into the Chambly was a rapid, or sault, "which flows with great swiftness, and there are a great many rocks."

It was at Chambly that Champlain discovered his European boat was of little use in American waterways, since its long oars made it cumbersome in the confines of narrow, tree-enclosed streams and its heavy, plank hull made it exceedingly difficult to lug over the trails around the rapids. For these reasons, Champlain abandoned his boat and continued in a light, portable birchbark canoe—that particular Algonquin creation which was to become the mainstay of the French transportation system.

Champlain found the portage path around the Chambly Rapids quite good, having been traversed by warriors' moccasins for hundreds of years. That night, because they were entering territory the Iroquois also frequented, the Algonquins decided to throw up a small fort. Champlain watched, impressed, as they "began to fell big trees for a barricade on the bank of the river. . . . They know so well how to do this that in less than two hours five hundred of their enemy would have had a good deal of trouble to attack them." [3] Later French voyageurs, learning from the Indians, would build such barricades whenever they traveled through enemy country.

Continuing up the Richelieu, they entered a long lake which Champlain named after himself. Then, as now, it presented an appealing vista with "many pretty islands, which are low, covered with very beautiful woods and meadows, where there is a quantity of game and animals for hunting, such as stags, fallow-deer, fawns, roebucks, bears and other animals. . . . There are also many beavers"—the last added with a significant undertone. And on each side of the island-studded water he viewed the pleasing contours of New York's Adirondacks and Vermont's Green Mountains, in which, so the Algonquins told him, "there were beautiful valleys and open stretches fertile in grain."

Southward they paddled through the winding, ever-narrowing waterway—advancing only at night to avoid Iroquois scouts. They steered by the stars, whispering to each other the contents of their dreams to discover whether their daring raid would be successful. Champlain himself had a dream in which he saw a group of Iroquois drowning. When he told this to the somewhat apprehensive Algonquins, "they no longer doubted that good was to befall them."

Despite their precautions, that very evening they were discovered by two hundred Iroquois, who announced their presence with fearsome war whoops. Both groups immediately beached their canoes near a long cape called Ticonderoga, or the land between two lakes, which dominated the well-traveled portage path connecting Lakes Champlain and George. As it was obvious that it was too dark to recognize friend or foe, each army decided to attack at dawn. "While we waited, the whole night was passed in dances and songs," Champlain wrote, with "endless insults" being shouted between the opposing camps.

When the sun rose, round and bloody, the Iroquois advanced. They were "strong and robust," Champlain noted, uneasily, and they moved with the "dignity and assurance" that made them feared and respected everywhere. As Champlain and his two companions loaded their arquebuses full of bullets, the Algonquins pointed out the three Iroquois chiefs conspicuous by their large plume headdresses. The battle now started:

> Our men (wrote Champlain) began to call me with loud cries; and, to give me passageway, they divided into two parts and put me at their head, where I marched about twenty paces in front of them until I was thirty paces from the enemy. They at once saw me and halted, looking at me, and I at them. When I saw them making a move to shoot at us, I rested my arquebus against my cheek and aimed directly at one of the three chiefs. With the same shot two of them fell to the ground, and also one of their companions, who was wounded and afterward died, for I had put four balls into my arquebus. When our men saw this shot so favorable to them, they began to make war cries so loud that one could not have heard it thunder. Meanwhile the arrows flew from both sides. The Iroquois were much astonished that two men had been so quickly killed, although they were provided with armor woven from cotton thread and wood, proof against arrows.[4]

The Iroquois, having never before seen a white man nor felt the fury of his strange weapons, pulled back in momentary surprise. Then, when a second Frenchman fired from a hidden position in the woods on their flank, the bewildered Indians threw down their bows and dashed off in full retreat—a sight few Algonquins had ever seen. After celebrating their tremen-

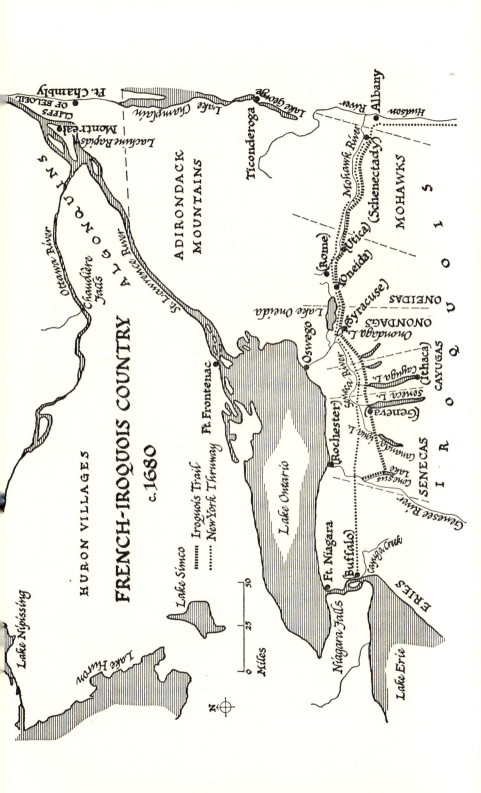

FRENCH-IROQUOIS COUNTRY
c. 1680

——— Iroquois Trail
············· New York Thruway

HURON VILLAGES

ALGONQUINS

ADIRONDACK
MOUNTAINS

Lake Nipissing

Lake Huron

Lake Simco

Ottawa River

Chaudière Falls

St. Lawrence River

Ft. Chambly
CLIFFS OF BELOEIL
Montreal
Lachine Rapids

Lake Champlain

Lake George

Ticonderoga

Hudson River

Albany

Mohawk River

(Schenectady)

MOHAWKS

(Utica)

(Rome)

(Oneida)

ONEIDAS

ONONDAGS

Onondaga L.

(Syracuse)

Lake Oneida

Oswego

Ft. Frontenac

Lake Ontario

Ft. Niagara

Niagara Falls

(Buffalo)

Cayuga Creek

ERIES

Lake Erie

SENECAS

Genesee River

Genesus Lake

(Rochester)

(Geneva)

Genesee River

Seneca River

Canandaigua L.

Seneca L.

Cayuga L.

(Ithaca)

CAYUGAS

IROQUOIS

50

25

0

Miles

N

dous victory with three hours of congratulations and dancing, the Algonquins hurriedly made their way back to the St. Lawrence, carrying with them the scalps of a dozen or so Iroquois for their women "to hang afterward to their necks like a precious chain."

But Champlain's victory at Ticonderoga was not what it seemed. By siding with the Algonquin tribes, Champlain had insured the wrath of the powerful Iroquois nation toward every Frenchman who would thenceforth travel the waterways of North America. Never again would two volleys put an Iroquois army to flight. Soon Dutch merchants established at Beverwyck, the Town of the Beavers (renamed Albany when the English took over), would provide the Five Nations with guns. Once this happened, the Iroquois would explode northward from the Mohawk Valley and Finger Lakes to devastate the French transportation lines.

Prior to the Iroquois outbreak, however, things seemed to be developing quite well for New France. In 1613 Champlain took the Ottawa River westward into lands unknown. Going around the seething barrier called the Chaudière, or boiling Falls (the site of Canada's modern-day capital, the city of Ottawa) he made contact with the friendly Hurons (a maverick Iroquois tribe) and more Algonquins. As a result, soon canoe caravans filled with furs began yearly voyages down the Ottawa to Montreal, which Champlain founded in 1611, for a trade fair held there in autumn.

But Champlain's plans called for even further expansion. Thus, he sent a nineteen-year-old French lad, Étienne Brulé, to live with the tribes along the Ottawa to learn their language and go with them on their hunting expeditions. This astute move resulted in Brulé finding the Lake Nipissing route to Lake Huron —resulting in another rapid extension of the French trade network. Then, in 1623, Brulé, paddling westward on Lake Huron with only a single companion, made the important discovery of the churning Sault Ste. Marie, that essential link leading to Lake Superior.

Eleven years later Champlain, now an old man with but a

year to live, sent another of his young explorers, Jean Nicolet, on a lengthy voyage with the yet-smoldering hope that he might chance upon the long-rumored passage to China. Guided by Hurons, Nicolet discovered the Straits of Mackinac and the body of water beyond called *Michi Gama,* or the large lake. Continuing expectantly down Lake Michigan, he stepped ashore twelve miles from modern Green Bay adorned in a "grand robe of China damask all strewn with flowers and birds of many colors." It must have been disappointing to be received by gawking Winnebagos rather than bejewelled emissaries of the Grand Khan, but Nicolet made the best of it. Enjoying a pleasant feast, which included that tender delicacy roasted beaver tail, he returned to Quebec with the news that distant Wisconsin was rich with pelts.

But now the newly-armed Iroquois launched a full-fledged campaign against the French and their Indian allies. Swarming down the Lake Champlain-Richelieu waterway, their war parties not only cut Quebec's lifeline with the interior but so terrorized the Algonquins that they fled posthaste to Wisconsin, leaving New France nearly depopulated. Not content with this, the Five Nations roared into the territory of the Hurons, who, though they were their own kinsmen, were virtually exterminated. Such was the fury of the Iroquois attack that Hennepin ventured the staggering (though characteristically overstated) opinion that this "insolent and barbarous nation, have shed the blood of more than two million people." They even raided to the very gates of Quebec itself, where a large number of French Indians were gleefully carted off for torture.

With the river system in shambles, the French empire tottered on extinction. Finally King Louis XIV, Europe's mightiest monarch, felt impelled to bestir himself if his colony was to be spared. In 1666 he sent the famous Carignan Regiment, fourteen hundred of the toughest soldiers in France, to subdue the rampaging Iroquois. The Carignans marched rapidly up the Richelieu trail, pausing only to erect three posts to protect their supply line (the site of the one at Chambly is currently occupied by the picturesque ruins of a slightly later stone fort). When the Carignans reached the Mohawk Valley, the Iroquois, not caring to use their antiquated muskets against Europe's finest weaponry, simply faded into the woods. The Frenchmen, unable to do battle, had to be content to burn the Indians' corn fields and their storehouses packed with food for the winter.

But the show of force succeeded. The next year the Five Nations called a temporary truce and a better era opened for New France.

2. The Necessity of Exposing My Life

Once the Iroquois were temporarily cowed, French traders again sought out the Algonquin tribes. But it was not so easy now, for the Iroquois had caused them to flee far westward. The route was long: up the St. Lawrence to the Ottawa, thence through four hundred miles of rapids and pounding water to Lake Nipissing and the turbulent passage to Lake Huron. Then across the northern shores of that seemingly endless body of water and either through the rough Mackinac Strait and down Lake Michigan to Green Bay or up the rumbling Sault Ste. Marie to the tribes along Lake Superior.

The Indians were overjoyed to see the French again, although they had difficulty understanding why they traveled so far and through so much dangerous water for the sake of beaver pelts. One of the first men to arrive was Nicolas Perrot, who opened up Green Bay and the important Fox River. When he reached the Potawatami, whose villages dotted the plains where the city of Green Bay now stands, the happy Indians "insisted on carrying him upon their shoulders . . . they did not dare look on his face. And the women and children watched him from a distance. 'He is a Spirit,' they said."

Perrot had no difficulty in drawing the Potawatamis and other tribes into the French web of commerce. All he had to do was show them his goods in a most casual manner: "He tossed them a dozen awls and knives," records a contemporary historian, "and said to them: 'Throw aside your bone tools; these French awls will be much easier. These knives will be more useful to you in killing beavers and in cutting your meat than are the pieces of stone that you use.' Then, throwing to them some glass beads: 'See, these will better adorn your children and girls.'" Immediately the word went out, and soon the streams were crowded with canoes bringing beaver skins.

But traders were not the only ones going to the most distant portions of the Great Lakes. The Jesuits, whose numerous missions among the Hurons had been destroyed by the Iroquois, were anxious to resume the task of saving Indian souls. These Jesuits were men of great fortitude who often regarded their missionary work even above their lives. Going into villages where the hardiest trader dared not venture, they were jeered at, robbed, beaten, tortured, and sometimes killed. Their efforts were at times almost superhuman, yet in the end they were unable to convert permanently more than a small proportion of the Indians, and more than one ardent Jesuit had to admit that "all our teachings are of slight effect."

Nevertheless, the Jesuit fathers played important roles in the development of North American trade routes, for not only were their frontier missions centers around which Indians and traders gathered, but often a Jesuit (or sometimes a member of a lesser known order, such as a Récollect or Sulpician) was the first European into a new area—thereby preparing the Indians for trade.

One of these religious pioneers was Jean Claude Allouez, who went with Perrot as far as the entrance to the Sault Ste. Marie, where they found bands of Chippewa spearing the delicious whitefish while driving their canoes through the rocky maze of foaming water (which modern tourists can bounce over via excursion boats). Although the lake had already received its name Superior, or upper, by Brulé or some other previous explorer, Allouez was the first to try to establish a permanent post on its chilly shores:

"On the second of September [1665]," he wrote, "after clearing the Sault—which is not a waterfall, but merely a very swift current impeded by numerous rocks—we entered Lake Superior . . . The form of this lake is nearly that of a

bow, the southern shore being much curved, and the northern nearly straight. Fish are abundant here and of excellent
quality; while the water is so clear and pure that objects at
the bottom can be seen to the depth of thirty-two feet. The
savages revere this lake as a divinity and offer it
sacrifices . . ." [5]

Allouez coasted along the southern shore of Superior, finding a place for his mission on Chequamegon Bay. Two years on
the wind-blasted outpost exposed to the insolence and thievery
of the Indians, for whom "the word of God was listened to only
with scorn and mockery," forced the Jesuit to return to the Sault,
where the mission he next established among the more friendly
Chippewa and St. Lawrence Algonquin tribes proved quite successful. Soon Allouez's mission became the gathering place for
traders paddling to and from the beaver-rich streams of northern
Minnesota. And it was here in 1671 that one of the most impressive ceremonies in New France was held.

Everyone was there: the Sieur de St. Lusson, representative
of the "Sun King", Louis XIV; Nicolas Perrot, foremost explorer;
Louis Jolliet, energetic trader whose star was on the rise; and, of
course, Father Allouez, somber in his black Jesuit robe, yet
inwardly glowing with pleasure. Around them were soldiers in
gaudy uniforms, canoe men with buckskin jackets and rippling
muscles, and Indians from nearly every tribe then residing in the
upper lake region. St. Lusson ascended a small height while the
missionaries chanted a hymn. Then, with his sword upraised and
shouting loudly to make himself heard over the rapids, he proclaimed: "In the name of the Most High, Most Mighty and Most
Redoubtable Monarch, Louis, the Fourteenth of the Name, Most
Christian King of France and Navarre, we take possession of
Saint Marie of the Falls as well as Lakes Huron and Superior,
the island of Manitoulin and of all other countries, rivers, lakes
and tributaries, contiguous and adjacent thereunto . . ." [6]

The pageant continued with Allouez explaining to the
open-mouthed savages that his King had "towns of his own more
in number than you have people." Then, according to a typically

phrased French report: "the whole ceremony was closed with a
fine bonfire, which was lighted toward evening, and around
which the 'Te Deum' was sung to thank God on behalf of those
poor peoples that they were now the subjects of so great and
powerful a monarch." [7]

Thus, amid the fragrant pines and bubbling water of the
northland, did France take formal possession of one of the
richest areas in the world.

One difficulty with St. Lusson's grandiose gesture was that
no one knew the extent of the territory claimed. A major mystery
was an important river called the *Michi Sippi* ("Great Water")
which was said to be not far distant. Should this river flow to the
west, it would connect with the Pacific. Then it would be possible to link up the spicy wealth of the Orient with the furs of
Quebec and the manufactures of Paris. France's commercial
empire would span the world!

In 1672 the Comte de Frontenac came to Quebec as Governor and immediately commissioned Louis Jolliet to seek out this
important river; and because it was customary that a priest go
along to sanctify such an undertaking, he selected Jacques Marquette, a Jesuit.

They were a strange pair, these two men who Frontenac
had brought together. Jolliet was Canadian-born, a hardy trader
used to a lifetime in the dense woodlands and coursing streams.
Only twenty-eight years old, he had been the first to discover the
Detroit Strait-Lake Erie alternative to the rapid-strewn Ottawa
River route to Wisconsin. Bold, even foolhardy, he was filled
with an insatiable love for adventure: "He has the courage to
dread nothing," wrote a contemporary.

Father Marquette, on the other hand, was a native of genteel France and had been in the rough New World for only a
few years. Sent to establish the mission of St. Ignace on the
northern shore of the Mackinac Strait, he found peace and
contentment in his life among the Indians. Eight years older
than robust Jolliet, he was slight and frail, and his health was

slowly deteriorating. Whereas Jolliet was avid for trade profits, Marquette cared nothing for material wealth—nor even for his own personal safety. "I was all the more delighted at this good news," he remarked upon learning he was going on the rugged expedition, "since I found myself in the blessed necessity of exposing my life for the salvation of all these peoples, especially the Illini . . ."

In one of the supreme ironies of American history, Jolliet, who had traversed thousands of perilous miles without incident, lost his journal (and very nearly his life) in the wild Lachine Rapids when in sight of Montreal: his journey's end—making the diary of Marquette, who cared nothing for fame, the only record of the epochal journey. Thus for future generations the name of Marquette became almost a byword; yet so little was known of Jolliet, who was the real leader, that his whole career, aside from references by Marquette, comprises less than a dozen sentences in the accounts of Frenchmen who knew him.

Yet in the spring of 1673, all this was ahead. When the ice broke, Marquette placed the voyage "under the protection of the Blessed Virgin Immaculate," then the two men and five voyageurs in a pair of birchbark canoes set off from St. Ignace into the world of dim, dangerous rumor.

They went along the limestone rocks of Upper Michigan, watching them glitter like sugar in the sun. Then down Green Bay, past locales long ago visited by Nicolet and more recently by Perrot and Allouez. From the foot of the bay, they began ascending the Fox River, which, although currently disfigured by the industry of the modern city of Green Bay, Marquette found to be "very beautiful . . . full of cranes, ducks, teal, and other birds, attracted thither by the wild rice of which they are very fond." A short distance upriver they came to the mission Allouez had started two years earlier at De Pere, where they paused for brief respite in this last outpost before the unknown.

Cautiously, now, they proceeded, past potentially hostile Indians who were fretful that they would open the way for future traders to bring guns to their enemies. But the party, ignoring tales of ferocious monsters and turbulent cataracts that the Indians swore were just beyond, continued up the placid, little river. They were enchanted by the scenery. At one point Marquette mounted a hillock from which he wrote that "one beholds on every side prairies extending farther than the eye can see interspersed with groves or with lofty trees." He also examined the good Wisconsin sod, and reported that it was "very fertile and yields much Indian corn." Noticing the Indians's crops, he found they "gather quantities of plums and grapes," [8] which he was certain could be made into highly flavorful wine —a thought which must have pleased his more lusty comrades.

At last the crucial moment arrived. Two Indian guides pointed out the short path which led from the creek-like Fox to the broad Wisconsin River, tributary of the mighty Mississippi. Hoisting their birchbarks onto their shoulders, they marched westward up a slight rise (modern Portage, Wisconsin) and a few moments later had passed over the Great Lakes-Mississippi divide. With pounding hearts and a prayer from Marquette, they placed their boats in the Wisconsin River and began the descent.

Navigating the Wisconsin was not easy, for "it has a sandy bottom which forms various shoals." Yet on the seventeenth of June, 1673, exactly one month after leaving St. Ignace, they reached the junction of the Mississippi—"with a joy that I cannot express," exalted Marquette. At this point the explorers may have clambered up the steep bluffs that are now part of Wyalusing State Park, for the vista Marquette describes is one that also impresses modern visitors:

> [The Mississippi] is narrow at the place where the Wisconsin empties; its current, which flows southward, is slow and gentle. To the right is a large chain of very high mountains, and to the left are beautiful lands.[9]

Down the easy current they went, two frail canoes piercing the wall of obscurity which had hidden the upper Mississippi from civilized man for uncounted ages. Soon they entered the prairie country of Illinois, where there were "hardly any woods or mountains." Deer paused at the water's edge to watch them furtively. Swans floated in the calm backwaters. Now and then a wildcat glared from a cattail ambush. From time to time monstrous catfish struck their canoes, once nearly caving in a side. And soon they came upon herds of buffalo, which, with their matted hair, huge heads, and disformed bodies, seemed hideous to the Frenchmen.

At one place they chanced upon a well-beaten path that ran from the river to an Indian village in the interior. Jolliet, with Marquette padding beside him, bravely set out on this road. After a short hike they came to one of the Illini camps. There they were given a fine welcome, for the Illini were eager to establish trade relations with the white race. "How beautiful the sun is, Oh, Frenchmen," Marquette quotes an Illini chieftain, "when you come to visit us! All our village awaits you." Marquette, finding the Illini so hospitable, vowed to return to establish a mission among them.

The voyage continued. Just above St. Louis they came to the Missouri. "I have never seen anything more dreadful," Marquette exclaimed. "An accumulation of large trees, branches and floating islands were issuing from the mouth of the river with such impetuosity that we could not without great danger risk passing through it. So great was the agitation that the water was very muddy . . ." [10]

Gradually other landmarks were passed: the Alton bluffs across from the Missouri, the wide sweep of the Ohio River, the fertile flatlands southward from Kentucky where the Mississippi began to meander through lush, semitropical land. About now swarms of mosquitoes plagued them, so that they were forced to construct over their canoes sweltering little cabins of canvas supported by sticks.

By the time they approached the mouth of the Arkansas (at a point near where De Soto had died more than a century and a quarter earlier), they were convinced that the Mississippi flowed into the Gulf of Mexico rather than into the Pacific. With this information, they decided to turn back rather than risk capture by the Spaniards who dominated the Gulf. The return trip was more difficult: they were forced to fight the strong current. But by taking a shortcut via the Illinois River and the Chicago portage, they arrived at the De Pere mission in September.

The whole journey had taken less than half a year, but in that short period of time the myth of an easy access to the Pacific was put to rest; and, by demonstrating that the Mississippi provided access to the Gulf, the basis for a trade empire in the interior of North America with ports on the Gulf as well as on the Atlantic was laid.

The monumental voyage over, Marquette spent several months recuperating, then set out with a caravan of Indian traders down Lake Michigan to fulfill his vow to establish a mission among his Illini friends. However, when his health gave out at the Chicago portage, he was forced to winter over in a lonely log cabin near the modern Damen Avenue bridge. Wracked by dysentery and hemorrhaging through his bowels, he managed to reach the Illini the following spring, 1674. But he was a dying man, as he well knew. On the canoe trip back to St. Ignace, the gentle priest expired amid the rolling sand dunes across the Pere Marquette River from Ludington, Michigan— where a cross marks the place of his death.

3.   Arrows Came Whizzing

While the journey of Jolliet and Marquette had been highly important, it involved no more hardship than hundreds of French voyageurs were experiencing on scores of waterways in France's expanding empire. The really difficult work of weaving the lakes, rivers, beaver creeks, and Indian villages into a unified whole was tackled by Robert Cavelier, Sieur de La Salle. La Salle, probably the most farsighted Frenchman in the New World, had been exploring since he arrived in Canada at the age of twenty-three. He was a proud, almost arrogant, man—so ambitious he would risk his life for success, self-assured to the point of conceit—precisely the kind of individual needed to challenge the hostile wilderness.

Even Governor Frontenac was impressed by the virile young man. In 1673, while his agents Jolliet and Marquette were coursing down the Mississippi, Frontenac put La Salle in charge of a strong fortification dominating the St. Lawrence as it emerged from Lake Ontario (at modern Kingston, Ontario). Fort Frontenac, as the governor humbly named it, plugged one of the main invasion routes to Montreal of the potentially hostile Iroquois.

But La Salle had even bolder plans than the governor— plans in which Fort Frontenac was only the first step. To help orient himself in the extensive trans-Appalachian area, he explored far westward along the inland sea that the Iroquois called *Ontario* ("Beautiful Lake") then southward through dense forests and rounded hills to the Ohio, the Iroquois' Beautiful River. Although he did not follow the Ohio much beyond the rapids at

Louisville, Indians along the way undoubtedly traced out the rest of the Ohio's course for him. Then, when Marquette and Jolliet ascertained that the Mississippi connected with the Gulf of Mexico, La Salle's magnificent scheme matured.

He would create an empire reaching from Montreal to the mouth of the Mississippi—bound together by lake and river highways. A string of forts would guard the important portage paths. A fleet of large ships would ply the Great Lakes carrying huge quantities of trade goods to the Indians and freighting a bounty of furs back to the canoe trunk lines, which in turn would speed them down the St. Lawrence to oceangoing ships at Quebec or—if his fantastic plan proved successful—down the Mississippi to the major port he would construct on the gulf.

La Salle's brilliant dream did not even stop there. Around his forts he would induce a large population of Indians to congregate. In the autumn, when the pelts were at their prime, they would fan out over the countryside to trap. During the warm months they would plant extensive fields of corn and other grains to live on during the winter. Once the Indians became sedentary, towns, even cities, would arise—their population augmented by immigrations from France. A Franco-Indian civilization would take root—a civilization that would make the narrow coastal colonies of the English pale in comparison. And over this all he would rule as the king's viceroy!

In 1677 La Salle sailed to France, his head spinning with the grandiose project. In a memorial which he set before all-powerful Louis XIV, he described the American Midwest with flowery phrases worthy of a chamber of commerce, which is what he was: "It is nearly all so beautiful and so fertile, so free from forests, and so full of meadows, brooks, and rivers, so abounding in fish, game, and venison—that one can find there in plenty and with little trouble all that is needful for the support of flourishing colonies." His ardor won the king, and Louis licensed La Salle as sole exploiter of the midwest and lower Mississippi for a five year period—with the neat little stickler that it would be La Salle, not Louis, who would bear the financial burden for building the forts and ships necessary to carry out the far-reaching enterprise.

With family and friends as backers, La Salle was soon engaged at Fort Frontenac gathering the supplies and carpenters he needed. In the meantime he sent eighteen men ahead to reconnoiter the area around the gigantic falls which the Iroquois called *Niagara* ("the Thunderer") where he wished to build his first fort. One of the men was Louis Hennepin, an adventuresome Récollet priest, whose journal provides us with Europe's initial view of the magnificent scene:

> We passed back by the great Falls of Niagara and spent half a day watching this prodigious cascade. . . . The discharge of so much water coming from these fresh water seas centers at this spot and thus plunges down more than six hundred feet, falling as into an abyss which we could not behold without a shudder . . . The spray of the water is so great that it forms a kind of cloud above this chasm.[11]

When La Salle arrived, he cajoled a band of Senecas, who had gathered below the falls to take advantage of the good fishing, into letting him construct a small stockade on the picturesque bluff overlooking Lake Ontario and the mouth of the Niagara River (where tourists now see the impressive battlements of a slightly later French fort). As soon as Fort Niagara was completed, La Salle and a portion of his men ascended the steep cliff at Lewiston, New York, and continued up the Niagara River until they found a sheltered place—probably the Cayuga Creek at Buffalo—at which to build the first large sailing vessel ever to float on the Great Lakes. Named the *Griffon,* in honor of the winged lion on Governor Frontenac's coat of arms, the ship, as large as many an oceangoing vessel, was intended to be an important link in La Salle's transportation system.

On the seventh of August, 1679, La Salle and his crew set off in the *Griffon* for the Illinois country and the next segment of his ambitious enterprise. The journey up the lake named after the vanished Erie, or Cat People, was uneventful and ten days later they had reached the *détroit,* or strait, which connects Lake Erie with Lake Huron. The passage was pleasant, Hennepin reporting that the site of modern Detroit was then "adorned with fine open plains. And you can see numbers of stags, does, deer, bears, by no means fierce and very good to eat." They also found "vines loaded with grapes, of which we made some little wine." Their rigging loaded with the venison they were drying, they passed through a wide lake, which they christened St. Clair after the saint whose day it was.

Continuing through Lake Huron in the midst of such a violent storm that even staunch La Salle believed them lost, they reached the Ottawa village at the Mackinac Strait. Here La Salle, instinctively knowing the art of impressing the Indians, dressed in a cloak of bright scarlet trimmed with gold lace and conferred with the chiefs as they came from services in Marquette's old mission. Then, as the splendors of autumn began tinting the encircling forest, he hoisted sail and glided down to the Potawatami settlement at Green Bay. He was well received there by the chief, who had been entertained by Governor Frontenac at Montreal in prior years.

It was now that La Salle made a fateful decision. "Contrary to our opinion," Hennepin grumbled, "the Sieur de La Salle, who never took anyone's advice, resolved to send back his ship from this place and to continue his route by canoe." The *Griffon* was loaded with the furs collected from the Ottawa, Potawatami, and other Algonquins encountered on their route, and, along with a large amount of supplies and trade goods which could not be carried in the canoes, set sail into the gray, glassy waters of Lake Michigan: her destination Fort Niagara. She fired a parting cannonade, then was gone. No man ever saw her again, for the proud ship, all her crew, and a large part of La Salle's fortune vanished without a trace.

But La Salle did not know the fate of his ship as he and fourteen followers crammed their four canoes with merchandise, weapons, food, and a cumbersome but essential forge to repair their guns and tools. Heading southward they were caught in a fierce storm (probably the same one that sank the *Griffon*). With huge breakers washing over the canoes, the Frenchmen considered themselves lucky to reach the shore. Wind, snow, and icy waves plagued them from then on. Their food almost gave out, forcing them to paddle with nothing more to sustain them than a handful of Indian corn each twenty-four hours. Their arms ached, their heads spun, and sickness made many weak. Passing the Pere Marquette River, they probably called out for succor from the dead priest, as was fast becoming the custom. But it appears that Marquette did not help them, for the bad weather did not abate. Still La Salle, a man of an iron will who, perhaps, expected too much of his weary men, pushed on.

It was November first when they reached the mouth of the St. Joseph River. Here, while La Salle awaited the arrival of Henri Tonti—his capable Italian lieutenant who had an iron claw in place of one hand—he constructed a stout fort on an eminence overlooking the river (the site of which is now a park in St. Joseph, Michigan). By the time Tonti reached them three weeks later, the men had grown sick of the fatty meat of bears, the only game animals left in the wintery dune lands; and there was much whispered talk of desertion. La Salle's inflexible determination alone held the group together.

Shortly thereafter the muttering voyageurs reloaded their canoes, which with the addition of Tonti's numbered eight, and paddled up the St. Joseph River past monstrous trees arching over the water to the site of South Bend, Indiana. Here a difficult-to-find portage trail ran two miles across a treeless marshland where, according to Hennepin, "we found a number of buffalo horns and the carcasses of those animals, and some canoes that the Indians had made of buffalo skins to cross the river with their load of meat." Then they paddled down the Kankakee ("wolf") River, while a whistling north wind sent snow buzzing like hornets about them. It was a desolate country: "as far as the eye could reach nothing was to be seen but marshes." Beyond the marshes were boundless prairies, the brown grass shaking in the wind. The men knew the Miami Indians were out there, for they could discern the grass fires they made to force the buffalo down routes lined with bowmen. But La Salle did not permit his hungry men to leave the dreary Kankakee, even though it was clear that the Miamis were feasting not far away.

During most of bitter December the thirty-two explorers drifted down the Kankakee, which became the Illinois when it was joined by the Des Plaines River forty-five miles southwest of Chicago. At Lake Peoria, a wide place in the Illinois, La Salle decided to debark. The populous and kindly Illini confederation figured highly in his plans, and here in the very center of their fertile country was an ideal location for his capital. But first he constructed a fort, for there was a persistent rumor that a strong Iroquois force was marching on the Illini. A low bluff was selected opposite the modern city of Peoria and soon the French-men had a pair of sturdy barracks and a stockade of sharpened timbers to protect themselves. La Salle named the fort Crève-coeur after an important European bastion; but, perhaps not unconsciously, he chose an appropriate title (the word translates into broken heart): not only were his men plotting desertion, but earlier someone had even placed poison in his food. Adding to his growing uneasiness was the lack of word concerning the *Griffon*.

Nevertheless, he pushed on with his plans. Even while Fort Crèvecoeur was taking shape, La Salle started work on a second ship the size of the *Griffon* to be used on the Mississippi. Con-struction of the hull went along on schedule, but when it came time for the sails and rigging, the project was stalled—since these items were part of the cargo of the *Griffon*. To secure the necessary supplies at Fort Frontenac, La Salle with only five companions started out across the thousand miles of wilderness —with the rivers icy and treacherous and reports of the advanc-ing Iroquois coming in ever more frequently.

Before he left, La Salle placed Tonti in charge of Crève-coeur and ordered a pair of voyageurs, with Father Hennepin as supercargo, to explore trading possibilities on the upper Missis-sippi. Both Tonti and Hennepin kept records of the next few months which contained enough adventures and hairbreadth escapes to last them both for a lifetime.

Hennepin's party was given a goodly stock of trading goods: "ten knives, twelve awls, a small roll of tobacco . . . two pounds of black and white beads, and a small package of needles." Then, on the 29th of February, 1680, they pushed out into the Illinois in a single birchbark canoe. Down the scenic canyon they went, passing at intervals bands of Illini in their slow, wooden dugouts.

Upon entering the Mississippi, they turned upriver, deftly guiding their fragile canoe around the menacing chunks of ice flowing about them. Yet they were accustomed to danger and were rewarded by a more than ample supply of food—easily shooting the buffalo, deer, beaver, and bears that were constantly swimming across the Mississippi. But, as they approached the mouth of the Wisconsin, their peaceful days were abruptly ended. Here a war party of a hundred and twenty Sioux in thirty-three birchbarks swarmed about them. They were on their way for a surprise attack on the Illini and Miami, but, when Hennepin blithely announced that he had seen the Miami far eastward, the angry Sioux abandoned their escapade and contented themselves with taking the three Frenchmen prisoners instead.

Carrying Hennepin and his companions upriver with them, they passed into Minnesota (Sioux homeland before the capture of Spanish mustangs permitted them to begin their adventures on the Great Plains). Hennepin, given as a slave to one of the Sioux families who had lost a warrior, lived a precarious existence, seldom having enough to eat and never quite sure whether the Sioux had plans of torturing him to death.

But captivity permitted Hennepin to spend the rest of the spring and part of the summer traveling with Sioux hunters to places in Minnesota never before seen by white man. Some of the least agreeable incidents of his forced exploration were periodic visits to a roaring cataract which he named in honor of St. Anthony of Padua. This place, now in the heart of Minneapolis, was then the Sioux' holiest of sites—their greatest spirit was supposed to live under the falls. Hennepin saw one Indian climb a large oak and cry out: "Thou who are a spirit, grant that the men of our nation may pass here quietly without accident, that we may kill buffalo in abundance, conquer our enemies, and bring slaves here, some of whom we will put to death before thee." Although Hennepin witnessed no human sacrifices here, the thought made him uneasy, for wasn't he himself a slave!

On his last trip down the Mississippi, Hennepin, with almost unbelievable luck, met the Sieur du Lhut and a party of *coureurs de bois*. Although Duluth always denied he had been engaged in illegal, unlicensed trade, he had been scouting, in a most suspect manner, the environs of Lake Superior and the spectacular bluffs where the city named after him would one day rise. Duluth, a genial and glib gentleman, convinced the Sioux that Hennepin and his companions must be released if the Indians expected any traders to bring them the muskets they craved for their perpetual battle with the Chippewa, their greatest enemy.

This episode was enough for the good father. Hennepin scampered back to Montreal, where Governor Frontenac was thunderstruck to see him—Hennepin's death at the hands of the Sioux had been reported many months earlier. His face gaunt, his cheeks hollow, his tattered Récollet frock patched with irregular bits of buffalo hide, Hennepin seemed a man risen from a dirt grave. Soon thereafter he boarded a ship for France, never again to live the hazardous life of a missionary in the New World.

While Hennepin was suffering at the hands of the Sioux and La Salle was on his sixty-five-day ordeal across the freezing wastelands, Henri Tonti, left in charge of Crèvecoeur, was having difficulties of his own. Soon after La Salle had departed, Tonti had taken a few men seventy miles up the Illinois to examine a circular butte called Starved Rock as perhaps a better place for a fort than the gullied environs around Crèvecoeur. While he was absent, the rest of the men, learning from a pair of newly arrived voyageurs that the Griffon was lost, creditors had seized Fort Frontenac, and La Salle was probably a ruined man, wrecked Crèvecoeur, stole all the gunpowder, furs, and provisions, and fled to Mackinac where they seized more of La Salle's furs claiming them in lieu of two years' wages.

Tonti, upon returning, had little time to be angered for at this moment, when only three French gunners and two Récollet priests remained, the Iroquois made their long-dreaded attack.

The fearful Illini sent their women and children hurrying beyond the valley for safety, then massed to resist the mighty warriors from the east. The Iroquois marched in battle array, six hundred muscular savages, their bodies dabbed with vermilion war paint. The air reverberated with their whoops and taunts. No longer did they fear the Frenchmen, for the Dutch and English traders were supplying them with guns and ammunition. Although the Illini numbered only four hundred and had no weapons other than stone-tipped arrows, they stood their ground.

At this point, with muskets already blasting and arrows whining, Tonti scooped up a few strings of wampum and a calumet and strode bravely toward the enemy, his hands outstretched with the twin symbols of peace. With him was Father Zenobius Membré, whose eye-witness report, along with that of Tonti written much later, provides us with a close account of what happened.

Tonti tried to bluff the Iroquois into calling a truce by telling them there were many French sharpshooters hidden in the Illini lines and that the Illini, in addition, had more than a thousand braves in the vicinity. "These proposals for peace did not, however, please some young warriors, whose hands itched for fight," Membré wrote. "Suddenly a volley of bullets and arrows came whizzing around us, and a young Onondaga ran up with a drawn knife and struck M. de Tonti near the heart." [12] As Tonti fell to the ground with blood gushing from his side, an Iroquois snatched his hat and hoisted it atop his gun barrel to show the Illini that the French leader was their prisoner.

But one of the more sober Iroquois chiefs shouted that Tonti, as the representative of Governor Frontenac and the power at his command, must not be killed. Tonti's life hung on a very slender thread, for, as he later wrote, "there was a man behind me with a knife in his hand who every now and then lifted up my hair." Yet somehow the friendly chief was able to prevail and, while the victorious Iroquois swept into the Illini villages, leaving complete devastation in their wake, Tonti, Membré, and the other Frenchmen were given a battered old canoe and ordered to leave.

Their trip to the mission at Green Bay was one of extreme hardship. Tonti, weak from loss of blood, managed to keep going, although he and his companions had no provisions and maintained themselves with wild garlic grubbed from under the autumn snow and a few handfuls of frozen corn found in an abandoned Indian village. One of the starving voyageurs even ate the dirt-ingrained leather from his shoes—the result of which made him so sick he nearly died. Their leaky canoe finally sunk forcing them to trudge over the frozen Wisconsin earth, which quickly cut their moccasins to pieces. They managed to stumble forward on bandages made from the cloak of one of the friars who had been killed by Indians while straying from camp during his meditations. Tonti's legs became so swollen and painful he could barely keep from stumbling. By the time they staggered into the Green Bay mission "not one of us could stand," wrote Membré, adding "we were all like skeletons."

But weak men did not go into the interior. Tonti recovered and La Salle, obtaining new financial backers and overcoming his shock at the desolation in the Illinois Valley, made still another attempt to found the empire he alone was capable of erecting.

After returning to the Midwest, one of his first actions was to call a conference at the South Bend portage between the Illini and Miami tribes: an effort to form an alliance which would discourage further incursions by the Iroquois. Here, under a large oak which still stands in Highland Cemetery, he brought the chiefs of both nations together and a treaty was signed. There was a touch of irony at the meeting, for the impressive ceremonies were watched by some of King Philip's warriors fleeing from the English, in possession of their former lands along the Boston Post Road. Now the eastern tribesmen, easily following the dialect of their cousins the Illini and Miami, were witnessing the destruction of the western Algonquins by members of their own race (the Iroquois) while white men were trying to save the Indians.

It wasn't for another year that La Salle was able to gather enough men and supplies to pursue his long-deferred goal: the discovery of the mouth of the Mississippi. Tonti was with him, as were eighteen Mohegans and other tribesmen displaced from New England and twenty-three Frenchmen—including Father Zenobius Membré keeping his ever-dependable journal. Tonti and Membré preceeded La Salle to the river which Membré, certainly in jest, called the Divine; but which the Potawatamis more accurately called the *Chicago* ("Bad Smell") after the wild garlic and onions which soured the air around the ofttimes murky swampland.

La Salle joined Tonti on the fourth of January, 1682. The Chicago River was frozen, so they had to drag their canoes and supply packs over the ice—past a lonely landscape now the throbbing center of one of the world's greatest cities. Frozen, too, was Mud Lake, that indefinite area where the waters flowing into Lake Michigan mingled during the spring floods with those of the Mississippi system (currently part of the Chicago Portage National Historic Site off Highway 43). Soon they reached the Des Plaines ("River of the Plains") and, passing the embankment that would one day support the heavy girders of a Tri-State Tollway bridge, eventually entered the Illinois River just southwest of the city later named in honor of La Salle's acquaintance Louis Jolliet (though for some unaccountable reason the Americans dropped one *l* from Jolliet's name).

It was not until they entered Lake Peoria, with the ominous ruins of Crèvecoeur standing bleakly on the bluffs, that the ice was gone and the canoes could be launched. A month after leaving Chicago they reached the Mississippi, whose still partially ice-choked waters kept them waiting impatiently for nearly a week. Then they moved southward again; but slowly, for their provisions were low and they had to make frequent hunting excursions ashore.

After passing the mouth of the Ohio, they paddled nearly

two hundred miles without stopping "because the banks are low and marshy, and full of thick foam, rushes and walnut trees," recorded Membré. Now, too, they noted the appearance of alligators, some fifteen feet in length, so vicious that no one dared "even put his hand out of the canoe." But beyond the swampy flatlands, they found the countryside to be pleasant, "covered with palm trees, laurels of two kinds, plums, peaches, mulberry, apple, and pear trees of every kind." Stopping at last atop the Chickasaw Bluffs, they built Fort Prudhomme (on the site of Memphis) near the very lookout from which De Soto had discovered the Mississippi one hundred and forty-one years earlier.

Continuing south, they found the Indians did "not resemble those of the north, who are all sad and severe in their temper; these are far better made, honest, liberal and gay." The Arkansas tribesmen, "the largest and handsomest men of all the Indians of this continent," gave them a three-day festival. Later La Salle and a portion of his company slept as guests of honor in the village of the Natchez, a powerful tribe fishing near the bluffs where white-pillared, Greek Revival mansions currently attract visitors.

Southward, ever southward, they voyaged. When the Mississippi turned brackish, the men roared with pleasure: they were approaching the sea! La Salle, nervous with anticipation, directed his fleet past the long mound where the levees, wharves, and bistros of New Orleans would one day rise. Then, on the ninth of April, three months after leaving Chicago, they sighted open water: the Gulf of Mexico!

Amid shouting and congratulations, the Frenchmen and the New England Indians headed their canoes into the mud and undergrowth, to step ashore where few if any humans had been before them. As a tepid breeze sent the chocolate water lap, lap, lapping against the hulls of their worn birchbarks, they shoved a large cross into the earth. Led by Father Membré, they sung the "Te Deum." Then La Salle, possibly dressed in the scarlet coat with the gold lace which he reserved for special occasions, marched forward. "In the name of the most high, mighty, invincible, and victorious Prince, Louis the Great, by the grace of

God, King of France," La Salle thundered, "I, this ninth day of April . . . do now take in the name of his Majesty and of his successors to the crown, possession of this country of Louisiana, the seas, harbors, ports, bays, adjacent straits, and all the nations . . . within the extent of the said Louisiana." [13]

The Indians watched in confused wonder and the Frenchmen in proud admiration, as their leader defined the gigantic territory to be known henceforth as Louisiana, after the king. It extended from the warm-water bay at which he was standing to the blustery northlands seen thus far only by Hennepin and Duluth . . . eastward up the Ohio to the kingdom of the unsuspecting Iroquois . . . and westward to the far reaches of Spanish New Mexico and the storied Rocky Mountains. La Salle's voice, muffled by the restless delta waters, carried but a few hundred feet. Yet it was sufficient to bring to France a subcontinent of undreamed of wealth.

After all the setbacks and heartbreaks, La Salle had achieved one of his primary objectives. With the mouth of the Mississippi definitely located, he could plant a great port city here—a port which would be ice-free, as Quebec was not, and which had a direct, cataract-free line of transportation with the interior. Not only furs, but deer hides, grains, dried fruits, and shipping supplies (such as tall mast poles to replace the stumpy little ones from France), would soon come down this broad water-highway, the Mississippi.

As La Salle gazed into the azure distances of the gulf, he must have imagined this was the beginning of the fulfillment of his dream. But he was wrong. It was in reality the end of his dream. Back up the Mississippi he went, leaving Tonti to construct a fort atop Starved Rock (now Illinois's most popular state park), around which the Illini and other Algonquins began to congregate in numbers approaching twenty thousand. Returning to France, La Salle was given four large ships, a hundred soldiers, and enough volunteer settlers (including girls of marriageable age) to found his city on the delta. Yet he overshot the Mississippi during a thick fog and ended up on Galveston Bay. The discouragement of his settlers increased as La Salle's notorious bad luck held and the ship bearing almost all their food and supplies was shattered on a reef just outside the harbor.

Soon famine struck. A half dozen persons died each day. La Salle, a man of volatile temper who in his entire life had called no more than two or three persons his friends, became even sterner, harsher, and often unjust. With the colony on the brink of disaster, La Salle determined to seek aid from his ever faithful Tonti up on the Illinois. Taking twenty men, including Anastasius Douay a Récollet priest, he started across the wide Texas plains, just turning green with advancing spring. But there was considerable discontent toward La Salle; many accused him (with a good deal of truth) of mismanaging the expedition. He was led into an ambush one day. From the underbrush two shots rang out. Father Douay, who was at La Salle's side, "saw him fall a step from me, with his face full of blood." He died an hour later in the weeping padre's arms.

Thus, too, died France's opportunity to create a permanent inland empire. Others would follow La Salle—brave men with special dreams of their own—but they were earthbound creatures who dealt with erecting forts, pacifying tribes, selling goods. They were not the kind to create a Franco-Indian civilization founded on agriculture as well as fur. The brilliant, overall strategy that a man like La Salle could give was gone.

And without it New France was doomed.

4.   No Life Is So Happy As a Voyageur's Life

Although the murder of La Salle in 1687 removed the only man who saw the necessity of founding an empire on a Franco-Indian agricultural society rather than upon fur trade alone, the French, nevertheless, successfully wove the Midwest into their Montreal-based transportation system. Often missionaries formed the first wedge of French penetration: Allouez, in particular, being helpful by attracting the Indians to the missions he established at the Sault Ste. Marie in 1668 and at La Baye Verte (as the French called Green Bay) the following year. Then Marquette founded the important mission of St. Ignace on the northern shores of the "Great Turtle" (Mackinac Straits) in 1671; and more tribes were drawn into the French sphere.

As traders began gathering about Marquette's mission to do business with the tribesmen (and their just-as-eager wives), the Canadian authorities decided to erect Fort de Baude immediately south of the mission church. It was an impressive structure according to Antoine de la Mothe Cadillac, one of the earliest commanders, with palisades "on the outside . . . as thick as a man's thigh and about 30 feet high." There was a "second row, inside . . . a foot from the first, which is bent over on to it, and is to support it and prop it up." And to make the fort practically impregnable, which it had to be since more than seven thousand fickle Ottawas and other tribesmen camped nearby, there was a third circle of sharpened palisades "four feet from the second, [consisting] of timbers three and a half feet in diameter standing 15 or 16 feet out of the ground." Fort de Baude, guarding the Mackinac Straits, was essential, said Governor Frontenac, "because it was through this place that all those tribes passed over whom the French were able to obtain complete influence."

In 1684 a fort was constructed at the mouth of the Fox River (on a site now spanned by the bridge on Highway 141 in Green Bay). With the river now protected, traders like Nicolas Perrot flooded into the interior, crossing to the Wisconsin River via Marquette's portage and establishing small posts along the Mississippi frontier. Perrot himself, had three posts: one at Prairie du Chien near the much-frequented mouth of the Wisconsin, a second where scenic Trempealeau Mountain squats in the midst of the Mississippi (the fort site is indicated by a marker in Perrot State Park), and a third overlooking majestic Lake Pepin (created by a natural dam across the Mississippi from the swift-flowing Chippewa River) near Maiden Rock, Wisconsin. It was at this last fort that Perrot conducted a formal taking-possession ceremony similar to that of St. Lusson at the sault some years earlier (the location of Perrot's festivities is indicated by a marker on Wisconsin 35).

Just as essential as the bastions at Mackinac and Green Bay, was the fort which Cadillac was ordered to build at the Detroit Strait in 1701. On a bright morning in July, Cadillac, vain and cocky, strode ashore with a hundred settlers, selecting a site on a low rise protected by a little stream, since filled in. Soon thousands of Indians gathered about the log stockade (which occupied the ground beneath the modern Veterans' Memorial Building in Detroit's Civic Center). Many of these tribes, including portions of the Sauk and Fox from Wisconsin, reached the fort by way of the Great Sauk Trail, a major Indian shortcut across lower Michigan (now U.S. 12).

At almost the same time, other Frenchmen were establishing themselves among the Cahokia and Kaskaskia bands of the harassed Illini. The first mission rose at Cahokia (opposite modern St. Louis) in 1699. Large groups of Illini gathered about the mission house and were joined by numerous Canadians attracted by the easy life along the rich Mississippi bottomlands. Soon there was an active French village, the administration of which was centered in the courthouse which, with its unique upright planks and white daubing, still stands.

Sixty miles down the Mississippi another Franco-Illini settlement rose at the junction of the Kaskaskia River. The French and Indians got along quite well. "We are more assured of the friendship of the Illini, than of any other Indian nation in Canada," wrote Pierre de Charlevoix, a Jesuit visitor, in 1721. "They are almost all Christians, of a mild disposition, and extremely well affected towards the French."

Charlevoix saw a promising future for Kaskaskia: "It is capable of becoming the granary of Louisiana, which it is able to furnish with corn in abundance. . . . The soil is not only extremely proper for wheat, but, besides, refuses nothing necessary or useful for human life." He believed it possible that the wild buffalos who roamed the Illinois prairies could be tamed, "and great advantages drawn from a trade of their wool and hides." The climate was far milder than rigorous Canada and the area was healthful—the only illnesses coming from what the priest disdainfully called the libertinism of the voyageur population, who obviously loved brandy and Illini maids more than the good Jesuit thought proper.

But why not enjoy Nature's bounty while one could? To live on the frontier was always perilous, what with tribes like the Sioux, Fox, Chickasaw, and even the distant Iroquois liable at any moment to sweep down upon them—not even withstanding the erection in 1720 of Fort de Chartres twenty miles up the river (the original wall bases and stone powderhouse are part of the modern state park). And so it was as Charlevoix noted: "The French in this place live pretty much at their ease."

On the other hand, the Illini were "very laborious"—a quality rarely found among the Midwestern Indians. "They bring up poultry," Charlevoix wrote, describing the Kaskaskian economy, "which they sell to the French. Their women are very neat-handed and industrious. They spin the wool of the buffalo, which they make as fine as that of the English sheep; nay sometimes it might even be mistakened for silk. Of this they manufacture stuffs

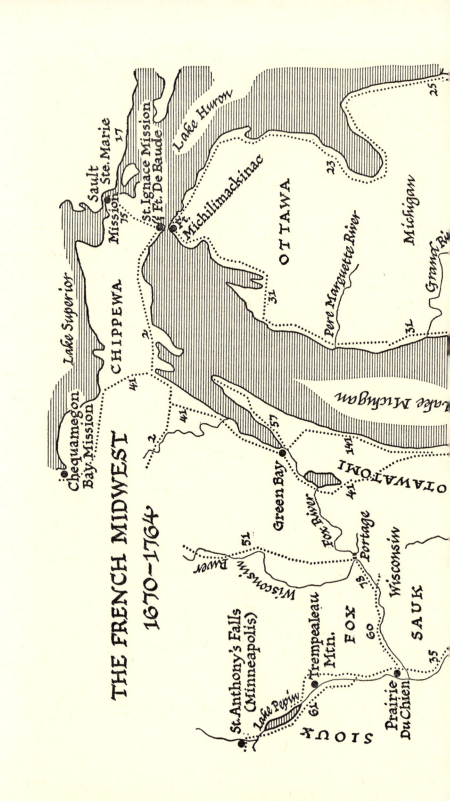

THE FRENCH MIDWEST
1670–1764

Lake Superior

Chequamegon Bay Mission

Sault Ste. Marie

Mission

CHIPPEWA

St.Ignace Mission (Ft. De Baude)

Ft. Michilimackinac

Lake Huron

OTTAWA

Pere Marquette River

Michigan

Grand R.

Lake Michigan

Green Bay

Fox River

Portage

Wisconsin

POTAWATOMI

St. Anthony's Falls (Minneapolis)

Wisconsin River

Trempealeau Mtn.

FOX

SAUK

Lake Pepin

Prairie Du Chien

SIOUX

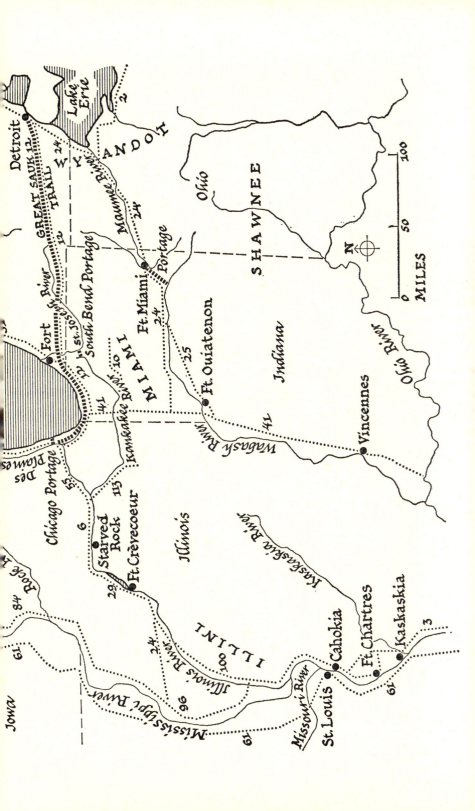

which are dyed black, yellow, or deep red. Of these stuffs they make robes which they sew with thread made of the sinews of the roebuck." [14]

Once established on the mid-Mississippi, it was natural that French traders should consider the furs up the untapped Missouri. Eventually French pirogues were approaching the Great Plains, area claimed by the jealous Spanish. To firm up French power, Fort Orleans was constructed in 1723 a full two hundred miles up the Missouri (the fort site is indicated by a marker a few miles west of Brunswick). But it was soon felt that the fort was too far from the main transportation routes, and it was abandoned a few years later.

Meanwhile, the French expanded in still another direction. When the Fox tribe, enraged by a French-inspired, but Indian-executed, massacre of one of their most populous bands at Detroit, retaliated by waging devastating, Iroquois-style warfare in western Wisconsin and northern Illinois, the French began using the Maumee-Wabash route in place of the exposed Fox-Wisconsin one to reach the Mississippi. As early as 1680 there had been a small trading post at the point where the portage trail left the Maumee to reach the Wabash twenty-six weary miles away (a marker in Fort Wayne beside the St. Marys River, a branch of the Maumee, indicates the location of this, Indiana's first white settlement). But in 1712 the French threw up a sturdier stockade named Fort Miami.

To guard the Wabash, Fort Ouiatenon was constructed a few years later five miles below modern Lafayette (a replica blockhouse marks the site). And about 1730, the Sieur de Vincennes erected a fort ninety river-miles from the Ohio. Although Vincennes met a fiery death at the hands of the fierce Chickasaws of the south, the village which bore his name eventually became the hub of a hundred French farms lining the Wabash. Generation upon generation of French farmers and their wives and children rode into Vincennes each Sunday to attend the little log church which for nearly a hundred years stood on the site of the picturesque cathedral which currently attracts visitors.

There was considerable commerce between the Midwestern villages and Montreal. Early in the spring, the Indians, along with French traders called *coureurs de bois* (forest rangers), to distinguish them from the voyageurs or canoe paddlers, would pack the beaver pelts they had obtained during the winter and guide their canoes along the rivers and lakes which led to Montreal, where the merchants arranged a great yearly fair to facilitate the exchange of goods. But because the cargo of each canoe was so valuable (a large birchbark could hold up to a thousand pelts valued at four thousand dollars), the Indians and *coureurs* preferred to make the long journey in a strong, easily defensible fleet. For this reason they usually gathered at Fort de Baude, or, after 1715, at better located Fort Michilimackinac, (a modern stockade occupies the site just west of the soaring Mackinac Bridge). Here one would find Chippewas from Sault Ste. Marie, Ottawas and Winnebagos from the Fox-Wisconsin route, Potawatamis and Sauks from the Chicago portage, Miamis from the St. Joseph River—and even a band or two of Illini from their retreat on the Mississippi. From farther west, via the Lake of the Woods, the Pigeon River (where there is an extensive reconstruction of the French fur post), and Lake Superior came Cree tribesmen and an occasional party of Sioux.

While the tribes gathered, the *coureurs* broke out casks of brandy; and, after songs were sung and wild dances performed, the *coureurs* would induce the drunken savages to part with some of their choicest pelts at give-away prices. Although in doing so the *coureurs* were breaking the king's law, which forbade any but licensed merchants in Montreal and Quebec to trade, the *coureurs* were so numerous (one estimate is that up to thirty percent of the Canadian men between eighteen and thirty-five were *coureur* outlaws) that the authorities dared do little against them.

When all the tribes were present, the flotilla set out. After passing the barren hump of Mackinac Island (the great fortress which delights visitors was not built until the British era), it turned south along the shores of choppy Lake Huron to pass by Fort Pontchartrain guarding the Detroit Strait. Here more tribesmen joined: eastern Ottawas and those few Hurons who remained after the Iroquois wars. Beyond Detroit was the mouth of the Maumee (modern Toledo) where traders from Vincennes, Ouiatenon, and Fort Miami, together with such tribes as the Wea, Miami, and Shawnee, joined the fleet.

By the time the caravan reached the Niagara portage there were often as many as four hundred canoes, with well over a thousand Indians and several hundred *coureurs* and voyageurs. Senecas and other Iroquois bands fishing along the rushing river could only watch in dismay as the fur riches passed, for the fleet was far too powerful to attack.

Four months after it had set out from Mackinac, the fleet came in sight of Montreal. Most of the populace ran along the shore shooting muskets and waving banners—for this was the grand event of the year. Sometimes, if the governor was in a good mood, the fleet was even "saluted with the thundering guns and batteries of the fort," so Pierre Radisson reported.

The two-week fair was well worth the long, difficult journey. As a backwoods Indian brave wandered past the dozens of booths set up between St. Paul Street and the St. Lawrence, he could not help but be dazzled by the fantastic assortment of goods and gewgaws that caught his unpracticed eye. He would see shiny new muskets, with which he could bring down either game or enemies far easier than using his short-range, inaccurate bow; pistols with fancy refinements such as twin barrels; steel knives so much better for skinning, carving, or fighting than the dull, chipped stones he had formerly used. His wife would probably have hounded him to bring her back some of the steel awls and needles that didn't break as did the bones she used to sew their clothing. Of course, they both wanted an iron kettle or two, so superior to the fragile clay pots of their parents' day. And steel hatchets were likewise a necessity now in the construction of a canoe or bark wigwam.

In addition, there were many other items not so essential but nonetheless desirable: bags of shimmering glass beads, necklaces and bracelets of gaudy metals, bells that jingled as he shook them, tin mirrors that caught his reflection and made him laugh.

There were gay plumes for his headdress, sashes to loop around his waist, vermilion paint to make his countenance fearsome. And, naturally, there were the hogsheads of brandy to turn each evening into a wild orgy. Yes, it was a new age for the red man, and to be part of it he must make the scene at Montreal.

When the trading and carousing were over and the hangovers easing off, the Indians would shuffle off to their canoes, carefully pack their new belongings, and push out into the river. The young *coureurs*, too, could not resist the call of the fur lands. They would kiss their weeping sweethearts one last time while scarlet maple leaves cascaded about them, then would step into their birchbarks to follow the Indians back to their river haunts.

The lure of the river road held an almost magical spell over the young men of New France. A disapproving elder wrote:

> This has come to such a pass that from the moment a boy can carry a gun, the father cannot restrain him . . . I cannot tell you, Monseigneur, how attractive this Indian life is to all our youth. It consists in doing nothing, caring for nothing, following every inclination, and getting out of the way of all correction.[15]

Yet it was understandable for from the moment the *coureurs* or voyageurs left Montreal they were no longer grubby peasants or humble craftsmen or unfavored younger sons. The tribes held them in awe, referring to them as spirits. Even from the days of Cartier, the Indians had nearly worshipped the Frenchmen, arriving as they did in gigantic ships that sailed fearlessly from the mysterious, heaving ocean. "They came closely about us," Cartier wrote, describing a welcoming which would be experienced by many Frenchmen in years to come, "making very much of us, bringing their young children in their arms to have our Captain and his company touch them."

French guns stupified the red men, who, though they feared

the bullets, were even more apprehensive about the explosion, which they were convinced was the angry roar of a demon who lived in the weapon. Even ordinary iron tools were beyond their ken. "Thou art one of the chief spirits, since thou usest iron," the Potawatamis exclaimed when Perrot entered their Stone Age village. "They adored him as a god," the account continues, "they took his knives and hatchets and incensed them with the tobacco-smoke from their mouths; and they presented him so many kinds of food that he could not taste them all." [16]

The lowly cooking pot was likewise an object of Indian veneration. "I had an iron pot with three lion feet," wrote Hennepin from Sioux headquarters, "which these Indians never dared touch unless their hand was wrapped up in some robe. The women had it hung to the branch of a tree, not daring to enter the cabin where the pot was." [17]

This feeling of reverence continued as the years passed and the Indians grew ever more dependent on French manufactured goods—for who except mighty spirits could make such things that had never appeared before, not even in legend!

Of course, there were exceptions, such as the Iroquois and later the Chickasaw and Natchez of the south, but these tribes had been brainwashed by the English who provided more manna than the French.

Otherwise, the *coureurs* had the trans-Appalachian Indians to themselves. One year a Frenchman might winter among the Chippewas beside the churning Sault, living with an ardent Indian maid whom he took to wife for the season. In the spring he might canoe over to the raucous carnival at Fort Michilimackinac, where he would swap yarns with friends who had shot buffalo with Miamis on the prairies of northern Indiana or traveled with the Sioux on slaving raids against the Pawnees on the Great Plains. Then, if he should decide to remain in the West rather than accompany the caravan to the Montreal fair, he might paddle to Green Bay and do some trading there, or perhaps drift westward down the Fox-Wisconsin to Prairie du Chien on the Mississippi. By autumn he would have dropped down the Mississippi to Kaskaskia to gamble over flagons of brandy with some of the garrison of Fort de Chartres or make love to an Illini girl on the grassy bluffs towering over the river. He could wander as his fancy directed him, knowing all the portage paths, unruly rapids, the favored camp sites on the vast water network that made the Midwest a Frenchman's private preserve.

The key to the fur empire was the humble birchbark canoe. It was not uncommon for a canoe man to make two hundred miles in a single day; and even such an indifferent paddler as Louis Hennepin, frantic to escape the hated wilderness, rocketed through the 330 miles of "frightful" rapids between Fort Frontenac and Montreal in two and a half days. To cover such a distance on the King's Highway, an Englishman would need more than a week.

To penetrate the wilderness, thickly matted with trees and undergrowth, a birchbark was essential. Floating in only three inches of water, such a canoe was able to glide up all but the tiniest creek—could sail on a heavy dew, the voyageurs liked to boast. And the birchbarks were light enough to be carried with ease over the few portage paths that linked this remarkable water system. Sioux canoes weighed only fifty pounds, and, although those of the Algonquins were heavier, one or two hardy voyageurs could tote a canoe and a load of baggage over the steepest path. Nor could rainy weather stop the canoe men, for, while English roads mired, the voyageurs sped down the swollen rivers with joyous rapidity. Even in the winter the French river system functioned: a cargo-crammed canoe could be pushed along a frozen stream nearly as easily as if it had been on runners; then, when clear water was found, the journey could be continued without difficulty. This was how Tonti and La Salle began the northern portion of their Mississippi River exploration.

Canoe-making was a special art that impressed Frenchmen from the days when Champlain first noted the graceful Indian vessels "made of birch bark, strengthened inside with little hoops of white cedar very neatly arranged." But the birchbark canoe

was not known to all tribes. It was mainly certain Algonquins—
the Ottawas, Potawatamis, and especially the Chippewas—who
perfected this delicate means of travel. The Iroquois, for example, had only clumsy imitations made of leaky elm bark; the
Sioux had puny craft, frail and ill-balanced; the Illini, along with
the Chickasaw, Natchez, and other tribes of the lower Mississippi, used slow, heavy vessels made from fire-hollowed logs; and
the Foxes simply went on foot.

Birchbark canoes gave the Algonquins, and the French traders who used them, enormous advantages when dealing with
potentially hostile tribes—including the formidable Iroquois,
since once the presence of an enemy was detected, the traders
could speed off in their canoes, knowing there was nothing faster
on the continent. Indeed, such was the value of a birchbark that
the French were willing to trade the Algonquin craftsmen a
twenty-five-dollar musket, worth five beaver pelts, for a canoe.
But it was a long-term investment, because a canoe usually
lasted five or six years, providing the nicks and split seams were
promptly mended with resin.

For local use the canoes were only eight feet long, but for
commerce on the arterial waterways they were more than twenty
feet. These held four men and nearly a thousand pounds of
equipment and trade goods. Their utility was matched only by
their lean grace, especially when etched against the turquoise
water of a placid northern lake. One explorer wrote of the
brichbarks: "I have found nothing here more beautiful"—and
such was the opinion of many.

But whether the voyageur thought his canoe beautiful or
not, he was well aware that the tippy little craft was sometimes
all that stood between him and death. So he had to take great
care not to lose it—which was often not easy. They were so light
that more than one traveler was forced to stand helplessly on
shore as his birchbark was blown off by a strong wind. Other
times rocks would stave them in, or jagged chunks of ice would
burst through a side which was "but the thickness of five or six
sheets of paper."

When a canoe was lost, the Frenchmen, used to skimming

the water highways, had to adjust to the danger and inconvenience of land travel. Packing their bulky trade goods into a secret cache, or hole lined with branches and covered with sod, they had to trudge mile after weary mile, ofttimes in hostile country. Streams that were once their friends had to be waded or swum —larger rivers had to be crossed by a raft, the construction of which required an entire day. Stones and gravel would soon shred their moccasins, and gradually their trail would be marked by blood from their tortured feet. If they were in an area unfrequented by game, they would quickly run out of food. Then their sustenance would be a few grains of dried Indian corn, roots grubbed from the earth, and, if they were lucky, the rotting carcass of some animal killed earlier by wolves. Is it any wonder that René Galinée, upon being stranded on the shores of Lake Erie without a canoe, lamented: "we could do nothing else than recommend the matter to God and prepare for great misery and suffering."

The small space available for cargo, combined with a trader's natural desire to carry as many pelts as possible, meant skimping on food, since it (hopefully) could be picked up on the way. But this was a gamble, for game was always unpredictable and the Indian villages were seldom in the same place twice. Indeed, the journals of many Frenchmen were filled with descriptions of extreme hunger. One of the most vivid is that of Pierre Radisson. He and his companions were taking the Ottawa River route to Lake Huron when their food gave out. They were able to catch a few scrawny fish, which they threw into a pot—"guts and all." Then they hopped from boulder to boulder peeling off the dirt-spattered lichen. After much labor, "the kettle was full with the scraping of the rocks, which soon after it boiled became like starch, black and clammy . . . I think if any birds had lighted upon the excrements of the said stuff, they would have stuck to it as if it were glue." An English colonial's complaint about food at a wayside tavern would have seemed hollow indeed to a voyageur.

Since there were no inns on the many thousand miles of French waterways, the voyageurs had to make do with what was on hand. The standard equipment for a journey included a mattress of woven rushes, to afford some comfort from the stony soil, and several blankets for warmth. In addition, the blankets could serve as a partial tent during bad weather: "We were forced to land on a bare rock," wrote Hennepin, "where we endured the rain and snow for two days, sheltered by our blankets and near a little fire which we fed with wood that the waves drove ashore." However, most travelers were luckier, as was Galinée who met inclement weather in a wooded area: "When it is wet, it is necessary to go and strip some trees, the bark of which you arrange upon four forks, with which you make a cabin to save you from the rain . . . Under these strips of bark I have passed days and nights where it was very cold, with three feet of snow upon the ground, without being extraordinarily inconvenienced." [18] When passing through hostile territory, it was prudent to construct a barricade of branches and timber, such as that described earlier by Champlain. However, if one cared to chance it, he merely scattered dry brush around so he would receive warning enough by a crackling twig to leap into his canoe.

While the voyageurs' highway was dangerous, it was also gay, tingling with excitement. The Frenchmen were always singing, with the rhythm set by the stroke of their oars—"fifty songs a day were nothing to me," one voyageur boasted. Then in the evening, gathered around a spiraling campfire, some of the Frenchmen would unpack battered old fiddles with strings of horsehair to scratch out an accompanyment to the singers. Most of the songs were happy, like "My Birchbark Canoe":

I take my canoe and send it chasing
All the rapids and billows acrost:
There so swiftly see it go racing,
And it never the current has lost.[19]

Still sometimes, when the campfire dwindled and the brooding forest closed in, the voyageurs would remember sweethearts waiting in far away Montreal, and their songs would take on a plaintive mood.

But solemnity had little place on the midland waterways. "I spent all my earnings in the enjoyment of pleasure," an old voyageur reminisced in the vein of all his brethren. "Five hundred pounds, twice told, have passed through my hands; although now I have not a spare shirt to my back, nor a penny to buy one. Yet, were I young again, I should glory in commencing the same career . . . There is no life so happy as a voyageur's life; none so independent; no place where a man enjoys so much variety of freedom as in the Indian country. Huzza! Huzza!" [20]

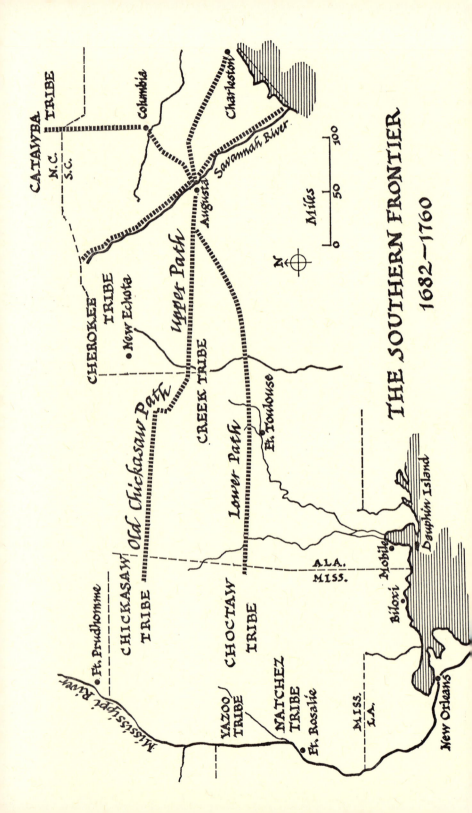

THE SOUTHERN FRONTIER
1682—1760

5.   Chickasaws Lying in Ambush

While the *coureurs* and voyageurs were making themselves at home on the Great Lakes and upper Mississippi, other Frenchmen were attempting to bring the lower Mississippi into the trade empire. But the mouth of the Mississippi—low, swampy, and unprotected from gulf blasts—presented a problem. As early as 1699 Pierre Le Moyne, Sieur d'Iberville, the son of a Montreal aristocrat, planted a small garrison at Biloxi, Mississippi, and from there proceeded along the gulf until he rediscovered the mouth of the Mississippi. The next year d'Iberville, along with his twenty-year-old brother Jean Baptiste Le Moyne, Sieur de Bienville, were back on the river scouting out a suitable site for a major post. At this time, to their great astonishment, they met Henri Tonti, paddling down the river with seven comrades from Kaskaskia in the distant Illinois country. The Mississippi linkage had begun.

The Le Moyne brothers inspected the narrow crescent of land over which a mile-long Indian path ran to connect with the lake that was soon to be named for Count Pontchartrain, the French colonial minister. "The savage I had with me," d'Iberville wrote, "showed me the place in which the Indians have their portage. . . . They dragged their canoes over a fairly good path; we found there several pieces of baggage belonging to people going one way or the other." But it was not an especially desirable location "half the way being through woods and water reaching well up on the leg." So they returned, disappointed, to Biloxi.

Yet neither was Biloxi what they wanted: "A worst place

than this could not have been chosen for the general quarters of the colony," wrote Pierre de Charlevoix, the perceptive Jesuit traveler. "The anchorage is not good, and is full of worms, which destroy all shipping." In addition "the whole coast is extremely flat, the merchant vessels not being able to approach nearer than eight miles and the smallest brigantines not nearer than four. These last are even obliged to get farther off when the wind blows from the north or northwest or else be left dry, as happened that very night I landed." [21]

For these reasons Biloxi was soon largely abandoned for Dauphin Island, a sandy key at the mouth of Mobile Bay, now connected to the mainland by a scenic toll bridge. A fort was erected there in 1709, storehouses constructed, and missionaries sent to the Alabama and other tribes to try to bring them into the French orbit. But the colony had difficulties: the Indians were hostile and some of the missionaries killed; the sandy soil would not support crops; and to crown their catastrophies an English pirate, according to Charlevoix, "ravaged Dauphin Island, plundered and burned the houses and stores, and wrecked unparalleled cruelties on the people."

Therefore Bienville (his older brother having died of the dread yellow fever) decided to return to the crescent-shaped mound along the Mississippi which, being 110 miles from the gulf, gave it protection from pirates and tropic winds. In 1718 the first shipload of settlers debarked and soon laborers were clearing the land of the enormous cypresses, digging ditches to drain the disease-breeding swamps, and throwing up crude huts to protect them from the voracious mosquitoes and almost incessant rain. Negro slaves were bought from the sugar plantations on the nearby West Indian islands, their price being paid in installments since the colony was far from prosperous. The tiny settlement was christened New Orleans, after the Regent of France, the Duke of Orléans, a quite unscrupulous man not worthy of the honor. Streets were laid out (most of them with the names still familiar in the old French Quarter) and Governor Bienville built a two story house near the river on an avenue he called after himself.

Yet New Orleans did not thrive immediately. Charlevoix found, in 1722, it consisted of a hundred shacks, a large warehouse built of timber, and "two or three houses which would be no ornament to a village in France" (presumably he includes the governor's, which was the pride of the city!). Church services were held at this time in the cluttered confines of a storehouse. The primeval swamp forest hovered closely around the struggling hamlet, Charlevoix stating: "This wild and desert place is at present almost entirely covered over with canes and trees."

The people of New Orleans were, for the most part, as disreputable as the environment. Many were taken directly from jails and workhouses. They despised the torrid delta country to which they had been deported and were generally of an unhealthy condition. As a result "great numbers died of misery or disease," Charlevoix commented, "and the country was emptied as rapidly as it had filled." Adding to the discontent was the hostility of upriver Indians who often closed the Mississippi to boats from Kaskaskia carrying the food upon which they were, partially at least, dependent.

The Indian problems were quite serious. Since New Orleans was intended primarily as a trade entrepôt similar to Montreal in the north, it was essential that she maintain her river-bound communication with the interior. To insure free passage, Bienville had built Fort Rosalie among the formidable Natchez tribe even before constructing New Orleans. Although Charlevoix calls the Natchez "naturally treacherous," it is clear that French blunders antagonized them (one soldier, for example, killed the son of a chief during a minor argument). It is also probable that the Natchez were desirous of establishing economic relations with South Carolinian traders who were pushing westward from their supply base in Charleston. Could the Natchez rid themselves of the French, then the cheaper British-made goods would be theirs.

The Natchez planned their uprising very carefully. The French garrison was strong—the strongest, in fact, of any in Louisiana. Secret meetings were held with the Chickasaws and Yazoos, who agreed to attack other French outposts at the same time. Then the Natchez brought a few leaders of the slaves, who made up about a third of the population at Fort Rosalie, into their plot. Lastly, they pretended so great a friendship with Le Page de Chepar, who commanded the garrison, that he put seven French settlers who warned him of the gathering revolt into irons!

When all was in readiness on November 28, 1729, the Natchez "scattered through the dwellings," wrote Charlevoix, "announcing that they were about to start for the hunt, careful to outnumber the French everywhere. Then they sang the calumet in honor of the commandant and his company. . . . A moment later, at a signal of three musket shots fired successively at the door of Chepar's quarters, they began the massacre at the same time everywhere . . . two hundred men perished in this way almost in an instant." A few days later the Yazoos, seventy-five miles upriver, rose against another unsuspecting French garrison and wiped it out too.

When news of the warfare reached New Orleans, the small colony was in panic. The new governor, a young naval officer by the name of Perrier, successor to Bienville (recalled on the false charge of malfeasance), had a moat and earthen embankment constructed around the town—following the inner courses of Esplanade, Burgundy, and Canal Streets: the modern French Quarter. Under total mobilization, the town's six hundred soldiers and militia kept a minute-by-minute watch for invading Indians. But when they didn't come, Perrier gathered an army of Frenchmen, Choctaw Indians, and some Negro slaves, and sent them against the Natchez. For a while the Natchez were able to hold out, even though, as Charlevoix notes "fifteen Negroes who were put under arms fought like heroes." It was only a matter of time, however, for the Choctaws were the most numerous tribe in the South. Eventually the Natchez were overcome and those few who were not killed or enslaved, joined the Chickasaw and the tribe passed out of existence.

Yet the French troubles continued as traders from Charleston continued to invade the southern piedmont. The main route linked Charleston by water with warehouses at Augusta, 140

miles up the Savannah River. Four major trails radiated from
Augusta, which, as the largest English trading town in the South,
was perpetually jammed with Indians, pack trains, rivermen, and
traders. One road eased northward along the fall line, crossing
the Congaree at Columbia (another roaring frontier post) and
moving into Catawba territory around Charlotte, North Carolina. A second trail bumped beside the rocky Savannah River
until it reached the misty vales of the Cherokees, an Iroquois-
speaking tribe ranging from the Great Smoky Mountains to the
hilly country below Chattanooga (a plaque two miles east of
Calhoun, Georgia, denotes the site of the Cherokee capital New
Echota).

However, it was the other two trails which most concerned
the French. The Upper Path went due west from Augusta to
reach an important segment of the Creek tribe below Atlanta.
From there, after the rum, muskets, and blankets which comprised most of the trade articles had been exchanged for deer
skins (there were no beaver in the South), many traders continued across the Georgia pinelands into the territory of the
Alabama division of the Creeks along the Tallapoosa and Coosa
Rivers. Most of the pack trains went no farther, for the arduous
journey had already taken a month of hot, dusty travel. But a
few, whose sights were on the distant Chickasaws, set out on the
Old Chickasaw Path, skirting the southern terminus of the Appalachians around Birmingham before arriving several weeks later,
weary and sore, at the villages of the small, but extremely
warlike tribe around Tupelo, Mississippi.

The other trail, known as the Lower Path, led southwest
from Augusta to seek out another Creek division just below the
falls of the Chattahoochee around modern Columbus, Georgia.
Other Creeks were near Montgomery; and beyond them, ranging
throughout central Mississippi, were the powerful Choctaws.
The path was not frequented in Choctaw country, for the venture took on a decided element of danger among that French-
allied tribe. Yet not all Choctaw divisions felt the same adhesion
to the French, and their eagerness for cheaper British goods was
a constant lure to the Carolinian traders.

As distinguished from the French, the English used only land routes, since no rivers flowed westward along their line of march. Their heavy, ofttimes bulky, goods were transported by packhorses, usually purchased from the Cherokees. Land travel was far more difficult than that by river. Whereas a pair of voyageurs could carry nearly a thousand pounds of cargo in their birchbarks and could make up to two hundred miles a day downstream, a Carolinian needed six or seven pack-horses to tote that much—and he would be lucky if he made fifteen miles after a day of sweating, cursing, pleading, and plodding.

An average trading outfit consisted of around thirty horses, four traders, and an equal number of hired ruffians to keep the horses moving and guard against stealing forays by the Indians. For distant, more dangerous ventures a number of outfits combined, and Charlevoix reported a caravan of 120 English horses arriving at a Choctaw village—a most distressing development, since that tribe was the mainstay of French power in the Louisiana territory.

Although the Carolinian traders offered the French stiff competition in Alabama and Mississippi, they were never able to challenge their supremacy seriously. For one thing they had troubles with the Yamasees, Creeks, and Cherokees on their own borders. For another, there were no major English outposts to compare with New Orleans, Mobile, or Fort Toulouse, which the French built in 1714 to contest British access to the Creek tribes around modern Montgomery. And lastly, the vast herds of deer, which supported the trade, were gradually decimated. (The killing was enormous: in 1748 alone 160,000 deerskins were exported from Charleston.)

New Orleans continued a slow but steady growth, both as the result of the deerhide trade with the Indians and from the mildly prosperous tobacco and rice plantations which sent their products to the Crescent City for export to Europe and the West Indian plantations. But the upriver trade never assumed the proportions it could have under the direction of a man such as La Salle. The connection with the northern beaver country was very weak. The fault lay not with the broad-flowing Mississippi, the continent's greatest natural highway, but with the pitifully ineffective organization operating up north—particularly in the Illinois country, the key to the success of Louisiana.

The main problem was with the Fox tribe, who not only ravaged Wisconsin for twenty-five years, but worse still, extended their raids into Illinois. The result was that the Illini, already deathly afraid of the Iroquois, feared to journey into the countryside in search of beaver.

However the Illinois country managed to survive and eventually several thousand Franco-Illini farmers turned Kaskaskia into the breadbasket of Louisiana, as Charlevoix had prophesied. Soon a more or less regular procession of trading vessels plied the Mississippi carrying Kaskaskia grain, buffalo wool, and handicraft products to New Orleans in exchange for manufactured goods.

Much of the traveling was done in pirogues: logs hollowed out by fire, the largest of which could accommodate eight men with their baggage. Charlevoix, voyaging down the Mississippi in a pirogue in 1721, gives us an excellent description of the boat and the reasons for its use:

> People do not chose to venture themselves in canoes of birchbark on the Mississippi, by reason that the river constantly carries down with the current a number of trees, or else receives them from other rivers which fall into it; and many of these trees stopping on some point of land or on some shoal, there is danger every moment of running foul of a branch or root under water, which would be sufficient to break these frail vehicles to pieces, expecially when in order to avoid an enemy or for some other reason you are obliged to travel by night . . .

> They must therefore substitute pirogues in place of canoes of bark, that is to say, trunks of trees hollowed, which are not subject to these inconveniences, but are bad going vessels, and not easily managed. I have one made of a walnut tree, but so narrow that it cannot carry sail; and my guides being accustomed to those little paddles made use of in canoes,

are far from being expert at the management of the oar.
Besides, if the wind rises ever so little, the water comes into
the pirogue; and this often happens at this season of the
year.[22]

Being round and having no keel, the pirogues were extremely tippy. Thus a larger flat-bottomed boat called a bateau
was often substituted where sufficient men or cargo warranted. A
bateau could hold up to twenty-four men; ten of whom rowed
and one of whom maneuvered the cumbersome wooden rudder.
Even more impressive were the demigalleys that could carry
fifty or sixty men. The advantage of such a sturdy ship was that
its high sides afforded protection from the arrows of the hostile
tribes who frequented the river.

The danger of Indian attack was not taken lightly—especially from the Cherokee and Chickasaw allies of the Carolinians
who supplied them with muskets. "Not long ago," Charlevoix
recorded in his journal while taking a pirogue from Kaskaskia for
New Orleans, "the Cherokees massacred thirty Frenchmen near
this place." Even more dangerous were the Chickasaws, as the
nervous Jesuit then added: "A few days after I passed, the
Chickasaws had their revenge of two Frenchmen who followed
me in a pirogue. These Indians lying in ambush among the canes
on the banks of the river, as soon as they saw the French
opposite to them, made a rustling among the canes without
showing themselves; the two men believing it was a bear or some
other wild beast drew near in to take it; but just as they were
going to land the Indians discharged their muskets at them,
which laid them dead on the spot." To this Charlevoix attaches
the uneasy statement: "I was very lucky not to be perceived by
the Chickasaw, for my rowers would lose no opportunity of
hunting."

Since the pirogue, because it was small and easily made,
was the primary mode of transportation on the lower Mississippi,
we are fortunate to have the record of one Father Du Poisson, a
missionary making the journey upstream in a pirogue in 1727:

"Our baggage and that of our oarsmen made a mass which was more than a foot higher than the sides of our two pirogues. We perched upon a pile of chests and packages, and were powerless to change our position." Paddling close to the shore to avoid the mid-river current, they were barely beyond New Orleans when one of the many overhanging branches smacked against a chest, which toppled onto one of the travelers who, in turn, barely saved himself from falling into the river.

It was slow going in the overburdened boats—barely twenty-five or thirty miles a day—far less than that when one took into account the looping course of the river. The heat was sweltering with day after day devoid of any refreshing breeze. To add to their discomfort, the perspiration running down their faces and soaking through their clothing attracted innumerable flies "whose sting is so sharp—or, rather, so burning—that it seems as if a little spark had fallen on the part that they have stung." The travelers, afraid to make any quick movement that might overturn the pirogue, had to endure the flies as best they could.

But this was not their worst complaint. What follows must surely be a classic in the lore of travel discomfort:

> The greatest torture—without which everything else would have been only a recreation, but which passes all belief and could never be imagined in France unless it had been experienced—is the mosquitoe. . . . This little creature has caused more swearing since the French came to Mississippi than had been done before that time in all the rest of the world. . . . We are eaten, devoured; they enter our mouths, our nostrils, our ears. Our faces, hands, and bodies are covered with them. Their sting penetrates the clothing and leaves a red mark on the flesh. . . .
>
> After having hastily eaten our supper, we are impatient to bury ourselves under our *baires* [shelters made of canvas supported by cane arches stuck in the earth], although we know we shall stifle with the heat. But with whatever skill,

whatever adroitness we slip under the *baires*, we always find that some mosquitoes have entered, and only one or two are needed to make us spend a wretched night.[23]

And so the years passed in this extensive empire knitted together by the liquid cords of the water roads. The St. Lawrence settlements took on permanent roots as a hundred and fifty years went by since their founding by Champlain. With a population reaching fifty-five thousand in the north and six thousand in Louisiana, with many generations of French and Indians living about Kaskaskia, Green Bay, Vincennes and a dozen or more lesser villages, and with the fur trade firmly in French hands it seemed as if the trans-Appalachian region would forever ring to Indian tom-toms and voyageurs' songs.

But while the empire looked impressive on maps, it was apparent to many that it was crumbling within. For one thing, neither the numbers of beaver nor of deer (the empire's economic bases) could keep up with the slaughter. Duluth told of having to hack his way through over a hundred beaver dams while making his way down a small river flowing into Lake Superior. Yet a generation later, the beaver were gone and trappers had to go farther west into the Lake of the Woods to find them.

For another thing, the French had never been successful in large-scale immigration—certainly nothing to match the tremendous influx of English into the coastal colonies. This wasn't the fault of the French kings. Louis XIV required every merchant ship sailing to New France to carry a certain number of colonists. Soldiers of the Carignan regiment and the garrisons of Montreal and Quebec were encouraged to remain when their enlistments were over by a grant of food, farmland and a tantalizing sum of money. But the lure of the midwestern Indian country was so great that a staggering proportion of the men who should have become the progenitors of large families preferred the exciting life of a voyageur or *coureur*. Thus while the population of New France barely inched upwards, the population of their English competitors rocketed beyond two million.

Most serious of all was the catastrophies overtaking the Indians. When Champlain made contact with the red men there were probably upwards to a hundred thousand Indians living between the Atlantic and the Mississippi—an effective bulwark against English expansion. But once the Europeans put muskets in their hands and goaded them into competing for beaver pelts, a most destructive warfare broke out. One has only to recall the horrible campaigns of the Iroquois, where entire tribes (such as the Hurons and Eries) were massacred, to understand the serious consequences of these Indian civil wars. And the Iroquois were not alone. Ottawas and Potawatamis killed a large portion of the Fox at Detroit—and the Fox in turn virtually destroyed the Illini. In the South the Choctaws broke up the Natchez; while the Chickasaws constantly killed Choctaw bands.

The French themselves were helping eliminate the people who were most essential to their trade empire. Charlevoix's journal is filled with descriptions of wild Indian drinking orgies. The Indians admitted to Charlevoix that they knew brandy was destroying them, but they could not resist it.

But it wasn't warfare or brandy which created the greatest danger to an Indian population that Charlevoix estimated to be just one twentieth of what it had been 150 years earlier. The main problem was sicknesses the white men inadvertently brought. Never having been exposed to such ills as smallpox, the Indian race had no resistance to the vicious disease. As a result whole tribes were decimated. Who can ever forget this picture drawn by Charlevoix of the demise of the Arkansas tribe—the people who had hosted La Salle and who the French spoke admiringly of as *les beaux hommes,* ("the handsome men"):

I found the village of the Arkansas in great desolation. Some time ago a Frenchman passing this way was taken ill of the smallpox. The infection was at first communicated to a few of the Indians, and soon after to the whole nation. The burial-place appeared like a forest of stakes and posts, on which was suspended almost everything in use amongst these Indians.

I pitched my tent pretty near the village and all the night I heard nothing but weeping, in which the men joined as well as the women . . .[24]

Thus neither by immigration nor by natural increase could the French and Indians keep pace with the English. Yet for many years the French and Indians, provided with amazing mobility and cohesiveness by their vast river-road transportation system, were able to hold their own against their more numerous, but far more divided adversaries. Indeed, the woodland wars that began in 1689 resulted in the virtual halt of English westward expansion.

Divided, the English colonists had no chance of victory. But gradually the King's Highway snaked down the coast, linking the major cities, and, by providing for an interchange of newspapers and mail as well as merchandise and statesmen, brought a degree of unity to the Thirteen Colonies. Then the English struck back with shattering decisiveness.

6.   Through Woods and Thickets

The English moved hesitantly and with great difficulty into the shadowy forest which bristled about them. It was "a hideous and desolate wilderness," William Bradford wrote, recalling his first impression as he stood on the deck of the sea-battered *Mayflower*. "The whole country," he continued, "full of woods and thickets, represented a wild and savage hue. . . . What could now sustain us but the Spirit of God and His grace."

The pious Pilgrims were not alone in beseeching God and the powers of righteousness to protect them from the "hideous" wilderness; the Puritans, whose settlements at Boston, Salem, and Cambridge soon had them outnumbering by many thousands the little hamlet on too-shallow Plymouth Bay, were even more fearful. The Puritans saw life as a perpetual battle between God and Satan; and, though the ultimate outcome would be the complete victory of God, the crafty Devil was certainly reaping more than his share of gains in the present.

Since nearly everyone believed in the machinations of Satan, often called the Black Man, it was not strange that this evildoer should adopt the dark, encircling forest as his haunt. The forests—omnipresent, mantling hill and valley—were moody and foreboding beyond all comprehension. The trees were virgin timber, rulers of the landscape since the last glacial ice seeped into the soggy earth some ten thousand years earlier.

75

They were huge, uncompromising creations, often towering fifteen stories, with massive trunks sixteen feet in diameter. Their
matted, outspread branches permitted only an occasional lance
of light to penetrate the gloom below. The ground was a tangled
conglomeration of rotting limbs and dense, nearly impenetrable,
thickets. Binding together the ponderous trees, the fallen timbers, and the sharp brambles was a maze of vines, many as thick
as a man's wrist, able to resist all but the keenest axe blade.

Because such a forest made travel extremely difficult, when
some of the earliest land-hungry pioneers set out from coastal
Massachusetts for the fertile vales of Connecticut, they went by
ship around Cape Cod. But the ocean was unpredictable. While
few colonists suffered the experience of John Smith and the
Jamestown settlers, who were becalmed for six long weeks, many
had difficulties similar to those of the Pilgrims who found it
impossible to get past the wild surf around Cape Cod: "they fell
(wrote William Bradford) amongst dangerous shoals and roaring breakers, and they were so far entangled therewith as they
conceived themselves in great danger . . ."

Thus, with the sea unsatisfactory, many New Englanders
fell back on land transportation. It was rough going for these
trailblazers. The only tracks through the hostile forest were
narrow footpaths made by Indian warriors—and a war party
walking single file, unencumbered by baggage, hunching beneath the overhanging tree limbs, did not make the kind of
roadway needed by white pioneers. One has only to read the
bare commentary of John Winthrop, governor of Massachusetts,
to see the difference: "June 30, 1636. Mr. Hooker, pastor of the
church of New Town [Cambridge] and the most of his congregation went to Connecticut. His wife was carried in a horse-litter.
And they drove a hundred and sixty cattle, and fed of their milk
by the way."

Here they are: nearly a hundred men, women, and children,
plunging into the mysterious forest, their cattle rambling around
them. The men would have their muskets primed and ready:
dangerous Nipmucks, Wampanoags, Narragansetts and other
tribesmen frequented these lonely paths.

For two long weeks the expedition forced its way westward (along a route that modern travelers on the Massachusetts Turnpike cover in less than an hour and a half). As each day ended, they would round up their cattle, post their guards, and try to sleep. At times like these, with the last embers of the campfire turning the thick tree trunks blood-red, the pioneers must have had uneasy thoughts about the witchery that was so much a part of the Puritan culture—perhaps remembering tales similar to that related by Nathaniel Hawthorne:

A story about the Black Man . . . how he haunts this forest, and carries a book with him—a big, heavy book with iron clasps; and how this ugly Black Man offers his book and an iron pen to everybody that meets him here among the trees; and they are to write their names with their own blood. And then he sets his mark on their bosoms! [25]

As conversation died, the pioneers would try to sleep—while the moonlight made spectral patterns across the forest floor and the hot, midsummer wind rustled the leaves like Satanic laughter.

But eventually they reached the site of Springfield on the rich Connecticut River bottomland. For persons used to the bleak, rocky soil of eastern Massachusetts, the lush valley must have seemed like a gift from God. "I have spent this morning in riding through Paradise," a later traveler wrote. "My eyes never beheld so fine a country . . . Nothing can exceed [its] beauty and fertility . . ."

Soon other groups, hearing of Connecticut's fabulous richness, began to follow what became known as the Old Connecticut Path. It started at Cambridge, continued west along modern U.S. 20 through Waltham, then branched off just beyond Weston on Massachusetts 126 (to this day called the Old Connecticut Path) to make its way past Westboro and Oxford to Springfield. Soon the trail was grooved by hobnailed footware and the iron shoes of the packhorses. Axemen chopped down overhanging branches, then felled the brambles, and finally widened the trail so that women on horse-borne litters could procede without being battered by the forest. Eventually, as the migration grew, a second and slightly shorter trail, known as the New Connecticut Path, was blazed to Springfield by way of South Sudbury and Worcester.

In a few years the Connecticut Valley was dotted with growing villages: Windsor, Wethersfield, and Hartford. And around them clustered hundreds of prosperous farms, slowly encroaching on the once-omnipotent forest. The mighty trees, though swathed in mystery and magic, were no match for the persevering farmers. To kill the giants, all the pioneers had to do was to cut a strip of bark from around the trunk. During the growing season the lifeblood of the dying titan oozed from the incision. The following spring, when the forest normally leaved out, the girdled trees remained lifeless, their towering forms, once so impressive, now gaunt, stark, ugly. Then the farmers planted corn and wheat on sunny land that had formerly been the preserve of ferns and trillium. And when the crop had been harvested in the autumn, they proceeded at their leisure to hack down the skeletal trees and burn them.

The Indians grew fretful as smoldering timber made the air hazy year after year, announcing that the forest hunting grounds were shrinking at an alarming rate. In 1675 hostilities erupted in the form of King Philip's War, the most vicious series of frontier battles that have ever consumed the continent. The Connecticut Valley was under siege. Blockhouses sprang up at every town, yet even so Northampton, Hadley, Hatfield, and Springfield were almost destroyed. Nevertheless, although the Indians and the whites were nearly evenly matched when it came to numbers, the Indians lacked the resources for a prolonged conflict. When a New England army burned the fields upon which the Indians were depending for winter food, all Red resistance collapsed.

With the Indians out of the way, land transportation was again free to develop. There were already trails between New Haven and the villages of her short-lived colony which extended along the coast to Stamford. As New York, which had been snatched from the fuming Dutch governor, Peter Stuyvesant, in 1664, increased in size and commerce, the need for dependable land communication with that town arose. Not only did New England merchants, farmers, and travelers wish for easier access to New York, but so did King Charles himself—it would help unite his northern provinces against the danger of attack by the Dutch or the French. Thus in 1672 the king wrote to Francis Lovelace, governor of New York, that he would be more than happy if it were possible for his "American subjects to enter into a close correspondency with each other." Lovelace, quick to know an order when he heard one, made a rough horseback journey to Hartford where he and Governor John Winthrop, Junior, drew up plans for a postal service to be established between New York and Boston.

Almost nothing is known of the initial mail journey—not even the name of the foolhardy fellow who braved the dangers of Indians and the hostile wilderness to reach distant Boston. His problems were amplified by the fact that the trail was so poorly marked that it was not uncommon for travelers (at least those reckless souls who ventured into the forest without local guides) to strike off on a false path and wander around completely lost for several days.

The official starting date was set for January 1, 1673; but the rider was forced to while away three weeks (presumably at some of the Dutch brandy shops which comprised nearly a quarter of New York's buildings) waiting for the arrival of dispatches from Albany. When at last he had his saddlebags filled, he spurred his horse past the wall the Dutch had built to keep their cattle from being hijacked by Indians (now Wall Street) and headed through the knobby hills of Harlem for Boston 260 miles away. His difficulties started almost immediately. Southern Connecticut was a hopeless obstacle course of wide rivers to ford, swamps to tramp through, and brambles to avoid. At Hartford he was ceremoniously welcomed by Governor Winthrop, who gave him a fresh horse in accordance with his agreement with Lovelace.

Onward, again, north past pretty farmlands scattered along the placid Connecticut, fording the river at Springfield, then east into the primeval timber, through Worcester via the New Con-

necticut Path, until he and his exhausted nag stumbled across
the billowing grasslands of the narrow neck of land which led to
Boston, then virtually an island.

Happy citizens saluted the postman at the town gates, twin
brick arches reaching across the neck from shore to shore, near
modern Blackstone Square. On down Washington Street he continued, passing cattle grazing on the Commons and Beacon Hill
where a tar basket had been placed atop a tall pole to be fired
upon the approach of a hostile force. At last he reached the
environs of the statehouse—a rickety wooden structure nowhere
near as impressive as the two and a half story brick building
constructed in 1713 which still stands. At a tavern near the
statehouse, possibly that of Richard Fairbank the distribution
point for local mail as early as 1639, he tossed his satchels
triumphantly onto the bar. There must have been cheers and
more than ample toasts. Only two weeks from New York to
Boston! Who could have believed it?

Although the Boston Post Road (better known as the King's
Highway until the Revolution made the name unpopular) was
now a fact, for many years it remained little more than a vague
trail through the hovering forest. About the only persons who
knew much about it (aside from the farmers and villagers familiar with the dozen or so miles in their own localities) were the
post riders. For this reason anyone leaving Boston in the early
days of travel made it a point to latch onto the mailman. One of
those who did so was a courageous lady by the name of Sarah
Knight, whose 1704 journal tells of experiences similar to those
which must have unnerved most first generation travelers.

Trotting her horse beside the trusty mailman, she left Boston
and headed into the gloomy forest. About two in the afternoon
they reached what passed for an inn, where Mrs. Knight received a lunch she never forgot:

Having called for something to eat, the woman brought in a
twisted thing like a cable, but somewhat whiter; and laying
it on the board, tugged for life to bring it into a capacity to

spread: which having with great pains accomplished, she served in a dish of pork and cabbage—I suppose the remains of dinner. The sauce was of a deep purple, which I thought was boiled in her dye kettle; the bread was Indian. . . . I, being hungry, got a little down; but my stomach was soon cloyed . . ."[26]

As soon as lunch was over, they were off—with unhappy Sarah's stomach probably still cloyed. Fourteen bumpy miles brought them to the next inn. As it was now nearly dark, Sarah had her choice of spending the night here or continuing on with the post rider, who had many more miles to make. Although he tried to dissuade her by warning of a river they must ford "which was so fierce a horse could sometimes hardly stem it," Sarah preferred to stay with him as guide rather than hazard the crossing by herself by daylight. And so the weary lady continued down the road.

As night came, the forest closed in around them, moody, formidable, eerie. There was no moon, and the only illumination was from the stars, whose pale rays were often blotted out by ghostly, wind-whining tree branches. In this uncertain light "each lifeless trunk, with its shattered limbs, appeared an armed enemy; and every little stump like a ravenous devourer. Nor could I so much as discern my guide when at any distance, which added to the terror."

In the midst of this menacing blackness, they came to the dreaded river. The post rider drew up close to Sarah and together they cautiously descended the steep bank. Sarah could not see the churning water until her horse started into it. She reports "[I] now rallied all the courage I was mistress of, knowing that I must either venture my fate of drowning, or be left [behind] . . ." Giving the reins to her horse, she let him pick his own way among the invisible, slippery rocks. The water bubbled up around her. One misstep by the animal and she would be swept down the river, lost in an instant from the helping hand of the post rider. But the river was safely crossed and Mrs. Knight continued on to Connecticut in safety.

Not only unbridged rivers made the Post Road dangerous. As frequent use pucked away the grass cover, erosion
exposed the maze of roots which underlay the soil. "Roots
crossed the path," wrote one concerned traveler, "some above
ground and some beneath, so that my horse's feet would frequently get between the roots and he would flounce and blunder, in danger of breaking his own limbs as well as mine." Since
there were many miles devoid of villages, inns, or even farm
houses, a wayfarer who pitched from a horse and broke his leg,
was in serious trouble. It might be days before anyone came
along. And the same element of danger was present should he
become snowbound by one of the many storms which descended
on New England without warning. Because winter was a favorite time to travel (since frozen rivers were easy to cross), this
was a disquieting factor to many horsemen on the road.

Gradually, however, the roots were chopped away, the road
graded to a degree, and in places (such as the segment between
Brookfield and Wilbraham) a crude stone pavement provided.
Then stagecoaches began appearing—and with them a great
increase in travel. At first the coaches were exceedingly uncomfortable devices, being merely springless farm wagons with a
canvas top tacked on to wobbly, wooden supports and hard,
backless benches to serve as seats. After a while paneled sides
were placed on the wagons, benches gave way to cushioned
seats, springs were added to the axles, and leather curtains were
hung over the openings to help keep out the weather.

Even so, stagecoaches were hardly pleasure craft. In the
summer, dust filled the interior with a soupy, nearly unbreatha-
ble brew. If one drew the curtains to shut it out, the heat became
unbearable. It was worse in the winter when passengers would
often find "the rain and snow descending through the roof, our
hats frozen to our capes, and our cloaks to one another." When a
large river was reached, the passengers had to wait for the ferry
(sometimes for several hours if there were stages ahead of them
—or if the boatman decided to take a long lunch). Then they sat
nervously while they and all their belongings were rowed across
the ofttimes swirling river in a make-do flatboat that might spin

out of control at any moment. Even where smaller rivers were spanned by bridges, one was not always at ease—as witness one account: "In the morning we crossed a bridge all full of holes, and were grateful to the Saviour for our safety as we considered the very apparent danger."

Foreign visitors were shocked at the condition both of American coaches and American roads. An indignant European proclaimed:

> I must repeat again and again that the American stage-coaches are untrustworthy, and often an insult to common sense. It is impossible to conceive the frightful inconvenience of these vehicles. You are fully exposed to inclement weather and soaked as if you were out of doors. You are crushed, shaken, thrown about, bumped in a manner that cannot adequately be described. Every mile there is a new accident and you must get out into the mud while the dammage is repaired. It is not unusual to see the coaches shattered, the passengers crippled, and the horses drowned. . . . The roads are truly breakneck, likely at any moment to upset you." [27]

Nevertheless coaches were the most popular means to reach New York. The journey usually began from Boston's Scollay Square at a bleary hour: "We started from Boston at half-past three Monday morning," ran one account, "with twelve passengers and their full complement of baggage on board. The way was very dark so that, though I rode with the driver, it was some time before I discovered we had six horses." The route led down Washington Street to Roxbury, then crossed the Muddy River (now a tastefully landscaped park) and turned northward through Brookline on Harvard Street until it reached the Charles River ferry to enter Cambridge.

Cambridge was a handsome town with many fine mansions, such as that built in 1759 on Brattle Street by Major John Vassall and now known as the Longfellow house. Harvard College was there too, of course: America's first university founded the same year that Reverend Hooker and his congregation left the town to forge the Old Connecticut Path. By the middle of the eighteenth century there were about ninety young men living, eating, and studying at Harvard Hall, Stoughton College and Massachusetts Hall—a trio of multistoried brick buildings that still stands on the modern campus.

At Cambridge the highway turned sharply west to Watertown and Waltham, from which point its route was identical with modern U.S. 20—still called the Boston Post Road in this portion of Massachusetts. Passing the Old Connecticut Path turnoff (now Massachusetts 126) a few miles beyond Weston, the stages clattered on to South Sudbury, twenty-four miles from Boston. It was about sunup by this time and a stop was now made for breakfast—usually at the famous Wayside Inn, open for business since 1716. A blast from the driver's horn while some distance away, announced to the tavern-keeper that hungry passengers were arriving; and as they began tramping into the barroom (which modern tourists can visit) maids were already loading the tables with food, which the travelers, jostled for nearly six hours, wolfed down.

Continuing on to Worcester, an "elegant and well peopled" town forty-eight miles from Boston, they had dinner at one of the many taverns—probably that kept by Levi Pease, one of the proprietors of the stage line. These dinners were spectacles of great bounty. John Adams lists a typical Colonial repast: "ducks, hams, chickens, beef, pig, tarts, creams, custards, jellies, fools, trifles, floating islands, beer, porter, punch, wine and a long etc." The price of such a feast was around fourteen cents, though presumably a penny or two more if the etc. was long enough.

After dinner the coach was back on the road, covering the twelve miles to Spencer before the first day of travel was over. Having bumped over sixty miles in seventeen hours, the passengers were only too glad to collapse into bed—even though there would be half a dozen snoring guests in the same room, two or more of either sex in a bed—as Sarah Knight discovered to her dismay. But "the beds were good and the sheets clean," wrote Jean Pierre Brissot, a young Frenchman touring the country.

At four the next morning the coach riders were on their way

once more. The forest was close about them now; but every so often they came upon a clearing where a stone fence and a tiny, one story farmhouse bespoke of a pioneer's battle against nature. They began entering hilly country and the road became very bad. Inexperienced travelers wondered why the carriage that had carried them to Spencer had been replaced by a crude wagon without springs. But as the wagon slammed over rocks and skidded down precipitous slopes the reason became clear: "By the time we had run thirty miles among the rocks," Brissot explained, "we were persuaded that a carriage with springs would very soon have turned over and crashed."

Slowly the scenery joggled by: Wheelock Hill, the hamlet of Brookfield (where breakfast was usually served), Marks Mountain, Palmer, and finally North Wilbraham. Here a change for the worse was made (yes, it was possible). The grumbling passengers would be herded out of the uncomfortable, though commodious, wagon and packed into a little chariot drawn by two horses. When Brissot's companions objected to the cramped conditions, the "conductor said . . . that there were so few travelers in this part of the road that he could not afford to run with more than two horses, since most of the traffic from New York ended in Connecticut and most of that from Boston in Worcester." Then they were off like lightning, speeding downhill at a throat-clutching speed, roaring into Springfield ten miles away in less than an hour.

Springfield was an important town, not only located at the main fording point over the Connecticut River, but also at the junction of the traders' trail coming in from Albany, the colonial fur metropolis. After dinner at Springfield, travelers boarded a handsome coach on the west side of the river and continued to Hartford in style.

The beauty of the Connecticut Valley impressed everyone who traversed it. "It is a fertile plain," wrote Brissot, "enclosed between two mountains which render difficult its communications by land with the other states. It is watered by the superb Connecticut River, safe and easy to navigate . . . It is really the paradise of the United States." As Hartford was approached, the

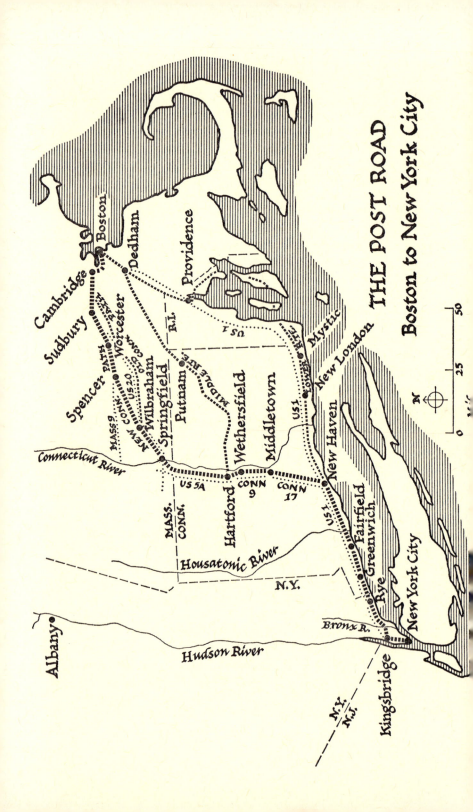

THE POST ROAD
Boston to New York City

Boston · Cambridge · Sudbury · Spencer · Worcester · Wilbraham · Springfield · Dedham · Providence · Putnam · Wethersfield · Middletown · Mystic · New London · New Haven · Fairfield · Greenwich · Rye · Kingsbridge · New York City

Albany · Hartford

Connecticut River · Housatonic River · Hudson River · Bronx R.

SPENCER PATH · MASS 9 · US 20 · NEW CONN · MIDDLE RD · US 1 · LOWER RTE · US 5A · CONN 9 · CONN 17

R.I. · MASS. CONN. · N.Y. · N.Y. N.J.

N · Mi's · 0 · 25 · 50

way opened up into "vast meadows covered with herds of enormous cattle destined for the market of New York and even
Philadelphia." Apple orchards grew close to the highway, fragrant and white in the spring, heavy with red fruit in the
fall—from which some of the most delicious cider in America
was made. Young colts frolicked through the grasslands, bliss-
fully unaware of their future as workhorses on torrid West
Indian plantations. The roadside inns boasted fantastic concoctions of cooling drinks made from Caribbean rum, particularly
favored by the grizzled coach drivers who, under the influence,
enjoyed demonstrating their skill at barely missing boulders and
skinning cattle shanks.

The prosperity of Connecticut had attracted a large population. "From Bissills in Windsor," reported John Adams in 1771,
"to Hartford ferry, 8 miles, is one continued street—houses all
along and a vast prospect of level country on each hand."
Hartford, the terminus of another, much less used thoroughfare,
the Middle Road coming in diagonally across Connecticut from
Boston, had some "very handsome and large houses." Nevertheless, the statehouse was a not so imposing structure, and was
replaced in 1796 by the pleasing brick and brownstone building
which still stands in its own park in the center of the city.

The next morning before dawn the coaches started out for
Wethersfield on what Adams considered "the finest ride in America." The fields of grain were so lush and green that one could
only gasp in wonder. Wethersfield was a booming town in
Colonial days, competing with Hartford for preeminence. Dozens of oceangoing vessels moored along her river docks loading
corn and onions. Many distinguished men had homes here—fully
140 of them still stand. Perhaps best known was the Webb house,
then called "Hospitality Hall, constructed in 1752 and used by
Washington while he planned the Yorktown campaign.

From Wethersfield the Post Road continued along the Connecticut River to Middletown, which John Adams referred to as
"the most beautiful town of all." Continuing, he wrote: "When I
first rode into the town, which was upon the top of a hill, there
opened before me the most beautiful prospect of the river, and

the intervals and improvements on each side of it, and the
mountains at about 10 miles distance both on the east and west
side of the river, and the main body of the town at a distance. I
went down this hill, and into a great gate which led me to the
very banks of the river." Passing through the gate, the road was
bordered by land that Adams thought as rich as the proverbial
soil of Egypt. "After riding in this enchanting meadow for some
time," Adams explained, "you come to another gate which lets
you into the main body of the town, which is ornamented, as is
the meadow I just mentioned, with fine rows of trees and appears to me as populous, as compact, and as polite as
Hartford." [28]

From Middletown the road left the Connecticut River to run
through Durham, where passengers were transferred to new
coaches with fresh horses. After passing the broad rampart
known as Trimountain (now a scenic state park), the stages
were on the coastal plain leading to New Haven. The road was
level here, well traveled, so safe that well-bred young ladies rode
far out into the countryside—something unheard of in other
parts of the continent. Brissot, a true French gallant, was quite
taken with the carefree maidens: "On the road you often come
upon these fair Connecticut girls driving a carriage or galloping
boldly alone on horseback and wearing fine hats, white aprons,
and calico gowns." But he could not suppress concern to find
"maidens hazarding themselves alone without protectors in the
public stagecoaches," viewing himself, no doubt, as an ideal
protector.

New Haven, at the junction of the Lower Road, which led to
Boston via Providence, was a charming town, settled as early as
1638 by Puritans and for twenty-six years thereafter the center of
her own independent colony which reached along the coast as
far as Stamford. Although most visitors to New Haven would
wish to see Connecticut Hall (built in 1752 and still standing),
home of famed Yale University, Brissot was able to remain in
New Haven only long enough for dinner, then resumed his
journey—now on the coastal portion of the Post Road along a
route currently followed by U.S. 1.

The ferry over the broad Housatonic usually delayed the coaches, but they could still make the last twenty-two miles to one of the many comfortable inns at Fairfield. Adams liked to dine at Bulkley's, whose tavern stood at 290 Beach Road and whose home (currently the residence of the town clerk) was across the street. Others chose the Sun Tavern, constructed in 1780 and standing today on Town Hall Green. Later travelers liked Benson's Tavern at the corner of the Old Post Road (it still bears this name) and Benson Road.

If anyone did not sleep well in Fairfield's snug taverns, it might have been because they knew what was just ahead. A shaken Brissot wrote:

> The agreeable part of our journey ended at Fairfield. From there to Rye, 33 miles, we had to struggle against rocks and precipices. I knew not which to admire most in the driver, his intrepedity or dexterity. I cannot conceive how he avoided twenty times dashing the carriage in pieces, and how his horses could retain themselves in descending the steep rocks. One of these is called Horseneck [at Greenwich]; a chain of rocks so precipitous that if a horse should slip the carriage must fall two or three hundred feet into a valley.[29]

Brissot makes no mention of a stop in Greenwich, which certainly held no pleasant memories for him as a result of his heart-thumping ride, but if he had he might have found Knapp's Tavern to be quite good. John Adams lodged here, as did many of the New England delegates going to and from the Continental Congresses in Philadelphia. The tavern, built in 1731, still stands, although now it is known as the Putnam cottage.

Brissot, wobbly from the harrowing ride, dined at Rye, three miles farther on. Prepared for the worst, he was agreeably surprised: "We stopped at one of the best taverns I have seen in America, kept by Mrs. Haviland. We had an excellent and cheap dinner. The air of the mistress was infinitely graceful and obliging; and she had a charming daughter, genteel and well educated, who played the piano very well." [30] Since John Adams and hundreds of travelers before and after him also enjoyed the hospitality of Mrs. Haviland (and her charming and, we hope beautiful, daughter), it is comforting to know that the ancient inn stands today in Rye, a most interesting museum.

The thirty-one miles from Rye to New York City were over a good surface, even and gravelly. The road (then as now called the Boston Post Road) followed much the same route as modern U.S. 1 from New Haven. When it reached the then-rural Bronx, it suddenly veered westward along Gun Hill Road to cross the Bronx River at William's Bridge. From there it proceeded one and a half miles farther on to Kingsbridge, where there was a tavern with some of the finest victuals around. And the setting was idyllic: "the Uncas River running before the door and verdant hills all around." After a repast, the coaches clattered down Broadway to the bridge which led over the Harlem River —at this point (before the channel was deepened and widened in recent times) more a muddy morass than the rather spacious inlet it became farther east. It wasn't until sixteen years after the Revolution that a bridge spanned the broader eastern portion of the river at Third Avenue to allow the Post Road more direct access to Manhattan.

Once over King's Bridge, the coaches continued down Broadway to the fork of modern St. Nicholas Avenue (just south of the George Washington Bridge). Here they angled across Manhattan along a route St. Nicholas still traces. The rugged terrain at Harlem Heights was surmounted at McGown's Pass (near Columbia University) and from there the road led through the northern edge of modern Central Park. Leaving the Park at 97th Street, the road meandered southward between Second and Fourth Avenues until it entered the city not far from Peter Stuyvesant's old farm or bowery.

Long before the travelers reached New York City, which huddled at the very tip of Manhattan Island extending not much beyond present-day Canal Street, they would pass large numbers of vehicle drivers: farmers with wagon loads of produce, teamsters carting in water (the only good supply was in springs some distance away), and dashing young men taking their ladies out for a spin in one-horse chaises. Many villas lined Turtle Bay not far from the United Nations Building. Here, in a sylvan setting, the young chaise-set enjoyed sumptuous turtle feasts. "These happen once or twice a week," observed Andrew Burnaby, a curious English preacher touring the middle colonies in 1760. "Thirty or forty gentlemen and ladies meet and dine together, drink tea in the afternoon, fish and amuse themselves till evening, and then return home in Italian chaises . . . a gentleman and lady in each chaise." As the Post Road reached a creek near the site of the Empire State Building, Burnaby tarried to peep at a quaint custom popular among the natives: "In the way there is a bridge, about three miles distant from New York, which you always pass over as you return, called the Kissing-bridge: where it is a part of the etiquette to salute the lady who has put herself under your protection."

Far out in the country the spire of Trinity Church was seen cutting into the sky (although now it is humbled into insignificance by the haughty skyscrapers of Wall Street). At last, entering the city, the coaches ground along streets filled with refuse, often with semiwild pigs barely escaping the horses' hooves. Yet this was not the case with the Dutch sections farther along. Persons, such as John Adams, who had never seen Dutch architecture, could not help but be impressed by the pre-English buildings which right up to the Revolution comprised half the town. "The houses are more grand [than those in Boston] as well as neat," Adams noted. And Washington Irving in his *History of New York* further describes the Hollanders' homes as made of "small black and yellow Dutch bricks . . . with an abundance of large doors and small windows on every floor, the date of its erection curiously designed by iron figures on the front." Then Irving added, with a characteristic twinkle, "and on the top of the roof was perched a fierce little weathercock to let the family into the important secret: which way the wind blew." [31]

After the coaches pulled into the depot near the present city hall, visitors might stroll south on Broadway to the rundown battlement at Battery Park. "From the Paradegrounds before the fort," Adams wrote, "you have a fine prospect of Hudsons River and of the East River or the Sound and of the Harbor." Or one might climb the steeple of one of the churches, as the overly energetic Adams did, "from which there is a very fine view." Others might just wish to saunter along the waterfront savoring the sea air and chatting with sailors and longshoremen loading the host of sailing vessels which made New York a rival of Boston, Philadelphia, and Charleston. The harbor was clear and unpolluted at this time, and Burnaby found enjoyment on a serene evening watching the "innumerable porpoises playing on the surface of the water."

However, there would probably be little thought for sight-seeing the first day—not after the bone-crunching four days and nights on the road. Certainly a person's first desire would be to locate an inn at which to recuperate. One of the finest was that run by Samuel Fraunces, a French-Negro from the West Indies (Fraunces' Tavern still stands at Broad and Pearl streets). Here the traveler would undoubtedly fall into a deep sleep, relieved that his ordeal on the Boston Post Road was over.

Yet for others the trek must continue on to Philadelphia . . .

7. Thirty Hours without Victuals

There had always been a road across Jersey—for the Lenni-Lenape, or Delaware, tribe who roamed the eastern Pennsylvania forests had a craving for the fish and oysters to be snared along the shores of New York Bay. Single file they went, gliding silently through the dense woodlands down a narrow but well-padded trail that skirted the rocky ridge of the Watchung Mountains. In good weather they slept under the stars. In bad they built bark shelters. Their food was what their arrows brought down or wild fruit picked along the way. Bronze as autumn leaves, stealthy as shadows, they were part of the forest. And their path, too, was part of the forest, detouring effortlessly around fallen timbers or mossy boulders, disappearing momentarily in swamps or meadows.

But then the white men came to straighten and rut the path so the forest could no longer claim it.

The first recorded use of the route was by the men of Peter Stuyvesant, czar of the Dutch in New York. The event was occasioned by the meddling Swedes, who plunked Fort Christina on a strategic overlook dominating the Delaware River where Wilmington would one day arise. More and more Swedish immigrants burrowed into the wooded countryside that Stuyvesant insisted was his alone, eventually establishing a dozen or so trading posts. This was irritating enough to the volatile Dutch commander. But in 1651 when the Swedes brazenly announced that their holdings reached upriver as far as the Trenton rapids, Stuyvesant conscripted a hundred and twenty traders, merchants, and mercenaries and sent them by sea and cross-country to terminate his antagonists' pretensions. Axemen cleared the way for the overland marchers with their packhorses staggering under the weight of guns, ammunition, and provisions.

Although Stuyvesant, operating from a fort he assembled on the site of New Castle, was successful in conquering the Swedes, he himself was shortly humbled by the English. Great Britain let the Delaware Valley and most of New Jersey lie fallow until an insistent Quaker named William Penn cajoled Charles II into donating a huge tract of land to him. In 1682 Penn braved the Atlantic to step ashore first amid the sullen Dutch at New Castle, then at the site he christened Philadelphia from the Greek for brotherly love. The name not only reflected his preoccupation with the peaceful philosophy of the Quakers, but was, perhaps, an unconscious attempt to remove the stigma of having Pennsylvania itself called after his father, a cannonading admiral whose wartime services to Charles II had disposed the king to grant William the territory.

The few grizzled Swedish traders squatting on the swamp and sand at the junction of the Delaware and the Schuylkill (hidden channel) must have grinned in amusement when proud Penn and his colonists had to live in dank riverbank caves while they constructed their first wooden homes. But the colony caught hold, and within three years there were six hundred sturdy structures facing the Delaware along Front Street.

Rapidly now the tide of immigration swelled as British and German farmers were lured to Pennsylvania both by Penn's astute propaganda and by favorable reports of his liberal constitution. The population of Philadelphia soared to twenty-five hundred by 1685, and quickly other towns sprung up along the path which was already being referred to as the King's Road. Postal service was commenced between Philadelphia and New York, but not all portions of the route were easy—and in 1696 the Pennsylvania Council recorded in its minutes the following complaint received from Andrew Hamilton, Post Master General:

It was formerly with great difficulty that the post could go to Philadelphia by land, to the great inconvenience of correspondence and trade; and that for remedy whereof and ac-

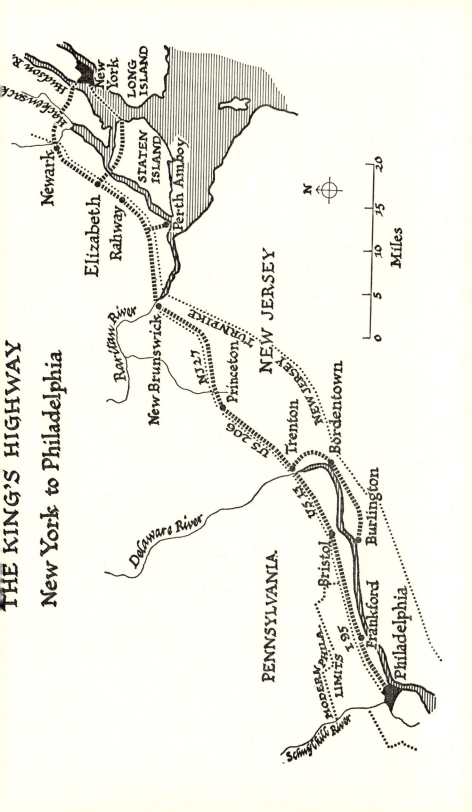

THE KING'S HIGHWAY
New York to Philadelphia

Hudson R.

Hackensack R.

New York

LONG ISLAND

Newark

Elizabeth

Rahway

STATEN ISLAND

Perth Amboy

Raritan River

New Brunswick

NEW JERSEY

NJ 27

Princeton

NEW JERSEY TURNPIKE

US 206

Trenton

Bordentown

Delaware River

US 13

Burlington

PENNSYLVANIA

Bristol

MODERN PHILA.
LIMITS

I 95

Frankford

Philadelphia

Schuylkill River

N

Miles

0   5   10   15   20

commodation of travellers a ferry had been erected on the
Jersey side at a great cost; but that the way was not yet made
from the landing on the Pennsylvania side to the King's
Road, to which is about three quarters of a mile and easily
cleared; and therefore requesting the Governor and Council
to approve the said road and give the necessary orders for
clearing it.

A sixty foot wide connection was accordingly made with the
Trenton ferry—while at the same time other thorofares feathered
into the countryside from the King's Road. And it was well that
the transportation system grew, for Philadelphia's expanding
population required good access with the interior. By 1700 the
city contained five thousand persons—and shortly it outdis-
tanced bustling New York and profit-minded Boston.

Our friend, Andrew Burnaby, arriving in 1760 when the city
had spiraled up to twenty thousand, spoke of it with awe:
"Philadelphia, if we consider that not eighty years ago the place
where it now stands was a wild and uncultivated desert inhabited by nothing but ravenous beasts and a savage people, must
certainly be the object of everyone's wonder and admiration." All
visitors were delighted by the broad, paved (!) streets which
bore the names of the trees which Penn himself had assigned
them. And there were even sidewalks for pedestrians! Wagons
crowded down to the riverside, where their cargos were sold to
merchants, who in turn exchanged them for the manufactured
goods carried to America by the great oceangoing argosies docking at the Front Street slips. Captains and merchants built neat
houses close to the waterfront—many of which can be visited
today on Elfreth's Alley, a most interesting and unique restora-
tion.

As Philadelphia expanded, it drew commerce from newly
emerging New Jersey farms as well as from the interior of
Pennsylvania—nearly nine thousand wagons were in use along
the scores of dirt roads which led to the dynamic city. Word
spread through the colonies that Philadelphia was the place for
bright up-and-comers, for men on the go, for the quick-witted;

and gradually the old Lenni-Lenape path was broadened by the tramping feet of potential tycoons.

But initially the way was not easy. From New York City one had to be ferried around Staten Island via the Kill Van Kull to Perth Amboy or, if one wished to extend the sometimes risky voyage, to New Brunswick fifteen miles up the Raritan. The trail across Jersey was about thirty miles long should one stop at Trenton, or forty-five if one chose to plod on as far as Burlington. From each of these two towns boats plied the Delaware to Philadelphia.

One of those who heard the call of booming Philadelphia was Ben Franklin, a youth of seventeen fleeing Boston from a distasteful apprenticeship under a jealous brother. In his autobiography Franklin gives a vivid account of the journey as it was during the days around 1723. His first adventure occurred just moments after boarding the ferry for Perth Amboy:

> In crossing the bay, we met with a squall that tore our rotten sails to pieces, prevented our getting into the Kill, and drove us upon Long Island. In our way, a drunken Dutchman, who was a passenger too, fell overboard. . . . When we drew near the island, we found it was at a place where there could be no landing, there being a great surf on the stony beach. So we dropped anchor, and swung round towards the shore. Some people came down to the water edge and hallow'd us, as we did to them; but the wind was so high, and the surf so loud, that we could not hear so as to understand each other. There were canoes on the shore, and we made signs, hand hallow'd that they should fetch us; but they either did not understand us or thought it impracticable, so they went away, and night coming on, we had no remedy but to wait till the wind should abate; and, in the mean time, the boatman and I concluded to sleep, if we could; and so crowded into the scuttle, with the Dutchman, who was still wet; and the spray beating over the head of our boat, leak'd through to

us, so that we were soon almost as wet as he. In this manner we lay all night, with very little rest; but, the wind abating the next day, we made a shift to reach Amboy before night, having been thirty hours on the water without victuals or any drink but a bottle of filthy rum . . .[32]

Although the ferry ride was the most dangerous portion of young Franklin's cross-Jersey hike, he experienced difficulties on land similar to those which must have affected many travelers. The evening he landed at Perth Amboy he contracted a fever. It could have been a desperate situation, with a minimum of medical facilities available, but Franklin drank cold water until his stomach bulged, sweated plentifully, and the next morning stumbled off, partially cured, into a pelting rain. By noon he had had enough. Weary from the effects of his fever and the constant sloshing through slippery mud, he stopped at one of the ramshackle little buildings which passed for inns that were sprinkled sparingly along the Jersey road.

After a worrisome night of persistent questioning by the innkeeper, who hoped Franklin might be a runaway bond servant for whom there might be a reward, Ben continued the next morning. Mile followed weary mile, the forest close about him, dark and malicious. Though the maples were flaming scarlet and the oaks just turning to mellow brown and maroon, there was a melancholy and unnerving mystery about the autumnal woodland that must have played on the young man's fears. He walked for hours on end seeing no inns or farmhouses—only the towering trees. The Jersey trip was nearly too much for him, and he found himself "beginning to wish that I had never left home."

He was more fortunate, however, in that night's lodging, for a Dr. Brown engaged him in a most friendly conversation. The next day Franklin arrived in Burlington, where he caught a boat headed for Philadelphia fifteen miles south. Yet his saga was not yet over:

. . . as there was no wind, we row'd all the way; and about midnight, not having yet seen the city, some of the company were confident we must have passed it, and would row no farther; the others knew not where we were; so we put toward the shore, got into a creek, landed near an old fence, with the rails of which we made a fire, the night being cold, in October, and there we remained till daylight.[33]

When chilly dawn broke, they discovered they were still slightly above Philadelphia. A few hours later they landed at the Market Street wharf and the young adventurer strolled ashore, his clothes dirty and frazzled, his stomach empty, and his sole stock of cash a solitary Dutch dollar.

But the King's Highway gradually improved. Soon freight wagons began creaking between Perth Amboy and Burlington or Trenton. The wagons, drawn by four to six straining horses, were especially designed for mud and mire, having iron-rimmed wheels nearly a foot wide. Sometimes the same rough-hewn vehicles hauled passengers. Then gaudy canvas tops were stretched across arching bands of wood and cushionless, backless oak benches were slapped down on the wagon floor. Although the transportation companies blandly advertised their conveniences as "flying machines," it took five days of agony to reach Philadelphia from New York.

However by the time Reverend Burnaby passed over the road in 1760, it was good enough for a chaise to be driven without bogging down more than a few times or hardly ever overturning. And when John Adams made the same trip to the First Continental Congress in 1774, the road could accommodate the largest carriage in reasonable safety, if not comfort.

Now there were several routes out of New York. "At nine o'clock," Adams wrote, "we crossed Powlus Hook Ferry to New Jersey—then Hackinsack ferry, then Newark ferry, and dined at Elizabeth Town." Burnaby, however, went via the Staten Island ferry, the nine-mile road across the island's top, then by scow to Elizabeth. This scow was half-rotten complained Peter Kalm, a thirty-two-year-old botanist sent to America in 1748 by the Swedish Academy of Sciences.

Kalm was favorably impressed with Elizabeth: "In and

about the town are many gardens and orchards, and it might truly be said that Elizabethtown is situated in a garden." Although few of the homes were particularly large since Elizabeth was merely a way point on the King's Highway, Boxwood Hall often caused travelers to pause in admiration—particularly when they learned it belonged to the eminent Elias Boudinot, later president of the Continental Congress.

Leaving Elizabeth and Boxwood Hall (which still stands), journeyers went over "as fine a road as ever was trod." The land was level; and as one angled southwest from Rahway, the musty air of New York Bay was replaced by zephyrs sweet with the fragrance of flax and hemp. Where there is now a maze of industries and a pall of smoke, Peter Kalm saw a clear and delightful vista of "houses, farms, tilled land, forests, lakes, islands, roads, and pastures." It was "exceedingly rich and beautiful," rhapsodized Andrew Burnaby.

After an enchanting ride through this elysium, New Brunswick on the Raritan was reached. The small town enjoyed considerable commerce. Several boats left daily for New York carrying "grain, flour in great quantities, bread, . . . boards, timber, wooden vessels and all sorts of carpenters' work." In addition, the King's Highway was always filled with travelers, who stopped in New Brunswick for food, lodging, or supplies—affording at the same time constant entertainment to townsfolk sitting on their verandas "to enjoy the fresh air and to watch the passersby"; so, at least, reported an amused Peter Kalm. As a result of New Brunswick's advantageous location a wealthy class arose, whose fine houses covered the banks of the Raritan and whose finely dressed daughters were equaled only by the Philadelphia ladies as the "handsomest women that I saw in America," according to the surprisingly quick eye of Reverend Burnaby.

The first night out of New York was usually passed in New Brunswick. Then wayfarers set out to the southwest (along a route now followed by New Jersey 27) through a dense forest which did not thin out until one arrived in the vicinity of Princeton, where all visitors were attracted to Nassau Hall, the largest stone building in America (it still stands). From its summit John Adams, as well as Princeton students, savored a vista eighty miles wide. Founded in 1746, the College of New Jersey, as Princeton was then known, boasted sixty undergraduates when Burnaby made the tally.

An easy afternoon ride took one to Trenton. The way was through a smiling land where a new farm appeared around every bend. It was October when Peter Kalm rode by: "Wherever we passed we were welcome to go into the fine orchards and gather our hats and pockets full of the choicest fruit," he reported. No longer was the route desolate and ominous as when Franklin had staggered over it. Indeed, even memories of those days were fast fading, although Kalm was accompanied for a while by an ancient who "assured me . . . that he could well remember the time when between Trenton and New Brunswick there were not above three farms."

Trenton was a long, narrow town with around a hundred homes, stores, and taverns lining the pair of streets which led toward the Delaware ferry. Trenton's prosperity revolved around transportation: "Their chief income [Peter Kalm noted] consisted in attending to the numerous travellers between Trenton and New York, which are usually brought by the Trenton yachts between Philadelphia and Trenton. But from Trenton to New Brunswick, the travellers go in wagons which set out every day for that place." [34]

Trenton's strategic location at the head of navigation made it an important gathering point for troops during the French and Indian wars which raged along the frontier periodically until 1762. The British government built a large, two story barracks there, which when Burnaby saw it was jammed with upwards of three hundred redcoats, mostly rough Irishmen. Although fourteen years later, John Adams, on his way to the First Continental Congress, found the barracks rented out for private dwellings, it would soon again fill with soldiers, this time those of the newly created United States. (The Old Barracks has been restored and contains an excellent collection of Colonial and Revolutionary firearms.)

Most travelers spent the second night out of New York in a Trenton inn. In the morning they gulped a mug of coffee at the ferry house, then crossed the Delaware into Pennsylvania. The ride was over a superb highway much frequented by young marrieds on weekend excursions from Philadelphia, thirty miles to the south. Many traveled in large groups of one-horse chaises, such as a happy congregation who treated Burnaby to food and merriment at Bristol, a riverside town opposite Burlington on the Jersey shore. Burlington was an important town, for in addition to being a central boat launching point for river commerce, it served as the alternate capital with Perth Amboy. The governor (who just prior to the Revolution was an illegitimate son of Ben Franklin) had his residence here.

Leaving Bristol, wayfarers had to pause at the Neshaminy Creek to wait for one of the ferries (the fare was three cents) then the road was clear to Frankford, a popular watering and dining spot five miles from Philadelphia. A short time later they pulled up at the City Tavern, America's most genteel public house according to John Adams, a tight man with compliments. Located on the west side of Second Street between Walnut and Chestnut, the City Tavern was only three blocks from the Pennsylvania state-house (Independence Hall) and so was a natural gathering place for local politicians and later delegates to the Continental Congresses. "Dined with the whole Congress at the City Tavern," Adams wrote—the feast sometimes consisting of turtle, Madeira wine, and such interesting items as "Flummery, Jellies, Sweetmeats of 20 sorts, Trifles, Whip'd Syllabubbs, Floating Islands, Fools,—etc."

Adams was impressed with Philadelphia: "The regularity and elegance of this City are very striking," he commented. He loved to wander the streets that William Penn had laid out nearly a hundred years earlier—and even enjoyed a repast with Richard Penn, popular grandson of the city's founder, who had a magnificent home on the south side of Market Street between Fifth and Sixth. At other times Adams would stroll along the Delaware admiring the long row of ships which brought goods from all over the world to the Quaker City. Or he might ride out to Frankford to visit his friend and distinguished fellow delegate John Dickinson, whose mansion Fair Hill commanded "a beautiful prospect" both of Philadelphia, strung like a necklace between the Delaware and Schulykill Rivers, and of the countryside gardens and farms to the north, all linked together by the King's Highway.

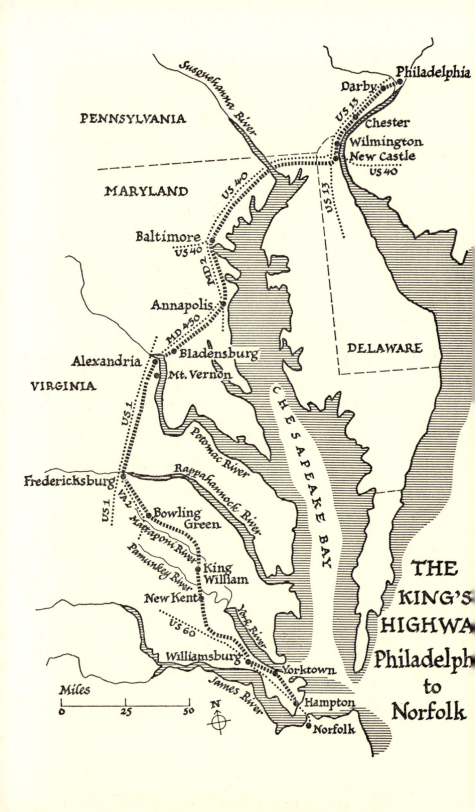

Susquehanna River

PENNSYLVANIA

MARYLAND

Baltimore
US 40
MD 2

Annapolis
MD 450

Bladensburg
Alexandria
Mt. Vernon

VIRGINIA

US 1

Potomac River

Rappahannock River

Fredericksburg
US 1
VA 2

Bowling
Green

Mattaponi River

King
William

Pamunkey River

New Kent

US 60

Williamsburg

York River

James River

Miles
0   25   50

N

Philadelphia
Darby
US 13
Chester
Wilmington
New Castle
US 40

DELAWARE

CHESAPEAKE BAY

Yorktown

Hampton

Norfolk

THE
KING'S
HIGHWA
Philadelph
to
Norfolk

8.   I Think We Shall Have a Crash!

The King's Highway southbound from Philadelphia was misleadingly good at first. "Nothing could be more pleasing than the ride which I had this day," reported Andrew Burnaby—for that portion of the Philadelphia peninsula which is now cluttered with industry was then a calm rural land "covered with villas, gardens, and luxuriant orchards."

William Penn, himself, had, in 1683, granted the first ferryman, one Philip England, exclusive authority to operate a boat across the Schuylkill near the modern U.S. 30 bridge, thereby connecting Philadelphia with Darby. But England soon had a competitor in the lucrative trade, and the ofttimes dull meetings of the Provincial Council were livened with the dispute that ensued. England was at last victorious in maintaining his monopoly, for we learn in the Council Minutes that it was decreed that "the said Nathaniel Mullinax be committed to the common goale of his county till hee give good and sufficient securitie to the Lieut. Governor that hee shall ferrie no more persons, horses, or cattle over the Skuilkill."

From Darby the well-traveled thorofare followed a primeval Indian path through Chester and on along the scenic Delaware River via a route officially surveyed under Penn's urgings in 1696. The way was relatively direct, for Penn had insisted roads in his province be "streight and commodious" and not be "turned about by ye planters, which is a mischief that must not be endured."

It was early summer when Burnaby made the trip, and the sun shown cheerfully through green leaves dancing overhead—

though if he had been earlier he would have marveled at the
banks of rhododendrons blooming in April or the rafts of dog-
wood and azaleas in May. Farmers had made significant dents in
the forest, and Burnaby described the landscape as "beautifully
laid out into fields of clover, grain, and flax." He passed through
"a very pretty village called Wilmington," where descendents of
the original Swedish pioneers could be seen going to Holy
Trinity Church, which stands to this day next to the site of New
Sweden's former bastion Fort Christiana.

Reverend Burnaby, evidently unaware of New Castle's
niche in history, called the town "a place of little consideration"
when he visited it next on his journey. However, modern travelers relish strolls down New Castle's quiet streets lined by ancient
Dutch homes and pause to enjoy the old brick court-house,
which from 1730 on was the capitol of Delaware Colony. Yet
even in Burnaby's time New Castle could not properly be called
a place of little consideration, for dozens of ships from Philadelphia regularly docked at the wharf at the end of Packet Alley—a
short, unpaved street which still leads to the riverfront. The
packets ran with great frequency for many persons would rather
ride the placid river than bounce along the King's Highway.
Anyone wishing to continue on to Baltimore, Annapolis, or Alexandria, however, had to debark at New Castle and proceed
either by stagecoach, or, if one was freer with his money, by a
rented chaise with a servant driver—as did Burnaby. Others who
could not even afford the stage purchased battered farm wagons.
Such was the case with a group of Germans on their way to
North Carolina. Let us leave Andrew Burnaby and his luxurious
chaise for the moment to recount the misadventures of this band
of less fortunate travelers.

Their problems began with the crossing of the Susquehanna,
fifteen miles down the highway from New Castle: "On the side
from which we approached there is a high sandy bank, and the
wheels of Conrad's wagon sank to the axle in the sand, and were
freed only after one and a half hours of work with levers and
extra horses." [22] It took two more hours to get their pair of
wagons and three riding horses across the river by means of the

ferry. This they considered quite lucky for "frequently travelers are detained here for an entire day."

They camped in tents that night since their finances did not permit the somewhat dubious comfort of an inn. But the next morning, being mid-spring, "it was so cold that we could scarcely keep warm at breakfast." Nevertheless by 6 A.M. the horses were hitched, the tents packed, and the party on its way. Almost immediately they had difficulties: "This morning in a rough piece of woodland, Conrad's wagon, in going down a hill, ran into a tree and crushed the left front wheel. We thanked the Saviour that the wagon and horses were not thrown to the ground, for it looked as if that might easily have happened." [35] After spending an hour repairing the wheel, they paused for some good beer, which they obtained from a nearby farmer. The following day "Hauser's wagon almost upset"—but that was routine by now.

Most travelers found the approach to Baltimore somewhat harrowing. "The road to Baltimore," wrote one irate man, "is frightful, built over clay soil, full of deep ruts, always in the midst of forests, and frequently obstructed by trees uprooted by the wind, which obliged us to seek a new passage among the woods. I cannot conceive why the stage does not often meet with disaster." [36] In addition to the deterioration of the road, the appearance of slaves now made Northerners uncomfortable. Thus the same account continues, "[We were depressed by] faces worn by the fevers and ague, naked Negroes, and miserable huts [which] are the most striking images to meet the eye of the traveler in Maryland."

Slavery was all too apparent in the little city of Baltimore, whose population was only a few thousand. "We stopped to dine at Baltimore," wrote Charles Dickens, who taking the King's Highway shortly after the Colonial era had much the same experiences as those going before him, "and, being now in Maryland, were waited on for the first time by slaves . . . Their condition is not an enviable one. . . . The presence of slavery filled me with a sense of shame and self-reproach." [37]

But slavery was not the only thing that made Baltimore

disagreeable. "There are stagnant waters in the town," complained Jean Pierre Brissot, "few of the streets are paved, and the great quantities of mud after rain indicate that the air must be unhealthy." John Adams, as was his fashion, wrote even more bluntly: "The streets [are] the muddiest I ever saw." Not content to stop here, he went on to state that the whole town was "the dirtiest place in the world." And from a man who had seen New York with semiwild pigs poking their snouts into the heaps of stinking refuse that were heaped in every gutter, this was quite an indictment.

Passing Baltimore's none-too-fragrant harbor crammed with a host of packet boats from Norfolk, New Bern, Charleston, and Savannah, the coaches rumbled off toward Annapolis, Maryland's capital. Annapolis's hillside location rid it of the stagnant water that so offended the more delicate visitors to Baltimore and, in addition, gave it "the finest water-prospect imaginable" —according to Andrew Burnaby.

An overnight stay in Annapolis could be quite appealing. Reynold's Tavern was uncommonly comfortable, and from there one could enjoy a leisurely walk along gently sloping streets leading to the picturesque harbor—where there was usually construction activity on three or four boats. Then one might wander back to the majestic statehouse which stands, now as then, on a crest in the town center. Later if properly introduced, he might visit the home of William Paca, who was to sign the Declaration of Independence, or possibly of the governor himself, who would complain that work on his huge royal palace was going so slowly it might as well be given to St. John's College— as it eventually was.

From Annapolis the King's Highway, or Great Coast Road as it was often called in this area, turned sharply west through Bladensburg to the Potomac, where a ferry transported vehicles to Alexandria—a port then nearly as active as Philadelphia. Travelers were deposited at the City Tavern, later known as Gadsby's, which rated with the Wayside Inn of Sudbury, Massachusetts, and Fraunces' Tavern in New York City (all of which still stand) as the finest public houses in the colonies. Clerks would undoubtedly point out the room where George Washington had his headquarters when he recruited troops for ill-fated General Braddock in 1754. Washington was well known in Alexandria; as a stripling of seventeen he had helped survey the town's nine original streets.

Although Alexandria was a good distance inland, there was an Atlantic tang about her Potomac waterfront. Sea captains, who lived in the neat riverside row homes still seen at the foot of Prince Street, congregated along the docks and taverns to swap yarns of adventures in the Mediterranean or along the Spanish Main. Market Square was an important trading area where tobacco from surrounding plantations was stored. Long wharves reached far into the river basin and the sails of oceangoing vessels dotted the water. Amid Alexandria's activity few thoughts were wasted on the swampy desolation across the Potomac that would one day be Washington, D.C.—since it was obvious it would never amount to anything.

South from Alexandria the King's Highway was for a distance called the Potomac Trail—an excellent road according to William Bartram. Travelers now entered the tidewater area, location of the largest plantations and finest mansions in America. Most of these were far removed from the highway for their commerce was primarily with England by means of the ships which sailed up the great tidal inlets to moor at the plantation docks. The James River in particular abounded with mansions, some of which still grace the waterway. Up on the Potomac were (and are) more. The Lee's owned magnificent Stratford Hall, sporting a quartet of massive tower platforms from which servants, and at times the master himself, watched for tobacco ships arriving from England. Farther up the broad river was George Mason's Gunston Hall whose drawing room of carved woodwork was the talk of Colonial Virginia. And above that was Washington's Mount Vernon.

Since Mount Vernon was just a short distance from the Potomac Trail, many travelers paused there to enjoy the hospitality of the gracious owner. "I hastened to get to Mount Vernon, the seat of General Washington, ten miles below Alexandria," writes Jean Pierre Brissot. "This route traverses a considerable wood, and after having passed over two hills, leads to a country house of elegant and majestic simplicity." Brissot goes on to describe the elaborate entrance way that typified many of the Virginia estates. His fancy-stepping horse pranced down a grassy mall, which Washington often used as a bowling green for the entertainment of his many guests. Shapely trees lined the road, framing in the distance the white walls of the two-and-a-half-story mansion. In front of the entrance was a wide, circular courtyard with gleaming white posts at which Brissot's horse was hitched by a uniformed slave (Washington had three hundred Negroes on his vast plantation).

Brissot makes little note of the thirteen work buildings, largely hidden by landscaping, which show modern visitors to Mount Vernon the complex nature of the plantation. There was a rambling garden house, the quarters for the servants, the ice-house, the spinning house (where a dozen or more clothesmakers worked), the gardeners' house, and the office from which Washington managed the affairs of his estate.

But the tidewater mansions did not give a complete picture of Virginia. While distinguished visitors, such as Andrew Burnaby and Jean Brissot, sipped juleps as they gazed over a "noble prospect of water, of cliffs, or woods, and plantations," others saw Virginia in a different light. Some of these were the German party who we remember breaking wheels near Baltimore. "Here and there in the woods," one of them wrote, "we saw Virginia cabins built of unhewn logs and without windows. Kitchen, living room, bedroom and hall are all in one room into which one enters when the house door opens." Life for travelers such as these became more difficult the farther south they went. Camping outdoors, "the ticks, whose acquaintance we had already made at the Susquehannah, now began to be very troublesome." In addition, there was the danger of thievery, mainly by destitute Negroes, whose owners seldom provided them with anything but the barest necessities. One morning the Germans were missing a flask of rum, some food, a bundle of farm tools, and all their spare clothing.

But the poor Germans did not have a monopoly of tribulations on the road to Fredericksburg. Here is Charles Dickens's experience while riding in one of the luxurious coaches in a later year:

> A tremendous place is close before us; the black driver rolls his eyes, screws his mouth up very round, and looks straight between the two [leading horses,] as if he were saying to himself "We have done this often before, but *now* I think we shall have a crash." He takes a rein in each hand; jerks and pulls at both; and dances on the splash-board with both feet. . . . We come to the spot, sink down in the mire nearly to the coach windows, tilt on one side at an angle of forty-five degrees, and stick there . . . [The persons inside] scream dismally; the coach stops; the horses flounder. . . . Then the following circumstances occur.
> BLACK DRIVER (to the horses). "Hi!"
> Nothing happens. Insides scream again
> BLACK DRIVER (to the horses). "Ho!"
> Horses plunge, and splash the black driver.
> GENTLEMAN INSIDE (looking out). "Why, what on airth—"
> Gentleman receives a variety of splashes, and draws his head in again, without finishing his question or waiting for an answer.
> BLACK DRIVER (still to horses). "Jiddy! Jiddy!"
> Horses pull violently, drag the coach out of the hole, and draw it up a bank so steep that the black driver's legs fly up into the air, and he goes back among the luggage on the roof. But he immediately recovers himself, and cries (still to the horses),
> "Pill!"
> No effect. On the contrary, the coach begins to roll back . . .[38]

Fredericksburg was a flourishing little town located where the river navigation ended below the falls of the Rappahannock. "Part of it is built upon an eminence," Burnaby commented, "and commands a delightful prospect; the rest [is] upon the edge of the water for the convenience of warehouses." Before continuing on to Williamsburg, most travelers of any means stopped at the still-standing Rising Sun Tavern (post office as well as inn) constructed by George Washington's youngest brother.

The road to Williamsburg was a miserable affair; and Benjamin Franklin, who made a grueling personal survey of the postal route, could curse it but could do little to improve it. The problem centered on flooding rivers which sometimes for periods of up to six weeks prevented even the hardened post riders from forcing their horses through to Virginia's isolated capital. This at a time when Philadelphia and Boston enjoyed weekly service.

Seasoned travelers preferred to go by horseback rather than chance an experience on the stagecoach such as described by Dickens. Burnaby rented three horses—one for himself, one for his servant, and one for his baggage—and made the 109 miles in four days. The route he took, which fell into disuse when Richmond superseded Williamsburg as capital in 1779, led to the hamlet of Bowling Green, then southeast until it reached the ferry over the Mattaponi, beyond which was a "disorderly and ill-kept" inn (called in Virginia an ordinary). The route continued southward from there, crossing the Pamunkey by a hazardous ford which nearly brought disaster to many, including twenty-three-year-old Thomas Jefferson, foolishly journeying in a chaise from Williamsburg to New York in 1766:

> In going through Pamunkey, [Jefferson wrote] being unacquainted with the ford, I passed through water so deep as to run over the cushion as I sat on it, and, to add to the danger, at that instant one wheel mounted a rock which I am confident was as high as the axle, and rendered it necessary for me to exercise all my skill in the doctrine of gravity in order to prevent . . . the upsetting of myself, chair and all into the water. . . . I confess that on this occasion I was seized with a violent hydrophobia.[39]

South from the Pamunkey ford was a comfortable rest in the fine New Kent ordinary, a handsome, colonnaded structure, now privately restored. Beyond New Kent there were no more major rivers; and, if the traveler did not care to spend an evening

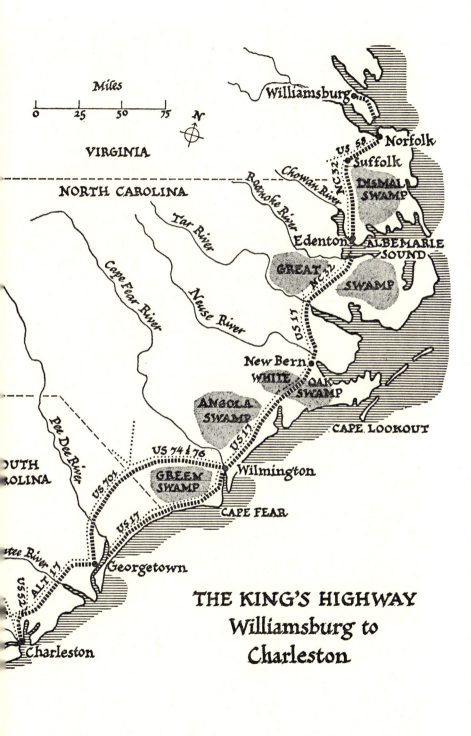

THE KING'S HIGHWAY
Williamsburg to
Charleston

playing cards and dice at Chiswell's in the village of Toano, he could be in Williamsburg by nightfall.

During most of the year Williamsburg was as unpretentious as the make-do road which led to it. "It consists of about two hundred houses," Burnaby observed, "does not contain more than one thousand souls, whites and negroes, and is far from being a place of any consequence." There were only three main streets, all of which were unpaved and very dusty. The center of the little town was the Raleigh Tavern, now reconstructed. Here Ben Franklin's carriers distributed their mail, while at a block outside, slaves brought from Africa were auctioned to planters who had made the long journey down the King's Highway from their plantations.

The tavern was especially active when the Virginia Assembly was in session. Then famous men from all over the colony took the highway to Williamsburg, staying at the Raleigh Tavern or at some of the now-reconstructed homes nearby. The evenings were enlivened by balls in the Raleigh's Apollo Room. One of these was attended by young Tom Jefferson, a student at William and Mary College down the street. Jefferson danced with his fair Belinda until late at night—but his love was spurned and the following morning he wrote to a friend that he was wretched. At other times the Raleigh was used by disgruntled legislators adjourning from the imposing capitol (once again standing in medieval grandure at the eastern end of the Duke of Gloucester Street). Patrick Henry, a firebrand from the western country, was one of these—and at such a meeting Virginia's revolutionary Committee of Correspondence was formed.

The Raleigh Tavern was a welcomed respite from the rigors of the highway, and the traveler could be excused if he preferred to remain more time than anticipated among the congenial planters, legislators, merchants, and sea captains. But there came a day when his departure could no longer be postponed. He must mount his horse (or carriage if he cared to chance an occasional overturning) and resume his ride south—a hazardous ordeal not to be undertaken lightly.

9. Much Fatigue and No Refreshment

From Williamsburg travelers trotted their horses southward through the capital's little port village of Yorktown (one day soon to gain everlasting fame as the site of the decisive battle ending the Revolution.) The road ended near the tip of the York Peninsula, where a ferry crossed the choppy waters of Hampton Roads to Norfolk, then a town of less than five hundred homes huddling around one of the most spacious harbors in North America. This harbor was always speckled with the sails of numerous packet boats servicing the southern coast, where swamps and broad rivers made land transportation exceedingly difficult. Indeed, most travelers preferred to brave the reefs off capes Fear and Hatteras rather than take the rugged four hundred mile overland trail which had been opened to Charleston in 1738.

The first intimation of the problems was gained in Norfolk itself. "Heat gives Norfolk a murderous climate," wrote Louis Moreau. "Bilious and intermittent fevers which stretch out through several years are common . . . the residents of Norfolk are so fearful of their city that all those who can afford it take a trip during the summer, even if it be only to sea." [40]

This was only a mild forecast of what was to come. From Norfolk the King's Highway, locally called the Virginia Path, passed through the hamlet of Suffolk, then skirted the Dismal Swamp (via modern Highway 32). The trip along the swamp lasted for thirty miles—two seemingly interminable days. "There are many pools of standing water," Moreau states, "that poison the air and breed swarms of insects which are a heavy trial even

115

in the daytime." And with the voracious mosquitoes came the danger of the dread yellow fever.

There were no inns along the lonely trek; and, should the traveler be unable to find a plantation to take him in for the night, he would be forced to pitch his little cloth tent (if he had one) on the marshy ground. A night in the swamps was unnerving. For one thing there were packs of wolves. "They go in great droves in the night to hunt deer," wrote John Lawson in 1709. "When they hunt in the night, being a great many together, they make the most hideous and frightful noise that ever was heard." And huge bears came to the swamp to eat acorns from the wide-spreading live oaks. They were unbelievably numerous. "Some years ago," Lawson exclaimed, "there were killed five hundred bears in two counties of Virginia in one winter." Large-clawed wildcats were constantly on the prowl. And there was often the ominous rustle of swamp snakes: some as thick as a man's leg. They were able to swim through the murky water "like an arrow out of a bow"; while others hung from branches, where they might be mistakened for vines. As a man passed, they would often drop, as happened to Lawson when he was canoeing across one of the many rivers: "I had the misfortune once to have one of them leap into my boat," he wrote. "The boat was full of mats, which I was glad to throw out to get rid of him, for they are reckoned poisonous." [41]

The first town in North Carolina was Edenton, on a low ridge of fertile land beside the Albemarle Sound. Although the town was small, it was surrounded by moderately prosperous plantations where the traditional Southern hospitality could not help but impress a traveler emerging from the desolate swamplands to the north. Lawson had many opportunities to enjoy a stay with the Albemarle planters, and he commented: "They give away more provisions to . . . guests who come to see them than they expend among their own families."

The town itself had (and has) considerable charm. Many of the pleasing Colonial homes still stand, such as those belonging to James Iredell, Richard Sanderson (now known as the Cupola House) and Thomas Barker (with a fine view of the sound). St.

Paul's Church (still slumbering in its tree-shaded park) had the oldest charter in North Carolina; and the fine Georgian-style courthouse gave Edenton an air of respectability that some thought it did not deserve since the inhabitants were a tough breed. Many of them had turned to smuggling when Virginia passed stringent laws against the exportation of North Carolina tobacco through her deep-water ports. "Rogues Harbor" the irate Virginians called Edenton and the other struggling settlements around the Albemarle Sound.

Mackey's ferry transported travelers across the three-mile-wide sound where they were soon threading their way through the great swamp along a route now taken by Highway 32. But by this time one would have grown accustomed to the dangers and could enjoy the unusual landscape through slaps at mosquitoes and surveilance for snakes. There were some small settlements along the Pamlico River, chiefly of French Huguenots, but the first real town beyond Edenton was New Bern, seat of the Colonial Assembly.

New Bern boasted one of the most impressive mansions in all America. Constructed by Governor William Tryon in 1770, the two-storied, brick building was set in six acres of meadows, trees, and tastefully landscaped gardens. Legislators would drive up through gigantic wrought-iron gates. Uniformed slaves would usher them into the magnificent council chamber where they could not help but be impressed with the exquisite Chippendale chairs, the rich Isfahan carpets, and the immense portraits of King George and Queen Charlotte—such at least are the furnishings in the modern Tryon Palace reconstruction.

Yet for all his splendor, Governor Tryon could not improve the unsatisfactory land travel in North Carolina. "It is a disagreeable reflection, my Lord," he wrote to an official in London, "that the chain of communication through the Continent should be broken within this province." Yet the British government was having enough financial trouble without tackling North Carolina's sweltering swamps, so the only action taken was to add a few more packets to the undependable, storm-wracked coastal route and to send out one Hugh Finlay to confirm the belief in the unfeasibility of the land route. After a most unpleasant sojourn in Carolina, Finlay wrote that the road "is certainly the most tedious and disagreeable of any on the Continent of North America. It is through a very bad country where there's much fatigue and no refreshment."

And so travelers guided their sweating horses past the White-oak and Angola Swamps, trying to enjoy the beauty and bounty of the North Carolina swamps. Live oaks bent protective arms overhead, screening out the torrid sun. Spanish moss swayed with a grace unknown to those who trod the starker northern woodlands. Palmettos soared to fifty feet or more, their fan-like leaves rattling pleasantly as one passed. Giant cypresses stood sedately in the wetter portions of the swamp (for much of the ground was merely marshy); the unusual symmetry of their trunks and the peculiar forms of their knees gave a traveler constant subjects for speculation.

Among the trees flew dense flocks of parrakeets, green and bright orange-yellow. Ducks rested in placid eddies; and graceful cranes on slender stilt-legs were constantly feeding in the water. Wild turkeys were everywhere eating acorns, edible also by humans. John Lawson frequently saw upwards of five hundred turkeys in a flock. A single one of these giant fifty-pound birds could provide sixteen men with a sumptuous meal, reported Lawson. And for a change of menu, scarcely a day passed without coming into rifle range of one of the hundreds of deer that leaped down the shadowy lanes.

In a few days one reached the environs of the Cape Fear River, a fertile valley inhabited by thousands of Scottish immigrants. Since the numerous farms were connected by a network of fairly serviceable roads, travelers might come across a Scottish lass out for a spin, perhaps even Miss Janet Schaw, who left us with this description of the Wilmington countryside in 1775:

> We were in a Phaeton and four belonging to my brother, and as the roads are entirely level, drove on at good speed, our guide keeping by us and several Negro servants attending on

horseback. During the first few miles I was charmed with the woods. The wild fruit trees were in full blossom; the ground under them was covered with verdure and intermixed with flowers of various kinds.[42]

As for Wilmington itself, because its location on the spacious Cape Fear River provided it with North Carolina's only deep-water harbor, it was the province's most important town. This, however, did not mean a great deal, since nowhere was the transportation system sufficiently developed to provide for the growth of large cities. Wilmington's eight hundred persons (the population during Miss Schaw's visit) lived mainly along Market Street, which was the town segment of the New Bern Road, as the King's Highway was called in this area. None of Wilmington's streets were paved, but that did not keep local boosters from extolling the virtues of their isolated metropolis: "I confess the spot on which it is built," wrote one enthusiast, "is not so level nor of so good a soil, but the regularity of the streets are equal to those of Philadelphia and the buildings in general very good. Many of brick, two and three stories high . . ."

From Wilmington a ferry led to a midstream island, where a short, though very bad, path met another ferry which completed the trip across the Cape Fear River. Here the King's Highway branched: one segment looping westward along the present U.S. 74 and 701 to avoid the Green Swamp, the other heading due south into the swamp over a bone-jarring horse-breaking corduroy causeway following the route now taken by U.S. 17. Alexander Schaw, Janet's brother, explained this corduroy construction: "The roads through swamp land are made by first laying logs in the direction of the road and covering them cross ways with small pine trees, laid regularly together over sod with which the logs are previously covered."

The Green Swamp was the abode of some vicious and powerful alligators. "He is indeed a frightful animal," Janet Schaw exclaimed, "of which a lizard is the miniature, and if you can raise a lizard in your imagination to fifteen feet in length with arms at least six feet and these armed at the end with hands and claws resembling the talons of the eagle and clothe all with a flexible coat of mail . . . if you have strength of imagination for this, you have our alligator." But though they were of fearsome power and encased in impenetrable armor, they were slow-witted and no match for the gangs of men that delighted in hunting them down. "The Negroes, who are very dextrous at this work," continued Miss Schaw, "presently pushed oars down his throat, by which means he was secured . . . he was at last overcome by pushing out his eyes and thrusting a long knife into his throat." But our lady did not enjoy the sport, for she added: "This sight, joined to the strong smell of musk that came from him, made me sick." [43]

The Green Swamp was North Carolina's parting shot, for just beyond the South Carolina border the road came upon forty miles of the finest beach in the world. The sand was shiny white; and the surf was alive with enough savory bass, trout, and pompano to make one wish to tarry week after week in the sea-tossed pleasure-land that has since become a major vacation hideaway. William Bartram, the world famous botanist, letting his horse romp down Myrtle Beach in 1777, found it "pleasant riding on this clean, hard sand paved with shells of various colours." However, Bartram was to have a little adventure that somewhat curbed his enjoyment of the oceanside ride:

> I observed a number of persons coming up a headland, whom I soon perceived to be a party of Negroes. I had every reason to dread the consequence; (for this being a desolate place—I was by this time several miles from any house or plantation,) and feared this to be a predatory band of Negroes; people being frequently attacked, robbed, and sometimes murdered by them at this place. I was unarmed, alone, and my horse tired; thus situated every way in their power. I had no alternative but to be resigned and prepare to meet them. . . . I rode briskly up; and though armed with clubs, axes and hoes, they opened to right and left, and let me pass peaceably. . . . I kept a sharp eye about me, apprehending that this

might possibly have been an advance division, and their
intentions were to ambuscade and surround me; but they
kept on quietly, and I was no more alarmed by them.[44]

A ferry took travelers over Winyah Bay to Georgetown,
center of the indigo country (the Indigo Society Hall of 1741 still
stands). The last segment of the journey led westward from
Georgetown to a favorable crossing of the Santee—a river which
John Lawson found to have such an incredible current that his
canoe-ferry was in danger of being swept away. But the road
became progressively better as it neared Charleston.

Seventeen miles after crossing the Cooper River near the
modern U.S. 52 bridge, the King's Highway met the traders' path
coming in from Augusta, a major frontier post 130 miles west by
northwest. Each spring the traders' path was crowded with
caravans of up to thirty horses each. They were loaded mainly
with deer skins obtained from Cherokees in the Tennessee mountains, from Creeks in mid-Georgia and Alabama, and even from
Choctaws and Chickasaws in the Mississippi Valley. Down the
long peninsula leading to Charleston the pack trains plodded,
accompanied by the cursing and shouting of the traders and
their hirelings. A dense cloud of flies and gnats hovered about
them undeterred by the loud clankings of the iron bells that were
supposed to drive them away.

But there was more traffic on the road than traders. Charleston, whose population reached twelve thousand by the end of
the Colonial era, not only approached Boston in size; but, with
more than 350 sailing vessels dotting the harbor and lining the
wharves along East Bay Street, the South Carolinian metropolis
actually exceeded Boston in total commerce. Charleston drew
from villages, farms, and plantations as far as North Carolina
and Georgia. F. A. Michaux, a French visitor, describing a scene
on the road into Charleston, wrote: "They carry the goods in
large four-wheeled wagons drawn by four or six horses, travel
twenty-four miles a day, and camp every evening in the woods."
In these wagons were bales of cotton, piles of tobacco, sacks of
hams, containers of candle wax, and huge bundles of bear skins.

(On the homeward trip these same wagons were loaded with a year's supply of pots and pans, tea and coffee, gunpowder and bullet lead, coarse cloth for work clothes and fine linen for go-to-meeting wear.) To add to the clutter there were great herds of cattle that coursed down the highway like a bellowing river.

To wayfarers used to the sleepy solitude of North Carolina's swampy stretches, the din, hustle, and jostle of the traffic funneling down the long arm of land leading to Charleston was quite an experience. At last the shipyards just outside the modern city limits were passed. Then marshes pressed on the highway as it edged by the distillery near the U.S. 701 bridge. A mile farther on, at what would become an earthen defense wall during the Revolution and would later be smoothed out and named Cannon Street, were the first buildings of Colonial Charleston. Here the King's Highway became known as King Street.

Continuing down King Street, one would notice a slight angular turn as he passed Beaufain Street. This, as an ancient map reveals, was the original town line dating back to the days when Charleston was founded in 1680. During this distant era, the inhabitants were justly fearful of attack both by Spaniards at St. Augustine, Florida, and by one of the many ferocious pirate bands based in the maze of coves in North Carolina. For this reason a massive wall was constructed around the early town. It was complete with bastion towers guarding each corner, a half-moon-shaped battery bristling with cannons dominating the sea approach, and a seven-foot-wide moat around the land sides. The strongest portion of the wall was that facing King Street, the main approach to the town. This segment rose twenty feet high, and its base became Meeting Street after the walls were torn down in 1718. Anyone wishing to enter the walled city had to venture over a creaking drawbridge that spanned the moat at Broad Street. Proud Charleston boasted of its streets paved with cobblestones, although if the surface of Chalmers Street—part of the original town—is any example, the rough surface was no special joy to ride upon.

After the wall and the moat (which had been an ideal

breeding place for the yellow-fever mosquitoes) were gone, Half Moon Battery remained the center of the growing town. In 1767 a handsome Exchange was built over the largely-demolished battery (the battery walls can still be seen in a former dungeon deep in the Exchange). At the Exchange, travelers weary from their trek on the King's Highway, could meet friends or business acquaintances and from them receive directions to one of the nearby inns, perhaps the Pink House, which is found now as then on Chalmers Street.

Modern travelers, too, can stand amid the Doric columns and Byzantine arches of the Exchange and gaze down Broad toward King Street three blocks away. Here was the terminus of the King's Highway: which had started in Yankee Boston thirteen hundred miles away. This was the road that had wound down the smiling Connecticut Valley, had terrorized coach passengers at the Horseneck Chasm and the ofttimes wild New York Bay crossings, had loped through New Jersey's gardens and pungent forests, had pushed through the smelly Baltimore harbor district and the mires that cut Williamsburg off from the rest of the world, had almost disappeared in North Carolina's murky swamps, had emerged along the lonely South Carolina ocean sands, and had finally crossed the treacherous Santee to merge with the traders' Augusta Road as the two descended the Cooper-Ashley Peninsula into bustling Charleston.

One can picture the saddle-sore wayfarers directing their dirt-splattered nags toward the Exchange. One can almost hear their sighs of relief as they wipe the perspiration from their foreheads, lumpy with mosquitoe bites.

"Well I made it!" One of their voices would croak out. "Yessiree," he would say a little louder, but still in disbelief. "I made it! I really did!" He would squint at the old Exchange building, rising before him. "Here I am. By gum!"

The French and Indian War, 1755–63

10.   They Threw Away Their Clothes to Run the
                                                                    Faster

Nemacolin, a Delaware Indian, raised his hatchet and swung. Bark splintered from the giant tree and a sharp noise, rather quickly muffled by the dense canopy of leaves, sputtered through the virgin timber. Nemacolin grimaced, then followed the almost imperceptible path to a nearby rise, where he again gouged out a wide chunk of bark. Captain Thomas Cresap of the Ohio Company walked closely behind the warrior as he descended to a small stream, drank from its crystal waters, then rose to whack out more bark.

Nemacolin's thoughts are easy to surmise. This was to be a white man's trail, for the Indians needed no axe-made scars to show them the way. Soon the traders would come with their pack trains. Then hunters would appear, killing the game on which tribesmen such as he must live. Eventually the trail would be widened and wagons stuffed with wives, children, and farm tools would rut the earth that had felt only the soft tread of red mens' moccasins. Yes, Nemacolin and his people had seen what happened in their native Delaware and Pennsylvania when white roads began slithering like snakes into their hunting grounds.

But the Indian kept an impassive face. "Thump," another blaze was made. He was beating the death knell of his race.

125

The power behind the little party edging westward along
the Indian trace which connected the upper Potomac with the
Ohio River was the Ohio Company, organized in 1748 mainly by
Virginians who hoped to participate in the lucrative western
trade, now largely in the hands of George Croghan and other
Pennsylvanians. They also expected to reap profits from settling
pioneers on their vast holdings which encompassed most of
modern West Virginia as well as a great piece of southwestern
Pennsylvania up to and including the site of Pittsburgh. Influential stockholders included Robert Dinwiddie, governor of Virginia, and Lawrence Washington, wealthy owner of Mount Vernon and a foremost member of the House of Burgesses, as well
as several highly placed advisors to the British government in
London.

Once Nemacolin's Path was blazed, Ohio Company traders
set out from the company's newly constructed post at Wills
Creek (Cumberland, Maryland) for the Indian country. One of
these traders was Christopher Gist, whose mission was to lure
the Indians away from the Pennsylvanians, who for more than
ten years had reached the Ohio country over the narrow Juniata-
Conemaugh Path or the rugged Raystown Path through Cowan's Gap (now a lofty state park just off the Pennsylvania
Turnpike). From the end of Nemacolin's Path at the Ohio Forks,
Gist continued eighteen miles down the Ohio River to a rambunctious Indian-trader village called Logstown, where suspicious Pennsylvanians threatened his life. Happy to leave Logstown to the traders, Indians, and fleas, Gist hurried westward
along the Great Trail (U.S. 30 and Ohio 80,) arriving after a not
too difficult few days at the important Wyandot town of Muskingum (Bolivar, Ohio). Here he came upon none other than
George Crogham, greatest of the Pennsylvania traders.

Croghan was in the process of building an extensive fur
kingdom. From his headquarters near Carlisle, Pennsylvania, a
constant string of pack trains threaded the paths to his active
post at Logstown, at the head of the Great Trail. Beyond Logstown, Croghan had formerly sent his men northwest across Ohio
to Sandusky Bay, near where the Great Trail turned due north

toward Detroit, its ultimate goal. Although the French had recently driven him from Sandusky, he was doing just as well by using the Pickawillany Trail across mid-Ohio, where the Mingos, Shawnees, and Miamis were won by the good prices they got from the English as compared with the French.

Gist found Crogham an amiable Irishman who regarded the Ohio Company as an ally in his struggle with the French. He permitted Gist to join his group as they led their pack train, bells a-jingling, down the scenic Tuscarawas (the drive on Ohio 212 and 16 is still most pleasant) to White Woman's Town, named for Mary Harris, once a prisoner but now remaining willingly with her Indian husband and half-breed children. Gist paused to speak with Mary, perhaps near White Woman's Rock, a natural landmark two miles north of modern Coshocton. "She still remembers," Gist wrote in his journal, "that they used to be very religious in New England, and wonders how white men can be so wicked as she has seen them in these woods."

From there the traders continued past the looming, mysterious earthworks of the vanished Mound Builders at Newark, then left the Appalachian plateau to ford the Scioto at a minor Shawnee village on the site of Columbus. A much-used Shawnee path led southward along the Scioto to larger villages at Chillicothe and around the mouth of the Ohio (where Croghan had more posts). But the main trail headed on across the Mad River (at Springfield) and the Miami River to Pickawillany: "the most important trading post in the West"—according to a marker in modern Piqua.

Perhaps Gist saw Pickawillany as the logical termination of Nemacolin's Path, which itself linked up with a trail leading all the way to Alexandria, Virginia, on the King's Highway. In any event he spent considerable time there with the strong-willed Miami chief, whom the traders called Old Britain after his attachment to the English. Gist found that Pickawillany was representative of Indian towns throughout Ohio, where English traders were welcomed and the Union Jack fluttered over wigwam and council hall. Indeed, by 1751 it appeared to Gist, Croghan, and the upwards of three hundred other traders who trod the Western trails that the entire trans-Allegheny country, perhaps as far as the Mississippi, would soon be tied by the tough cords of these trails to Pennsylvania and Virginia.

The only problem was that the French did not agree.

Word of the expanding English influence sped rapidly over the winding waterways of France's inland empire. When Charles Langlade, a fiery young trader married to an Indian maid, heard at Green Bay about the British aggressions, he rounded up 250 of the fiercest, most loyal Ottawa and Chippewa adventurers, led them through the Mackinac Strait, and, after a brief pep talk from the commandant at Detroit, paddled up the Maumee and the St. Marys rivers. From there he moved quietly over the Loramie portage and descended in surprise and fury on Picka-willany on a summer morning in 1752. Most of the Miami braves were on an extended hunting trip, as were all but eight of the fifty Pennsylvanian and Virginian traders who could have made things hot for Langlade from their fortified warehouse. The town was devastated; Old Britain was boiled and served for dinner; and the entire stock of English goods, carried with so much difficulty from Philadelphia and Alexandria and valued at about fifty thousand dollars, was hauled off as spoils of war.

It was a blow from which the Ohio trade never recovered.

The French acted in other ways, too. Using Fort Niagara as a base, their traders appeared with ever more frequency on the French Creek-Allegheny route to Logstown. The Indians were wooed with gifts and fed vivid tales about English designs on their land. And to further discourage the trade, a thousand dollars was offered to any warrior who lifted Croghan's scalp.

The Marquis Duquesne, warlike governor of New France, still was not satisfied. He then ordered the upper Ohio permanently sealed by the erection of a series of strong forts extending from the excellent harbor formed by a long spit of land known as Presque Isle ("nearly an island") to the strategic Allegheny-Monongahela forks (Pittsburgh). Accordingly, in the early spring of 1753 a host of fifteen hundred Canadians appeared in a

mighty canoe fleet, stunning Iroquois scouts with their numbers
and greatly concerning the English garrison at Fort Oswego on
Lake Ontario. Soon the Frenchmen had erected Fort Presque
Isle on the site of Erie, Pennsylvania, and were busily chopping
a road through the dense woods to French Creek, a tributary of
the Allegheny.

The road to French Creek, or *Riviere aux Boeufs* (River of
the Buffaloes) as the French called it, was the first true road ever
constructed in the Midwest. Twenty-one feet wide, it ran thirteen miles (along modern Pennsylvania 97) to Fort LeBoeuf,
which had been hurriedly built to guard the road's southern
termination (a marker in Waterford indicates the fort site).
However the dirt roadbed was nothing to boast about: not with
the great craters that filled with several feet of water after each
rain.

Nevertheless there was much activity along this muddy,
bumpy path, since all the armament and supplies to erect the
forts farther downstream had to be carted to boats and rafts
waiting on French Creek. As autumn approached fifty men were
sent to construct the third fort at Venango on the vital junction
of French Creek with the Allegheny. As it was soon too cold to
continue working, the commander wintered over in the deserted
cabin of an English trader John Fraser (who had providently
decided to relocate on the Monongahela) and waited until
spring to complete the post, a 75-by-105-foot parallelogram with
five two-story barracks.

With forts at Presque Isle, LeBoeuf, and Venango, the
French now massed their forces for the grand finale: a bastion at
the Forks (Pittsburgh), key to the entire Ohio Valley. Increasing
numbers of supply wagons began crunching over the pock-
marked road from Presque Isle to French Creek, where artillery
and powder were floated down to Venango preparatory to the
descent on the Forks.

In the meanwhile Nemacolin's Path in the south was nearly
as active as the LeBoeuf road in the north. Gist and other Ohio

Company traders escorted long pack trains to Logstown, where the bribe-happy Indians agreed to the erection of two English forts in their territory—one of which was to be at the Forks. Then in September, 1753, the company called an important summit meeting with the Indians at Winchester, the western-most Virginia town. The chieftains and their retinue streamed down Nemacolin's Path eager for the liquor and guns with which the Virginians hoped to buy their friendship. After several festive days, the Indians were on their way back to Logstown, having exchanged bland promises of eternal fidelity for what to them was a fortune in English goods.

With France and Great Britain clearly on a collision course in the Ohio Valley, Robert Dinwiddie, bellicose governor of Virginia, decided to play for time. As an interested shareholder in the Ohio Company, he knew it was essential that the French should not control the Forks, thereby plugging the route to the Indians at Logstown and the Great Trail country beyond. There-fore, as his company rushed plans for a post of their own at the Forks, Dinwiddie summoned a half-brother of his friend Law-rence Washington to Williamsburg. Even though this George Washington was only twenty-one years old, he had had some experience with surveying teams on the frontier. In addition, he was a muscular and determined young man. Besides no one else had volunteered for the dangerous spying mission Dinwiddie had in mind. The governor gave Washington a brusk message to be delivered to the French commander warning him to cease and desist from erecting any more forts on territory clearly given Virginia by her royal charter, at the same time confiding to Washington that he should make careful observations of French strength in the area.

On October 31st, 1753, Washington took the King's High-way from Williamsburg to Alexandria where he procured sup-plies, then he set off on the pioneers' road to Winchester (now U.S. 50), crossing the Blue Ridge Mountains through the tower-ing cliffs of Ashby Gap. From Winchester he followed a newly cut road (U.S. 50 and Md. 28) through the frowning mountains to the company post at the junction of Wills Creek and the

Potomac (Cumberland, Md.). Christopher Gist met him there. With this experienced woodsman and six other companions, Washington struck out on Nemacolin's Path into the dangerous territory under dispute.

Icy November rains splattered about them, soaking their clothing and laying a slippery glaze over the rocks. The climb around Savage Mountain was exhausting and that past the hulking, cloud-covered bulk of Negro Mountain even more wearing. The weather grew progressively worse. By the time they reached the zigzag course over Laurel Hill, blinding cascades of snow stung their eyes and drifted over the path so that only Gist's intuition and the half-obliterated blazings left by Nemacolin kept them from becoming irretrievably lost. Chestnut Ridge, the last mountain before the rutted plateau which led to the Forks, was snowy and menacing; but the party wearily surmounted it and reached the hut of John Fraser (recently of Venango) eight grueling days after setting out from Wills Creek.

Fraser greeted them hospitably and loaned them a canoe to carry their baggage to the forks which was only ten miles downstream. From the deserted forest-enveloped site of Pittsburgh they continued to Logstown, where Washington held council with the chiefs. Although he found a friend in Half-King, an elderly Indian with considerable influence, most of the wily red men would not commit themselves to the English cause. Why should they? They had already gotten their gifts at Winchester; and besides, weren't French gunners at Venango, only four days march, boasting they would rout all Englishmen from the West with the coming of spring? Nevertheless Half-King and a few of his warriors agreed to act as guides.

Although Washington refers to the Venango trail as a road, it is clear that it was merely a typical Indian trace. Weaving through the gullied countryside on a course much the same as U.S. 19 and Pennsylvania 8, the narrow path looped around swampy areas, skirted swollen creeks, and meandered through forests and meadows. Alternate paths radiated out at various intervals, to be taken or not depending on the condition of the land or one's inclination at the moment. Venango "lies near north sixty miles from the Logstown," Washington wrote in his journal, "but more than seventy the way we were obliged to go." What with fresh snow constantly obscuring the path, they were lucky to reach the French post at all.

The genial Venango commander Philippe Joncaire told Washington that Dinwiddie's message must be delivered to his superior at Fort LeBoeuf sixty miles upriver—a statement which must have both delighted and dismayed the exhausted English spies. More rain and snow harrassed them as they butted their miserable way up the eastern shore of French Creek (along modern U.S. 19 and 322). Several tributaries had to be crossed, with the scrawny ponies swimming the icy water and the men rafting over. After tramping "through many mires and swamps," they arrived at LeBoeuf on December 11th. There the commandant, a one-eyed old army man named Legardeur de St. Pierre, scoffed at Dinwiddie's pretentious demand and declared flatly that he and his men not only intended to remain but would resist any attempt to dislodge them with "exactness and resolution."

With St. Pierre's written refusal in his satchel, Washington took a canoe down French Creek to the Allegheny, then borrowed some horses from Joncaire and proceeded down the Venango trail. When the horses gave out and his companions could not make fast enough time on foot, Washington, with Gist, left them and hurried ahead, anxious that Dinwiddie should quickly receive St. Pierre's refusal together with their own even more important report of French war preparations.

The going was as rough as before; but now the Indians, possibly encouraged by the French, took a hostile attitude. With Half-King remaining at Venango to care for one of his sick braves, Washington and Gist were deprived of any red allies. While near a place with the sinister name of Murdering Town (modern Evans City), Washington very nearly lost his life as a French Indian's gun, leveled at point-blank range, misfired. The two white men sped into the forest to escape pursuit, and continued at a killing pace both day and night until they reached the Allegheny near where Pennsylvania 8 turns west along the river. Here, trying to cross the river on a raft which they had spent a whole day constructing, another disaster nearly overtook them:

> Before we were half way over [Washington wrote] we were jammed in the ice in such a manner that we expected every moment our raft to sink and ourselves to perish. . . . With all our efforts we could not get the raft to either shore; but were obliged, as we were near an island, to quit our raft and make to it. The cold was so extremely severe that Mr. Gist had all his fingers and some of his toes frozen.[45]

They spent a teeth-chattering night on the island (probably that spanned by Pittsburgh's 31st Street Bridge). When bleak dawn broke, they found the danger they had courted had been unnecessary as the river had frozen over. Crossing on the fragile, crackling ice, they struck out on Nemacolin's Path to their friend John Fraser's, who offered them the first warm shelter since leaving Venango nearly a week earlier. Obtaining horses from Fraser, they resumed their weary march. A day and a half's distance from Wills Creek they came upon the Ohio Company's fort-building expedition under the leadership of William Trent, one of Croghan's associates. Though the English crew of only forty men was puny compared with what Joncaire would soon muster, would the French dare push Trent out of the Forks when the two countries were not formally at war? That was the question which would be answered when the ice broke on the *Riviere aux Boeufs* in a few months.

By January 12, 1754, Washington was on the King's Highway, arriving in Williamsburg four days later—thus completing two and a half months of "as fatiguing a journey as it is possible to conceive."

Once at the governor's mansion (which still stands), Washington not only gave Dinwiddie a complete verbal description of all he had seen, but presented him with the day by day journal he had kept. Because the journal contained the first accurate account both of the military possibilities of the Forks and the

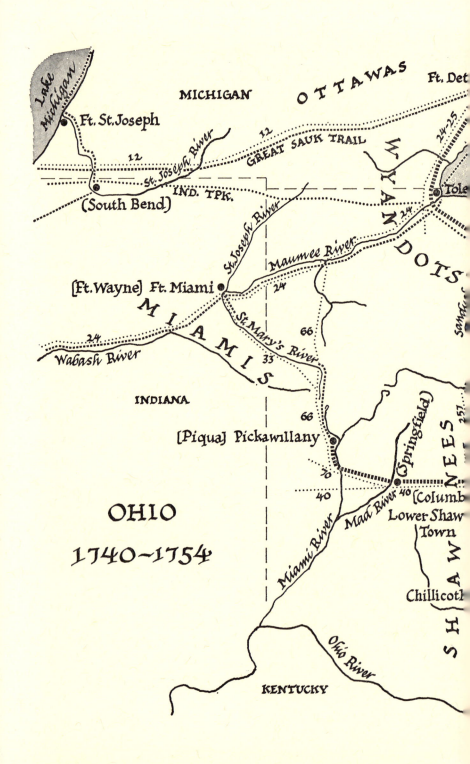

Lake Michigan

MICHIGAN

OTTAWAS

Ft. Det

Ft. St.Joseph

St. Joseph River

12

GREAT SAUK TRAIL

12

WYANDOTS

24-25

12

Tole

St. Joseph River

IND. TPK.

(South Bend)

24

Maumee River

24

[Ft. Wayne] Ft. Miami

St. Joseph River

MIAMIS

St. Mary's River

66

Wabash River

24

33

66

INDIANA

66

[Piqua] Pickawillany

(Springfield)

WYANDOTS

Sandu

SHAWNEES

257

70

40

Mad River

40

[Columb

OHIO
1740~1754

Miami River

Lower Shaw
Town

Chillicoth

Ohio River

KENTUCKY

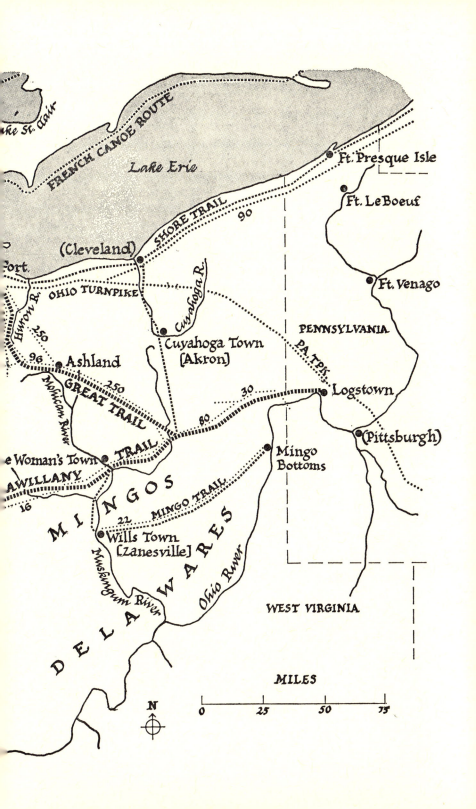

strength and disposition of the French forces, the governor rushed it into print. The journal quickly became a best seller not only throughout the aroused Colonies but in England itself. Instantly the name of the twenty-one-year-old frontiersman was known to everyone. Thus the cruel trek on Nemacolin's and the Venango Trails began the train of events which were ultimately to make Washington the foremost personage on the continent.

Because Dinwiddie was now convinced the French meant to take forceful possession of the all-important Forks, he promoted Washington to lieutenant colonel, gave him 150 men, and told him to quickstep westward to protect the post that Trent was building. By April Washington and his tiny army were on the road from Alexandria through Winchester to Wills Creek. They had hardly arrived at the company post when they heard the chilling news that a thousand French troops in sixty batteaux and three hundred canoes had dropped down from Venango, sent Trent's token force packing, and were already hard at work on a major fortress at the Forks—which they named Duquesne after their energetic governor.

Although it was obvious that there was little Washington and his paltry army could do against such overwhelming odds, he decided to lead his men over the mountains to keep the vacillating Indians from coming over to the French. But it was slow going, for Nemacolin's Path was no longer satisfactory; Washington had to widen the trail and bridge some of the streams to accommodate his supply wagons. Though all hands were put to work converting the trail into a road, the forest was so dense that they could make only four miles a day—where a trader's pack train could cover twenty and a scout on foot thirty.

Yet Washington gradually moved past the landmarks that were becoming familiar—foreboding Savage Mountain and the gloomy forest beyond, soon to be called the Shades of Death; Little Meadows with its quavering grasslands; and the Great Crossings of the upper Youghiogheny, a major obstacle which took several days to bridge. All the while he and his wary men were forced to keep a close lookout for Indian ambush from the thick underbrush that walled in the narrow road. Yet they continued westward, and on May 24 the army and their supply wagons (the first wheeled vehicles ever to cross the Alleghenies) emerged onto the Great Meadows, a marshy opening between Laurel Hill and Chestnut Ridge. Seventy miles ahead of them (via U.S. 119 and a series of county roads) were the hostile French at Fort Duquesne. Fifty miles behind them (via U.S. 40) was the weak post at Wills Creek, their only source of aid.

Hardly had Washington made camp than a runner from Half-King, his guide to LeBoeuf, informed him that a body of Frenchmen were skulking only five miles away in a hidden cove on Chestnut Ridge. Fearing an attack, Washington took forty of his best men and that very night set out for the Indian camp at Half-King's Rocks. There the chief warned him of his peril and they decided to advance on the French rather than wait to be surprised themselves. In a fierce quarter hour battle the entire French party of thirty-three was either killed or captured—save one lone survivor who bolted to Fort Duquesne with the news. Among the killed (or murdered, as the French were to put it) was the leader, de Jumonville, a young officer who it was claimed was merely on a reconnaissance mission similar to Washington's six months earlier.

And so here in the now-peaceful little cove modern tourists know as Jumonville Glen a hot-headed Virginian fighting a minor skirmish in a virtually uninhabited wilderness triggered a major war between the world's two mightiest powers. Repercussions were felt almost immediately in the courts of London and Paris, and soon France had the support of the populous Austrian Empire and Britain that of brilliant Frederick the Great, ruler of Prussia. Eventually Russia, Sweden, and Spain joined the fray and armies began battling in Africa, India, and the Caribbean as well as in Europe and North America.

Washington himself was the first to experience the fury of war. As soon as word of Jumonville's death reached Fort Duquesne, Captain Louis de Villiers was dispatched with six hundred French and a hundred Indians to avenge the killing of Jumonville, his brother. Using batteaux and canoes, the French ascended the Monongahela as far as Redstone Creek (now the site of Brownsville) where an Ohio Company trail connected with Nemacolin's Path. Advancing east over this trail, Villiers came to Gist's Plantation (now Mount Braddock), a small cluster of buildings that the Ohio Company hoped would become the nucleus of numerous settlements. Then Villiers turned south to cross Chestnut Ridge over the windy pass currently used by U.S. 40. There he spotted the circular stockade and V-shaped outlying entrenchments that Washington named Fort Necessity (now reconstructed as part of the Fort Necessity National Battlefield).

Both sides opened fire about noon in the midst of a pelting rain. The fight continued until twilight, by which time over a third of Washington's men were either killed or wounded. But the French, too, had suffered and when Villiers reluctantly proposed a surrender which would permit the English to return to their own country keeping all their weapons except their artillery, Washington knew he could do no better than accept. Accordingly, on the morning of July 4, 1754, he led his bloodied soldiers out of Fort Necessity and down the dreary road to Wills Creek.

Although he had been beaten, he had given a courageous account of himself, and stories of the violent little engagement increased Washington's stature and roused the ire of the Colonies.

With war now a reality, the duke of Cumberland, in charge of British preparations, decided to dispatch Edward Braddock, a sixty-year-old taskmaster, to tend to the destruction of Fort Duquesne. Since Braddock would have two Irish regiments of five hundred men each, to be augmented by seven hundred or more men recruited in the Colonies, it was deemed plausible that he would not only reduce Duquesne but would also continue north to aid in the destruction of Fort Niagara, which was the goal of another English-Colonial army.

By February, 1755, Braddock was in Williamsburg conferring with Governor Dinwiddie. Towards the end of March the two men, accompanied by their aides, servants, and much fanfare, took the King's Highway to Alexandria where the troops had already landed. Here a temporary camp was set up and Braddock, locating in the still-standing mansion of John Carlyle, invited Washington, who had just moved into Mount Vernon upon the death of his brother, to join him as one of his three aides-de-camp. Washington accepted and made Gadsby's Tavern (now restored) his headquarters for the recruiting which was his first duty.

From Alexandria Braddock ordered his army up the Potomac to Wills Creek, where a square, picket fort, sagaciously named in honor of the duke of Cumberland, was constructed. But it was easier to erect the fort than to assemble the wagons necessary to transport the army's food, equipment, and gunpowder across the formidable mountains. Since the source of supply was the prosperous farms around Lancaster and Harrisburg, all logic would have had Braddock advance on the Forks via Croghan's Raystown Trail, which, following the general route of the Pennsylvania Turnpike, was also some thirty miles shorter than Nemacolin's Path. But certain Ohio Company stockholders who were prominent advisors to the British government, realizing that the avenue Braddock must make through the forest would also provide them with a fine highway to attract settlers to their isolated transmountain domain, convinced the ministry to order him down the company's trail.

So from the beginning Braddock had problems. Pennsylvania farmers were reluctant to hire out with their wagons in return for Braddock's promises to reimburse them in full should they be lost. Indeed, had it not been that Benjamin Franklin, a frequent and quite jovial guest at Braddock's table, pledged his own personal credit to the farmers, it is doubtful that the campaign would have started at all.

In order to secure the essential wagons, Franklin posted the following advertisement in frontier Lancaster:

April 26, 1755. Whereas, 150 waggons, with four horses to each wagon, and 1500 saddle or pack horses are wanted for the service of his majesty's forces now about to rendezvous at Will's Creek, and his excellency General Braddock having been pleased to empower me to contract for the hire of the same, I hereby give notice that I shall attend for that purpose at Lancaster from this day to next Wednesday evening . . .

The pay Franklin promised for a driver and his wagon was "a very considerable sum": around $15 per day (modern valuation) in gold or silver. In addition, he assured the hesitant farmers that "the service will be light and easy, for the army will scarce march above twelve miles a day" (would that it did!) and that they would not "on any account be called upon to do the duty of soldiers." However, he ended his notice with the ominous statement that "waggons and horses must be had" and that if the Pennsylvanians did not furnish them voluntarily "violent measures will probably be used"—namely the invasion of British foraging troops, which, "considering the temper they are in, and their resentment against us, would be attended with many and great inconveniences . . ." Even so, it wasn't until early June that 150 wagons with their four-horse teams had made it to Fort Cumberland over the new road from Chambersburg.

At last, on the tenth of June, Braddock and his army, swelled with recruits to twenty-five hundred men, moved out of Fort Cumberland and marched down the Wills Creek canyon toward their rendezvous with disaster. Three hundred axemen and carpenters led the way, laboriously chopping down the massive trees and clearing the thick underbrush to a width of twelve feet. In addition, much effort was required to remove the great boulders that blocked the path, to grade the roadbed around the steep mountain slopes, and to build sturdier bridges to replace the flimsy structures that Washington had thrown up a year earlier. The pace was unbelievably slow, for in addition to the construction work, wagons were constantly breaking down and dozens of the five hundred packhorses were habitually wandering off.

Nonetheless the army inched forward along a route now marked with plaques beside U.S. 40. It took Braddock a week to reach Little Meadows, a bare twenty-five miles from Fort Cumberland. Here, realizing he had underestimated the transportation difficulties, he asked Washington's advice. Upon being told that the only solution was to leave most of his stores and baggage behind under the command of Colonel Dunbar and strike out with thirteen hundred of his choicest troops, Braddock seemed to consent. But even so he took thirty wagons, rather than relying solely on packhorses as Washington urged. "I found that instead of pushing on with vigor without regarding a little rough road," Washington complained, "they were halting to level every mole-hill and to erect bridges over every brook—by which means we were four days in getting twelve miles."

About this time Washington came down with such a severe case of dysentery that he could barely stay atop his joggling horse. Finally at the Great Crossings of the Youghiogheny, which was reached on June 23, Braddock insisted that Washington remain behind under doctor's care until he recovered. It was somewhat dangerous, since French Indians had been lurking on the army's flanks, murdering and scalping whenever they could. But Dunbar's contingent was close by, so Braddock moved on.

Crossing Laurel Hill the next day was an arduous job, with each of the four eight-inch howitzers requiring a nine-horse team to crunch up and over the obstacle. But it was done and soon Braddock was passing the ominous ruins of Fort Necessity, about which some Indians hovered, fleeing when British horsemen charged them. The next morning Chestnut Ridge was surmounted at Half-King's Rocks (a mile northeast of the present U.S. 40 pass), but not without the back-wrenching task of lowering the wagons down the steep hill by means of blocks and tackles.

Fording the Youghiogheny at Stewart's Crossings (now Connellsville), Braddock proceeded cautiously—with Croghan, Gist, and a few friendly Indians scouting ahead. The army was in high spirits when it reached the Monongahela on the eighth of July. It was here that Washington rejoined them, although he was still so weak that he rode in one of the covered supply wagons rather than on a horse. He considered himself lucky to be in on the kill, since it was commonly believed that the fort would fall on the morrow.

At sunrise the next day, Braddock had the men turn out in bright battle-red uniforms. With bayonets sparkling in the sunshine, colorful banners dancing in the air, and drums and fifes

playing loudly, the army presented such a thrilling sight that
Washington was to remark on it many times in later life. But
Braddock had more in mind than empty pagentry. He was well
aware that Indian spies were watching his every movement and
he wished to convince them of the folly of trying to test arms
with such an invincible juggernaut.

His plan nearly worked. The French at Fort Duquesne were
paralyzed by indecision. The garrison was seriously under-
manned; and the Indians, who some days numbered over a
thousand, had a disheartening way of melting when the odds
shifted against them. But morale rose when Charles Langlade,
conqueror of Pickawillany, reached Duquesne with his fierce
upper lakes tribesmen (including, possibly, the great Ottawa
chief Pontiac, most ferocious of them all). Even so it wasn't until
the very morning when Braddock made his final movement
toward the fort that Captain Daniel de Beaujeu was able to
inspire 650 Indians into accompanying his 250 French troopers
on what was commonly believed a mere delaying action against
Braddock.

Informed by Indian scouts that Braddock had decided to
ford the shallow Monongahela twice to avoid ambush along the
section of Nemacolin's Path which descended into the Turtle
Creek gorge, Beaujeu hastened to meet Braddock while he was
so engaged. However the French leader soon learned that he
was too late: Braddock had already reassembled his army—with
its cumbersome artillery and numerous wagons, packhorses, and
herds of cattle—beside John Fraser's deserted cabin.

The British force moved confidently ahead in two sections:
an advance guard of three hundred men under Lieutenant Colonel Thomas Gage (later British commander at the Battle of
Bunker Hill) and the main body under Braddock. Gage had
expected the French to attack at the ford, and when they did not
do so he imagined their strategy was to hold out within the fort,
a sturdy five-pronged earthwork. For this reason he carelessly
marched past a strategic hill to his right without securing it with
a platoon as was customary.

Suddenly Gage ran head-on into Beaujeu. The British

opened fire immediately, killing Beaujeu on the spot. As the redcoats cheered "God Save the King!" the French and Indians quickly fanned into the dense forest on both sides and up the vital hill and began shooting back. Here in the words of Captain Robert Orme, riding with General Braddock, is what happened as the fighting evolved:

> We heard an excessive, quick, and heavy firing in the front. The General, realizing the advanced parties were very warmly attacked . . . [had] eight hundred men detached from the line, and four hundred were left for the defence of the artillery and baggage. . . . The General sent forward an Aide de Camp to bring him an account of the nature of the attack, but the fire continuing, he moved forward himself. . . .
>
> The enemy had spread themselves in such a manner that they extended from front to rear, and fired upon every part. The place of action was covered with large trees, and much underwood upon the left, without any opening but the road, which was about twelve foot wide. . . . No enemy appeared in view; and nevertheless a vast number of officers were killed . . .
>
> [Gage's] advanced detachments soon gave way and fell back upon Lieutenant Colonel Burton's detachment, who was forming his men to charge a rising ground on the right [the essential hill]. The whole were now got together in great confusion. . . . The General ordered the officers to endeavour to form the men . . . into small divisions and to advance with them; but neither entreaties nor threats could prevail. . . .[46]

Washington was there, riding through the midst of the holocaust, shouting encouragement to the bewildered Britons, who were completely unprepared for this manner of fighting. Four bullets blasted through Washington's coat and two horses crashed dead to the earth beneath him. But he miraculously came through unscathed.

Braddock doggedly remained in the center of the fray until a bullet in the lungs sent him down. Then, with their general incapacitated, the men "threw away their arms and ammunition, and even their clothes to escape the faster," according to Captain Orme. What had, only two hours earlier, been a splendid war machine was now a broken, panic-blinded, leaderless mob. Down the road they fled, passing in minutes obstacles which had taken them hours to clear on their outward march.

The frantic retreat continued all the way to the supply camp where Colonel Dunbar was waiting expectantly to learn of Fort Duquesne's capture. By the time Braddock was brought there dying, Dunbar's contingent, which itself far outnumbered the defenders of Duquesne, was in confusion and terror. Already the road to Wills Creek was jammed with deserters—one of whom was twenty-year-old Daniel Boone, later to open a road of his own into the wilderness. Braddock, disconsolate at the utter disintegration of his once-proud army, muttered over and over "Who would have thought it? Who would have thought it!" In his dispair he had even tried to shoot himself with a pistol from George Croghan, who, with Washington, was at his side.

On the evening of July 13, 1755, the general mercifully died. After Washington read the funeral service, Braddock's body was buried in the center of the road he had hacked out of the forest with such sanguine hopes a week earlier. Then the few remaining troops marched back and forth over the grave (now indicated by a marker beside U.S. 40) to disguise it from the Indians. It was an ignoble, yet fitting, end to a calamitous campaign.

With Braddock gone and the exultant French firmly in control of the Forks, the road began reverting to the Indian path it had been. Dense weeds covered the wagon ruts. Thick underbrush moved forward from the shadows. And soon saplings pricked through the roadbed.

The dying trail was like a broken arrow pointing feebly at the heart of the French empire.

But there was another arrow in the English quiver . . .

11. I Will Sleep in Fort Duquesne or in Hell Tonight!

The new moon rested for a moment like an Indian scalping knife on the crest of Blue Mountain on Pennsylvania's frontier. The pale, half-light sparkled one last time on the snow which lay in thin patches over the valley floor. Then the moon sliced into the mountain and was gone.

As darkness enveloped the quiet fields around the hamlet of Shippensburg, a chill November wind sprung up, rustling the dead leaves and sending the powdery snow curling upward like phantom warriors.

A farmer, his wife, and their frightened children ate their supper in silence, listening nervously to the rattling leaves. At intervals the farmer, rifle in hand, would move to the door, slip open the heavy wooden bolt, and squint into the haunted night.

In the distance a wolf howled, to be answered by another . . . and then still another. The wife dropped her tin drinking cup and gathered the children close about her. The man clasped the cold rifle barrel tightly. But there was little he could do if the wolves were actually Shawnees on a scalping raid. His only chance was that they would attack one of his neighbors first; then he would see the flames of the burning cabin and could dash with his family to Fort Franklin at Shippensburg. This might save their lives, but the Indians would kill his plow horses, break his tools, and carry off all the food he had stored to last him and his wife and the little ones over the ferocious Pennsylvania winter.

The weary pioneer stood guard the entire night, remembering the words of William Trent, the Indian trader, who had told

him that forty-two bodies had just been found on Patterson's
Creek. This was in addition to the more than a hundred persons
murdered and scalped near Fort Cumberland. John Harris,
whose growing settlement was already being called Harrisburg,
said that fifteen hundred Ohio Indians led by Frenchmen from
Fort Duquesne were on the Susquehanna and reports from as far
east as Reading told of their atrocities.

The sun had barely risen in a bloody smear over South
Mountain when the farmer saw a half-dozen wagons heading
east over the Harrisburg Road. Ever since Braddock's horrible
massacre white families had been abandoning the farms they
had wrenched from the forest with such toil.

The farmer sighed. A man could only stand so much. If one
more homestead was burned or one more neighbor scalped, he
too would join the destitute throng trudging eastward.

Although such fears predominated all along the exposed
Appalachian frontier, Pennsylvania and Virginia, easily reached
by war parties taking the fine road Braddock had so conven-
iently provided, were the most seriously affected. In August
1755, young George Washington, survivor of Braddock's debacle
a month earlier, was placed in charge of Virginia's defense.
Making his headquarters in a log-and-stone house which still
stands in Winchester, he soon had his men busy erecting Fort
Loudoun (part of the earthwork remains today) and a series of
blockhouses along the South Branch of the Potomac.

Yet it was impossible with barely fifteen hundred troops to
defend two hundred fortifications against an enemy who could
attack at will with overwhelming numbers. White scouts from
Fort Cumberland estimated that as many Indian warriors were
taking Braddock's Road eastward as British soldiers took it westward six months earlier. Washington was in despair. "Every
day," he wrote, "we have accounts of such cruelties and barbari-
ties as are shocking to human nature. It is not possible to
conceive the situation and danger of this miserable country.

Such numbers of French and Indians are all around that no road is safe." And Washington's laments were verified by a French observer with an Indian war party: "They kill all they meet, and after having abused the women and maidens, they slaughter or burn them."

It was at Fort Duquesne that the Indians and French gathered to begin their bloody sorties on the Colonial farmers. The Indians came from all over New France. Some were from as far distant as Wisconsin and Minnesota, paddling by the fort guarding the Mackinac Straits to the bustling staging point Detroit. Others came from Illinois by way of the Great Sauk Trail which connected the Chicago portage with Detroit. And still others would course up the Wabash, past the forts at Vincennes and Ouiatenon, cross the low divide to the Maumee, and continue down that river to the fort on Sandusky Bay.

From Sandusky all the Midwestern warriors joined together to flood down the Great Trail that arched across Ohio to the Ohio River. And as they marched up the Ohio to Fort Duquesne, they would undoubtedly grunt in approval at the French regulars and Kaskaskian militia coming upriver in large batteaux from New Orleans and the Illinois settlements on the Mississippi.

Fort Duquesne drew from other regions, too. Tribes from Ohio streamed over the Pickawillany Path, once a safe highway for George Croghan and other English traders. From the north, up the St. Lawrence from Montreal, came Canadian tribesmen. Forts Niagara and Presque Isle were constant hosts to scalp-crazed savages on their way to Duquesne. And the Venango Trail, only recently traveled by Washington, was alive with painted warriors who would murder an Englishman in as little time as it took to flick their French muskets to their shoulders.

Once at Duquesne the Indians camped in huge wigwam villages on the Pittsburgh plain, thumping their tom-toms impatiently while waiting for presents and for marching orders from the commandant. He was their leader, of this there was no doubt. The great fort, which was his palace, held them in awe. An English prisoner fortunate enough to escape wrote:

It is square [and] has bastions at each corner. . . . The
bastions are filled with earth solid about eight feet high; each
bastion has four cannons . . . [The fort] is about fifty yards
wide—has a well in the middle, but the water is bad. About
half the fort is made of square logs, and the other half next to
the water of stockades . . . [It] has two gates, one of which
opens to the land side and the other to the water side, where
the magazine is built; that to the land side is, in fact, a
drawbridge, which in day-time serves as a bridge for the
people, and in the night is drawn up by iron chains and
levers. . . . The river waters sometimes rise so high [in the
moat] that the whole fort is surrounded with it, so that
canoes may go around.[47]

The Indian encampment along what is now Stanwix Street
had once been densely forested, but the trees had been felled
leaving the stumps to rot off later. Dozens of English prisoners
—men, women, and children—were paraded between the bark-
slabbed wigwams accompanied by the jeers and often the blows
of their tormentors. No place on the continent was filled with
such savagery as what is now the heart of modern Pittsburgh.
Petty chieftains strutted about in the tattered uniforms of Braddock's slaughtered officers, and along the Allengheny River were
the stakes where the captured were burned to death. There was
always brandy to enliven the evenings, and during the daytime
various tribes displayed scalps of whites and boasted of their
daring exploits along the Susquehanna or Shenandoah.

"I have succeeded in ruining the three adjacent provinces,
Pennsylvania, Maryland, and Virginia," boasted the commandant—and he was not far from wrong.

The Pennsylvanians, as well as Washington and his Virginians, fought back as best they could. The pacifistic Quaker
legislature was jarred into action when a group of angry frontiersmen, arriving in Philadelphia with a wagon containing the
bodies of friends and loved ones recently murdered by the

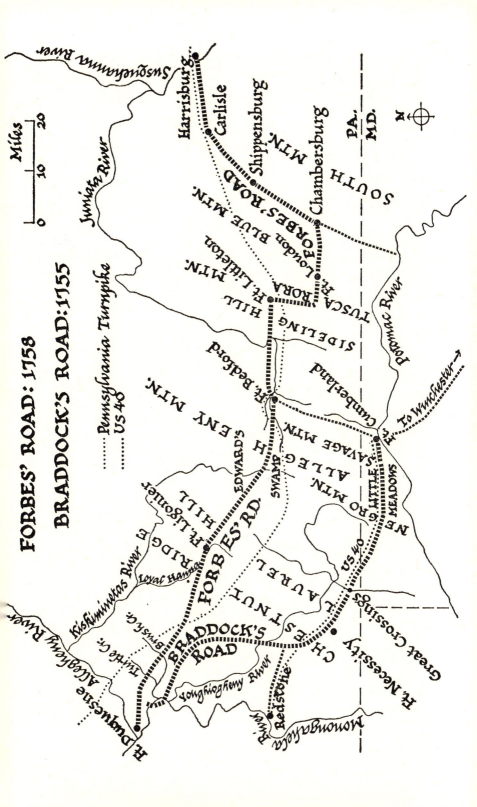

Indians, parked at the door of the Assembly House and vowed
not to leave until something was done. The Assembly, led by
Benjamin Franklin, provided the funds for the erection of forts
and blockhouses in the area under siege. At Carlisle, Fort
Lowther was repaired; and at Shippensburg, Fort Morris replaced delapidated Fort Franklin. Farther west Fort Loudon
was erected at the strategic location where the old traders' path,
having skirted Blue and Kittatinny mountains, began ascending
the rugged Tuscarora highlands (along a soaring route followed
by U.S. 30). Fifteen miles beyond Fort Loudon, at the other end
of Cowan's Gap (now a state park) was Fort Littleton, a lonely,
extremely perilous outpost attempting to guard that portion of
the traders' path which had been somewhat widened as far as a
projected settlement called Raystown (Bedford).

Nevertheless the tide continued to go against the Colonials.
William Trent, the tough old trader who had been building a
post at the Forks when the French rudely brushed him aside to
begin Fort Duquesne, wrote from Carlisle: "All the people had
left their houses betwixt this and [Blue] Mountain . . . They are
moving their effects from Shippensburg; everyone thinks of
flying. Unless the Government falls upon some effectual method,
and that immediately, of securing the frontiers, there will not be
one inhabitant in this valley one month longer." [36]

An emergency was clearly at hand.

Into the bloody and burning land stepped John Forbes, a
youngish Scot who had once thought he would become a doctor.
Forbes was a refined warrior, well-mannered and well-read, yet
with a disdain for ceremony and a quickness to adapt himself to
new modes of fighting which set him several heads above Braddock, his predecessor. It was, perhaps, because of this military
suppleness that William Pitt, the astute politician newly in
charge of Britain's war effort, appointed him to his challenging
post.

Although Forbes was to be allowed an army of six thousand
men (comprised mainly of Pennsylvanians, Virginians, and Scot-

tish regulars) against which the French and Indians could muster only half that number, his was an exceedingly difficult task.
In the first place, since his army would be strung out for many
miles along a narrow road that he must chop through the thick
forest, the enemy could attack any segment in strength compara-
ble to his. In the second place, the road itself would present a
gigantic problem, since the tremendous bulk of food, supplies,
and equipment for his soldiers must be carted westward over
this slender, still-unsurveyed lifeline. And in the third place,
Forbes was not certain that such a diverse group of men, many
of whom would be used predominantly for road and fort construction, could be shaped into an effective enough fighting
machine to match Indians used to a lifetime of forest warfare.

Nonetheless, by April of 1758 Forbes was in Philadelphia,
Pitt's directive in hand, but his army scattered about the Colonies. Once again he realized the immensity of his task. With
only twelve hundred men coming from Great Britain, he must
argue, cajol, even beg the provincial assemblies into furnishing
the troops his government had blithely promised him. To do this,
the assemblies in turn had to pass the necessary recruiting laws,
provide tax funds for supplies and transportation to Philadelphia, and let contracts for uniforms, weapons, horses, and military vehicles. Since Fort Duquesne had to be captured before
next winter's snows closed the mountain passes, there was from
the beginning a sense of urgency about the campaign.

Even before his troops began arriving, Forbes was running
newspaper ads for supply wagons. Then he started gathering the
innumerable items necessary for his men. There were the obvious things: barrels of gunpowder, lead for musket balls, cannon
shot, bayonets, pistols, and swords. Of course, he must have
ample supplies of whiskey, for nights were long and lonely on
the frontier. He also needed tremendous amounts of hay, since
the horses had little forage in the forest. And he couldn't forget
six or seven thousand canteens, complete with stoppers and
strings. He needed tents and blankets and heavy coats for the
mountains. Shoes—yes every man must have ten or more pairs.
And they would need such little items as sewing needles and

thread, extra buttons, handkerchiefs, combs, eating utensils. He must remember, too, soap and towels and such commonplace necessities as chamber pots. The list ran on and on—as did the merchants, private contractors, and shifty-eyed politicians with whom he and his quartermaster had to deal.

By the end of April Forbes was sending the first supplies across eastern Pennsylvania via the Lancaster Road (U.S. 30 and 230) to Harrisburg, where they were ferried past John Harris's fine Georgian mansion (still proudly standing at Front and Washington streets). From there, the supply wagons rumbled over a rocky road paralleling the Pennsylvania turnpike to Carlisle, the first storage depot on the frontier. Colonel Henry Bouquet, a Swiss soldier of fortune and Forbes's second-in-command, was in Carlisle to attend to the assembly of supplies and the bivouacking of the troops that Forbes had trudging into the little village by May.

On May 20 Forbes wrote Bouquet concerning the development of their campaign: "You will march Col. Armstrong's regiment to Fort Littleton and Loudon upon Mr. Burd's people coming to Carlisle. [Then] you will push both these regiments forward to Raystown, leaving at proper distances, escorts for the provision wagons." Bouquet soon mustered 120 supply wagons and moved out of Carlisle, reaching Fort Loudon early in June. The wagon segment of the road ended here. To aid him in extending the wagon route westward, Bouquet had Colonel George Washington—assembling the Virginia troops at Fort Cumberland, Braddock's old training ground—send six companies north on the newly constructed Chambersburg Road (U.S. 11).

Bouquet pushed his laboriously broadened road over the rocky shoulder of the Tuscarora Mountains to Fort Littleton, then wormed it up the treacherous incline of Sideling Hill. Once Sideling was surmounted, Bouquet pushed down the little maroon-rocked valley of the Raystown Branch of the Juniata River (the drive on U.S. 30 is a pleasant experience) through a gap in the Great Warrior, or Tussey, Mountain. Here in a vale between Great Warrior and Wills Mountain, Bouquet found the amazing

John Fraser, ahead of the frontier as usual, calmly conducting trading operations in a sturdy building that still stands in Bedford at the corner of Routes 30 and 220. Bolstered by frequent drinks at Fraser's tavern, Bouquet and his men quickly threw up Fort Bedford, destined to become Forbes's most important supply base and point of rendezvous for his troops.

Fort Bedford, named in honor of the duke of Bedford under whom General Forbes had once served, actually consisted of four squarish, stockaded enclosures with diamond-shaped bastions protruding from strategic points along the timber walls and surrounding dry moats. The main enclosure, on a low bluff overlooking the Juniata (at the place where a modern partial-reconstruction exists), was used mainly for storing the gigantic stockpile of goods to be used for the operations in the wild western mountains. The other three stockades protected the troops from the ever-present danger of an Indian hit-and-run attack.

About this time Washington and Bouquet began a series of heated arguments concerning the route to be taken to Fort Duquesne. It had originally been assumed that Forbes, after tapping Pennsylvania for wagons and grain, would drop thirty-one miles down the new Wills Mountain trail (U.S. 220) to Fort Cumberland, then continue westward over Braddock's Road. However Bouquet was convinced that a completely separate path should be cut directly to Duquesne, since the way was fifty-four miles shorter and there were no major rivers to cross. But Washington countered that the added time it would take to construct this road would make it impossible for them to reach Duquesne before winter snows smothered the army.

Forbes soon discovered that there was more to the dispute than military tactics. Pennsylvanians deluged him with demands that he make a road through their territory to aid in the later development and settlement of their western country. Virginians, on the other hand, wishing to have no competition for the area they claimed around Pittsburgh, urged that Braddock's Road be used.

And so, in addition to his complicated problems in logistics,

Forbes found himself in the midst of a vicious intercolonial squabble. In a letter to Bouquet, Forbes urged him to reconnoiter the traders' path across the Alleghenies, regardless of the Virginians' insistence that the way was far too rough. "I find we must take nothing by report in this country," Forbes warned, "for there are many who have their own designs in representing things." As for Washington's forceful protestations, Forbes was disturbed that his "behavior about the roads was in no ways like a soldier." To add to Forbes's difficulties, he now suffered the first of a series of debilitating dysentery attacks.

Bouquet sent several scouting parties from Fort Bedford to determine the feasability of widening and grading the Pennsylvania path to accommodate cannon carriages and supply wagons—and also, nearly as important, to ascertain if the meadows contained enough grass for the horses (lacking on Braddock's Road). He was particularly concerned with Allegheny Mountain and Laurel Hill: the two main barriers before Duquesne. When his men returned, Bouquet wrote Forbes that "they are convinced that a wagon road could be made across Laurel Hill [that would be] not so bad as that from Fort Littleton to this place, and there is water and grass all the way." Then, he added, that even though the matter of the two routes had not been decided, "Major Armstrong will set out with a party of 100 volunteers to mark out the road, and will send me a man every day (or every two days) to inform me of his progress and observations . . . if the report he makes of his route is favorable, I shall send 600 men to take a post at Loyal Hanna Creek, which I conceive to be the proper place for the chief depot. . . . I hope you will be here before the main detachment marches." [48]

By July Forbes had most of his army on the road west, and on the fourth was himself in Carlisle. Here his dysentery made him violently ill, yet from his sickbed he continued with his innumerable and wearing duties. The friendly Indian scouts were impressed with his driving will. Head of Iron they called him, referring to his unalterable determination. A constant crew of scribes were kept busy writing his long letters. One of these was that sent to Colonel Bouquet which settled the matter of the route: "[Forbes] thinks that no time should be lost in making the new road," the scribe wrote. "He has directed me to inform you that you are immediately to begin the opening of it."

Thus on August 1, 1758, Bouquet sent out his choppers (on what is now U.S. 30) and the final drive against Fort Duquesne was on.

The first obstacle was reached almost immediately: the frowning rampart known as Allegheny Mountain. "Work to be done on this road is immense," wrote the distraught supervisor Sir John St. Clair, from a camp at the foot of the massive ridge of stone. "Send as many men as you can with digging tools, this is a most diabolical work, and whiskey must be had." He estimated it would take five hundred men laboring most strenuously for the better part of a week to get them just a rudimentary trail over the mountain.

Felling the trees was the first problem, of course. Before the behemoths could be toppled, daring lumberjacks had to climb to the most lofty pinnacle to hack off the top and most of the larger side branches. But even after the tree had been sheared into a towering pole and the trunk had been axed through and the monster came thundering down, it would often crash into other trees which crowded nearby. Then more daredevils must clamber up the precariously swaying trunk to disassemble it. And when it finally thudded to the earth, swarms of sawyers must spend hours cutting the trunk into manageable proportions which could be rolled down ravines or left to rot on the margins of the road.

Grading the highway was even more difficult. First the tree stumps had to be loosened from the stony soil by spades and axes, then rooted out by straining teams of horses. Next the rocks and boulders had to be wrenched out of the earth. And finally a roadbed had to be forced twelve feet into the mountain side, on as level a line as the rock outcroppings permitted. Also, it was essential that some sort of reinforcement be provided to keep the outer portions of the road—and the wagons that would soon be on it—from slipping into the canyon far below.

Bouquet, seeing summer slipping away, became impatient with St. Clair's slow progress. Bothered by Washington's warning of being snowbound in the mountains, the Swiss mercenary detailed more and more troops for construction work—until there were fourteen hundred men laboring on Allegheny Mountain, with an equal number deployed in the woods to guard against a surprise attack. But here one of Forbes's clever stratagems paid off. By having Washington and his men sortie constantly out of Fort Cumberland and part way down Braddock's Road, the French and Indians were completely deluded into believing this was the route which Forbes planned to take. Thus Bouquet could proceed during these moments of greatest exposure with none of the harassment which could have been so devastating.

Although by mid-August St. Clair was breathing the exhilarating air that screamed over Allegheny Mountain's "aerial heights," his pleasure was short-lived, for at the base of the mountain he found himself plunked in the middle of Edward's Swamp, "a dismal place perplexed with laurels, logs, and rocks, covered with weeds or brambles interwoven with young locust." The only way for wagons to traverse such a wasteland was over a corduroy causeway—logs laid crosswise over the muck. This took additional time that Forbes had not counted on. But the evil swamp was finally bridged; and on August 23, St. Clair wrote from Stoney Creek (a plaque on U.S. 30 marks his campsite) that "three wagons have got to this place"—quite an accomplishment.

With the good weather still holding, Bouquet hurriedly dispatched Colonel James Burd and sixteen hundred soldiers on packhorses past St. Clair and over Laurel Hill to Loyal Hanna Creek, where they began constructing Fort Ligonier, the last fortification before Duquesne fifty miles distant. It was a bold step, since these troops might be exposed to the full fury of a

French and Indian attack which had annihilated Braddock's army that had numbered only a few hundred less. Yet the enemy as yet had no inkling of the existence of Forbes's Road, and work on the strategic fort went on without incident.

However Fort Ligonier, supplied solely by the trickle of goods that could be hauled by pack train, would be useless offensively until the wagon road reached it. "The slow advance of the new road and the cause of it," Forbes wrote to Bouquet, "touch me to the quick." Agreeing with Bouquet that St. Clair lacked the grit to drive his workers to their fullest, Forbes rose from his sickbed and set out from Carlisle to tend personally to the matter. But when he reached Shippensburg two days later his strength gave out. He collapsed onto a cot, writhing with "excruciating pains," so weak he could barely lift his head to take nourishment. For nearly a month—at the most crucial period of the campaign—he was prostrated. His once-handsome face grew hollow and gaunt. Lines of worry and agony daily became more etched around his mouth and eyes. He watched the summer flowers fade, to be replaced by autumn asters and goldenrod. Soon the September sun tipped the birches amber. The days were mellow but the nights were cold, and they came too early. He could see that each day had ever fewer precious hours of light for construction work on the road.

He knew he was needed at Bedford, for although Bouquet was an excellent officer, no man could operate at such a pace and with so many unforseen problems without losing his judgment somewhere along the line. So as Forbes's dysentery attacks kept him confined, a foreboding feeling hovered over him like a threatening cloud.

On September 7, 1758, Colonel Bouquet arrived at Loyal Hanna Creek, exhausted from his rugged horseback journey over towering Laurel Hill (modern travelers are still impressed by the spectacular ascent on U.S. 30). There were many details to take care of. Work on Fort Ligonier, a rambling stockade (currently reconstructed), was proceeding at a confused pace and hundreds of foremen came to him for orders and instruction. In the midst of the disorder Bouquet was cornered by Major James Grant, an impetuous Scot thirsting for fame. Scouts, Grant confided, thought the French strength vastly overestimated. Grant urged Bouquet to permit him and eight hundred troops to make an in-force reconnaissance of Fort Duquesne. They just might frighten off the small number of Indians believed to be remaining there during the summer hunting season, and surely they could capture a prisoner or two whose information would be invaluable. Bouquet, forgetting his usual caution, gave his permission.

Grant confidently marched out of Fort Ligonier and off down the winding traders' path leading to Fort Duquesne. Although he had told Bouquet he would merely reconnoiter the fort, it seems clear from his subsequent actions that he imagined his flying column, without artillery or adequate intelligence reports, had the strength to take the French bastion. Three days later, having covered all but eleven of the fifty miles to Duquesne, Grant had his little army rest until mid-afternoon. Then he advanced.

By two in the morning they sighted the unsuspecting fort. Silently they moved forward. Even when they reached the rise thereafter known as Grant's Hill (now Grant and Forbes streets in the center of Pittsburgh's business district) just half a mile from the fort, no sentries challenged them—nor were there any Indians encamped in their usual grounds outside the fort.

With his information about the weakness of the garrison now seemingly confirmed, Grant hit upon what ordinarily would have been a brilliant plan. He posted a hundred Pennsylvanians among the trees to his right and a strong detachment of Highlanders to his left. Then, concealing himself and the rest of his men in the underbrush atop the hill, he sent a company of kilted Scots marching brazenly into the plain in front of the fort, banners flying and drums beating.

It took only a moment for the astonished French troopers to

leap out of bed. The Duquesne drawbridge clanged down and the first sleepy-faced Frenchmen tottered out to meet the small Scottish force. The Scots caught them with a blast of gunfire which momentarily stunned the French. But as more French and Indians scurried through the gate, the Scots began falling back toward the forested hill where Grant and his grinning ambushers eagerly awaited them.

The marvelous plan was working perfectly . . . except for the fact that Grant's intelligence report had not been quite accurate. Grant watched in dismay as the enemy kept pouring out of the fort. Soon the field was flooded with them, and still they kept coming! They crested the hill and swarmed into Grant. It was Braddock all over. The Scots fought bravely, but their leaders had not taught them the most elementary North American tactics. "The Highlanders exposed themselves without any cover," went a contemporary newspaper report, "and were shot down in great numbers. . . . Major Grant exposed himself in the thickest of the fire and endeavored to rally his men, but all to no purpose, as they were by this time, flanked on all sides."

When the fighting was over, 273 British and Colonials, including Grant himself, were killed, wounded, or taken prisoner —over a third of the army. The Indians in triumph sliced the heads of many fallen Scots and stuck them on poles with their kilts draped derisively around them.

When word of the disaster reached Forbes, who had finally dragged himself to Fort Bedford, the general could barely control his anger. "Your letter of the seventeenth I read with no less surprise than concern," he wrote Bouquet, "as I could not believe that such an attempt would have been made without my knowledge and concurrence." He ended this letter prophetically: "My friend Grant most certainly lost his wits, and by his thirst of fame brought on his own ruination and ran great risk of ours." [49]

And ruination was right, for now the French and Indians at last realized the direction of the true danger. Drums beat at Fort Duquesne summoning the tribesmen. Scalp dances were performed. Knives were sharpened. Ammunition checked. Then

some of the most skillful forest fighters in history filed eastward:
their destination the vital, yet exposed, fort on the Loyal Hanna.
The decisive battle for control of the Ohio Valley was at hand.

The French were desperate. In August Fort Frontenac, a
major supply depot at the mouth of Lake Ontario, had been
captured by the British; and a tremendous amount of essential
food, clothing, and military equipment destined for Duquesne
had been destroyed. But even more important: the nine armed
vessels that made up France's Lake Ontario fleet were either
burned or hauled off for English use. This meant that the French
had lost control of the lake, and with it, of their long supply
route to the West. Fort Duquesne and the interior were strictly
on their own.

Around eleven o'clock on October 12, shots rang out from
the black forest surrounding Fort Ligonier. Not certain what this
signified, two parties of British were ordered to investigate. As
soon as they were lost from sight in the woods, the firing increased. Realizing this was the expected attack, Bouquet sent
five hundred men—nearly half the garrison—charging to their
support. But the French and Indians blasted them with such
effectiveness that the troops were forced back into the fort.

Bouquet then ordered his artillery to open up. During the
rest of the afternoon the wooden timbers of Ligonier shook with
the cannons' roar. But the French kept up a bitter return-fire
from behind the trees to pin down the garrison while the Indians
butchered the food cattle and the packhorses so essential in
transporting supplies from Fort Bedford, the main depot fifty
miles east. But the French had been unable to bring artillery
over the crude traders' path, and for this reason were unable to
breech Ligonier's stout wooden palisades. When morning came
they were gone.

While they had not been able to take the fort, the sharp
well-executed attack not only resulted in considerable and, in
many respects, irreparable damage, but also caused a slowdown
on road work, since after this the crews had to be protected by

increased patrols. To add to the troubles, the weather turned bad. Pelting torrents of rain eroded the way over Laurel Hill so that it was soon referred to as "the Bugbear." The flooding water caused Edward's Swamp to become virtually impassable. And even normally easy rises and level meadows became so slippery and muddy that no wagons and few pack trains could slush over them. In reply to Bouquet's pessimistic evaluation of the situation, Forbes wrote back: "Your description of the roads pierces me to the very soul."

The rains continued through the last weeks of October. Day after dismal day dirty clouds poured cascades of water mixed with snow down the mountain sides. "If the weather does not favor me," Forbes wrote in despair to William Pitt, "I shall be absolutely locked up in the mountains. I cannot form any judgment how I am to extricate myself." Forbes's situation was indeed desperate. The army, living in rotting tents or log huts that seemed to leak in every place at once, was fast becoming discouraged. Morale dipped dangerously low. Insubordination was a problem. All wagon transportation ground to a halt and provisions grew scarce. With nearly six thousand men every day growing more susceptible to a flu epidemic, a crisis of truly calamitous proportions was clearly at hand.

Early in November Forbes took the rain-scarred road over the soggy heights of Allegheny Mountain, where patches of snow were beginning to form, and then up the dizzy, dangerous switchbacks of Laurel Hill, the great bugbear. Arriving at Fort Ligonier wasted away by illness and fatigue, Forbes called a council of war among his officers. One by one the discouraged men recommended the abandonment of the campaign. Forbes, the "Head of Iron," looked at the quagmire that was to have been the grand encampment from which his army would be launched against Fort Duquesne. With great reluctance he bowed to their wishes.

The campaign was over.

Yet the very next day the unbelievable happened. A small French party attempting to kill some horses and cattle, was

captured. Under insistent questioning one of them revealed that
both the lack of provisions due to the fall of Fort Frontenac and
the conviction that the victory over Grant and the destruction of
horses and supplies at Fort Ligonier had effectively stalled the
British until winter snows made any advance impossible, had led
the French commander to send most of his three thousand
French and Indian troops home until the following spring. Instantly Forbes was on the offensive. Bad weather or not old
Head of Iron would have Fort Duquesne! With twenty-five
hundred picked men, unencumbered with anything except muskets, blankets, and food for but eight days, Forbes struck out on
the rocky trail as Washington, commanding the lead, broadened
it before him. Excitement ran high. In one day they were at
Chestnut Ridge. Continuing along modern U.S. 30 as far as
Greensburg, they followed what is now Pennsylvania 130 along
the margins of Brush Creek until they reached the camping
ground which is currently Bushy Run State Park.

With their goal just thirty miles off, Forbes proceeded more
cautiously—fearful of the type of action which had cost Braddock and Grant so heavily. Carried on a litter slung between two
horses, Forbes reached the vicinity of Turtle Creek two days
later at a point not far from the fatal field where the skeletons of
Braddock's fallen stared out with sightless, warning eyes.

As twilight gathered and the frosty November wind rustled
like advancing warriors through the gaunt trees, Forbes posted
his sentries with extra care. He knew there were French Indians
in the woods, but the question was how many? Possibly his
captive informant had been sent on the mission especially to
mislead him into making an attack against a strong garrison
which had had months to prepare an effective ambush.

Blackness came. The men slept on their arms, ready at an
instant to jump into action. An owl hooted in the distance. A dry
leaf skittered down a tree limb. Then there was a heavy, almost
oppressive, silence. Forbes, twisting in pain, tried to sleep.

Suddenly a deep rumble thundered about them. The soldiers sat up and fingered their weapons. Could it be that the

French were blowing up their fort? Were they going to retreat without a fight? Or was it just another trick?

The next morning tension prickled like static electricity. Someone advised Forbes to delay his march so the area could be reconnoitered. The General glared back. "I will sleep in Fort Duquesne or in hell tonight!" he roared. And so the army moved toward the Forks over the trail that would one day be named Forbes Avenue, but then was an Indian path dotted by posts topped with the gory heads of Grant's dead. The angry troops lusted for vengeance, but there were neither French nor Indians to be seen. Rounding Grant's Hill, they came upon Fort Duquesne, once the pride of New France, now merely a smoking ruin.

Forbes was carried to an improvised shelter where, two days later, he wrote a letter to William Pitt. The heading told the story: "Pittsbourgh 27th November 1758." The French were gone forever. The strategic site now bore the name of England's great war leader.

Forbes, weary yet satisfied, fell back on his bed. He had at long last removed the French and had opened the way to the West with a broad highway that would soon be thronged with thousands of land-hungry pioneers. His mission was over.

Four months later he was dead.

12.   Decision at the Thunderer

William Johnson, his young Indian wife, and his bodyguard
of swarthy braves guided their horses up the Iroquois Trail. It
was early spring, 1759, and the waxing sun slanted through the
budding trees, dappling their trunks with amber. On the left was
the Mohawk River, bubbling and gurgling as its water, flooded
with melted snow, lapped hungrily at the muddy banks dotted
with clusters of hepatica—white, pink, and purple.

The Indian girl hummed softly while she watched her man
riding ahead. How often she had passed along this trail. She
knew every bend, every lichen-covered boulder, every glen
where the coals of uncountable fires marked the campsites of the
stream of delegations that had once come from as far as the
Seneca lands to the stone mansion that her husband called Fort
Johnson. But for the past two years the delegations had slacked
off, until her husband and his trusty Mohawks, her people, had
been all that prevented the mighty Iroquois League from renouncing their traditional friendship with the English. Yet when
General Forbes had driven the French from the Ohio Forks, the
Iroquois had agreed to meet with her husband at Canajoharie,
the principal Mohawk castle and her childhood home.

As the pleasant afternoon wore on, the rhythmic tread of her
horse lulled the girl into memories of the past. How well she
remembered the day William Johnson had first appeared at her
father's longhouse, a tall young man fresh from the place called
Ireland. His eyes were a piercing blue-gray, the color of a
musket barrel; and though they glinted with determination and a
strong will that made her shudder, there was nothing of the

usual traders' deceit in them. His face had been fair as ermine, but now it was as dark as a Mohawk's; and although he had bested many a Mohawk in games and in the hunt, the tribesmen grew to love and trust him—and he them. Not only had he been the only trader, aside from the crafty French Joncaire brothers, invited to the Iroquois' sacred council meetings at Onondaga, but the Mohawks had adopted him into their tribe as a war chief —an unheard of honor for one not of Iroquois blood.

Soon they came to the fording place. The slope to the river was gentle, having been smoothed by centuries of moccasins. Now the horses grunted up the opposite bank and before her rose the huge longhouses of her people. She was astonished at the activity. Groups from all the Five Nations had gathered there: Mohawks from local villages, Oneidas from the rounded hills near the Great Carrying Place, Onondagas from the country of the sacred council fire; Cayugas from their lake as slender as a maiden's finger, and Senecas from the land near the awesome gorge of the Genesee River. Wherever she turned there were chieftains, their scalplocks bristling with bear fat, their faces painted many colors, their jackets fringed with scalps taken in battle.

She looked longest at the Senecas, for they rarely traveled the trail to Mohawk country. There were sixty of them, distinctive with triangular stones dangling from their nostrils. Their sentences were sprinkled with French phrases learned from the Joncaire brothers, Philippe and de Chabert, whose constant stream of presents and flattery brought the Seneca closer to the Canadians than any of the other Iroquois. Since Iroquois law proclaimed that no tribe could commit the Five Nations without the approval of all the others, the Seneca warriors were essential in her husband's plan to bring the confederacy into the war on the British side. So concerned had William Johnson been to obtain the Senecas' goodwill that he had sent one of his most trusted interpreters galloping far up the trail to be certain that the suspicious Dutch and German settlers in the area around Fort Herkimer, recently devastated by Canadians and Algonquins, treated the Senecas with courtesy and deference.

At Johnson's approach a howl of welcome rose from the assembly. Known as *Warra-ghi-yagey* ("the Man of Great Undertakings"), Johnson was as much a celebrity to them, whose daughters he had loved and whose braves he had bested, as with the periwigged folks of the Colonies. His traders, led by skilled George Croghan whose thirst for adventure had won and lost him a trade empire on the Pennsylvania frontier, were everywhere on the Iroquois Trail—whether it be over the forest path (now taken by the New York Thruway) or the Seneca River-Oneida Lake route. And the Mohawk River was constantly flecked with Johnson's bateaux plying between the Great Carrying Place (now Rome) and the *schenectady* ("way through the pines"), the cutoff that linked the Mohawk River with Albany, bypassing the rough Cohoes Falls.

Johnson's trade goods—knives, guns, blankets, rum—items that Hiawatha, traditional founder of the Confederacy, never dreamed of—had become necessities to the Iroquois. And Johnson's agents were paying fair prices for the pelts that the Iroquois trapped—or that they had stolen from the weaker tribes on their flanks.

Yet there were many things that had worked to Johnson's disadvantage in dealing with the Iroquois—and these items played on his mind as he conversed freely with his old friends in the Mohawk dialect. Glancing to one side, he noted the gambrel roof of Martin Van Alstyne's house (which still stands). Up the river was Fort Herkimer surrounded by German homesteads; and at the other end of the Iroquois homeland was Schenectady, surrounded by a well-built stockade and containing scores of sturdy homes (most of which still grace Church and Front streets). Yes, Europeans were gradually encroaching on Iroquois territory and he had heard rumblings of dissatisfaction among his Indian clients.

At the same time the pioneers were antagonizing the Iroquois the British were generally demonstrating their ineffectiveness at arms. The Braddock debacle in 1755 had been particularly humiliating to the Five Nations, for the Algonquin Ottawas, Chippewas, and other western tribes had ridiculed them for their attachment to such miserable warriors. Although, two months later, Johnson had done much to counteract the damage by his well-fought victory over a French invasion force at Lake George. The previous year, the brilliant Montcalm had completely shattered a gigantic British army that outnumbered him four to one at Ticonderoga—this as Johnson and his Mohawks watched impotently while stationed by the incompetent General James Abercromby atop nearby Mount Defiance where their muskets were ineffective but where cannons, many of which Abercromby still had on the road, could have reduced the fort with ease. Although Forbes had taken Fort Duquesne in November, that victory was not so important as it seemed, since the French army was unbeaten and was poised at Venango waiting for spring to pounce upon the English garrison, still small due to the difficulty of hauling food over Forbes's Road. It was both to meet the threat of this French army and to end the dominance of the French traders at Fort Niagara that Johnson had called the meeting at Canajoharie.

Johnson held council with the colorful array of grunting, guzzling, gesticulating chiefs. That evening a pair of huge oxen were boiled in five black kettles, and as the Indians tore the tender meat between their teeth, their drummers began beating out dances. Finally a muscular Seneca chief called Old Belt rose ponderously. With the campfire forming grotesque designs on his heavy face, he announced that his tribe—who had originally granted La Salle permission to construct a trading post on the land near the mighty Niagara ("Thunderer"), were now convinced that this fort should be destroyed.

The encampment was in an uproar. Red wampum belts signifying a vote for war flew from hand to hand. The drums broke into a more frenzied cadence. Warriors bellowed out their battle cries, and quickly the chiefs and their followers were prancing around the spiraling fire. At long last the French and their Algonquin allies would be driven from Iroquois land. And there would be plunder at Fort Niagara. Much plunder!

The dancing and shrieking lasted all night. But when dawn

seared the sky, the warriors were back on the trail, carrying the war message to their tribes.

The only difficulty was that the Man of Great Undertakings had neglected to inform his jubilant compadres that General Jeffrey Amherst, his British superior gathering troops at Albany for a push at Montreal, had no intention of diverting part of his force for the Niagara operation.

To rectify this stupendous oversight, Johnson dashed off a letter to Amherst:

> I take the earliest opportunity to acquaint you that all the material business at the meeting here with the Indians is finished. . . . It is with great pleasure I can inform your Excellency these Confederate Nations have, with every mark of unfeigned zeal and sincerity, declared their unanimous resolutions of joining in the present war against the French . . .[50]

Then the next day he dispatched another urgent letter to Amherst in which he stressed the necessity of prompt action: "No time should be lost as the transportation to Lake Ontario grows more and more difficult as the summer advances."

Waiting for a reply, Johnson nervously paced the grounds of his sturdy stone mansion guarded by cannons. (Fort Johnson may be visited today just outside Amsterdam, New York.) What if Amherst should decline to take part? The whole undertaking would become nothing more than an empty boast. The Iroquois would laugh him right out of the Mohawk Valley. All pretense of British influence in upper New York would vanish.

His concern growing when no reply came, Johnson bade his wife Molly farewell and headed down the Iroquois Trail for Albany. Turning his horse into the stockaded town, he passed through the gate-blockhouse. Although Albany was the center of most trading activity in the north, it was only about four streets wide and six long, with one main thoroughfare paralleling the

Hudson and another (now State Street) climbing a low hill to the small fort which stood on the grounds of the modern-day state capitol.

Jeffrey Amherst, lean, cool, and aristocratic, merely listened quietly to Johnson's urgings. Although his orders from William Pitt were to move on Montreal at the same time that James Wolfe advanced along the St. Lawrence to attack Quebec, Amherst could see that if Johnson bottled up the western water road at Niagara, Algonquin and voyageur aid to the Canadian cities would be thereby eliminated. Yet Amherst was not a man of quick decisions, as would be amply demonstrated in the miscarriage of his advance on Montreal; and Johnson was made to wait so long for an answer that he gave up in despair and had already returned home when Amherst's messenger pounded up the trail with a despatch. "The assurances you have given me," it ran, "both by letter and in conversation that the Confederate Nations of Indians had . . . declared their unanimous resolutions of joining in the present war against the French, have determined me to pursue [your] plan . . ."

The drive against Fort Niagara was on!

Oswego was the rendezvous point. While British regulars under the expedition's leader Colonel John Prideaux rebuilt the fort, Johnson, second in command, tended to the Iroquois. By canoe and foot and horseback they came: boasting of their adventures on the Seneca River, of the bear or wolves they had killed near the Great Carrying Place, of the storm on Oneida Lake, of the wild Oswego rapids—of a thousand incidents that made travel over the trail exciting.

By June 30, with nearly a thousand Indians assembled, Prideaux and Johnson decided to move. Leaving half of the forty-four hundred British and Colonial troops to guard Oswego, their all-important link with the long supply route to Albany, the two leaders set out on Lake Ontario in a fleet of small boats and canoes. It was a risky undertaking: not only could one of the many summer storms scatter the squadron beyond recall, but had any of the Indians been French spies, a corvette from Niagara could blast them out of the water.

So they continued nervously down the lake shore, camping the first night at Sodus, the next near Rochester, the third at a bay Prideaux called after himself, and the fourth at a creek which still bears Johnson's name. Each day they feared that the hazy clouds on the horizon might be the threatening ship. But when on July 6 they made camp at the open roadstead just below Fort Niagara, they knew this segment of their operation had been a complete success.

Fort Niagara was virtually impregnable to direct assault—as modern visitors can surmise. More than three quarters of a century had passed since the Sieur de La Salle had built a pair of crude wooden stockades joined by a shaky palisade. Joncaire de Chabert had been responsible for duping the Senecas into granting him permission to construct a stone house for trading— which, though he designed it to resemble a harmless chateau, had massive, bullet-proof walls, many loopholes, thick shutters that could be slammed over the windows, and a battery of powerful cannons hidden on the third floor.

This chateau formed the nucleus around which the royal engineer Captain Francois Pouchot perfected one of the most formidable fortresses in North America. Not only did he throw a great stone wall completely across the wedge of land dominating the Niagara River, but he added a monstrous V-shaped outer work complete with a deep, dry moat guarded by flanking guns which made any attempt at scaling the walls suicide.

Pouchot himself was in command when Prideaux and Johnson appeared. With five hundred well-fed men in his garrison and plenty of ammunition, he felt he could hold out for a long time. Nevertheless, he realized that his fortified bastions could eventually be taken by a well-planned siege, so he sent couriers speeding to the army at Venango (already mobilized for the descent on Fort Pitt) urging the commander, gruff old Francois de Ligneris, to hurry his rugged voyageurs, Ottawas, Chippewas,

Shawnees, and Wyandots to his aid. This done, Pouchot and the Joncaire brothers relaxed, confident de Ligneris would arrive in time to send the British screaming back to civilization.

Prideaux and Johnson made camp beyond the range of Pouchot's cannons. Then siege operations began. First, the men were employed digging a deep trench which angled toward the walls. When this trench approached close enough for the French to bombard it, work was done only at night. The earth was hard and the work was slow. But eventually one quarter-mile was covered . . . then another. During the daytime the French artillery ploughed up the diggings, wrecking the labor of hours. Yet even harder on the morale was the fact that the English gunners, lacking the protection of the French, were kept silent back at the main camp.

The orderly book, which still exists, kept track of the monotonous entrenchment proceedings: "The officers which command the working parties constantly attend to see that the men . . . are not idle," went one order. "An officer and 200 men always to be posted at the Tail of the Trenches to prevent any shirker from quitting," went another—which was further amplified: "such mean and unsoldier-like shirkers as shall quit the Trenches without leave from their officers shall be punished in a most exemplary manner." However things were made a little brighter by the judicious distribution of such rum "as the General will think fit, and he himself will see the delivering of it."

And so the mole-like pace continued. Another quarter-mile was burrowed toward the fort. Yet still the English guns were kept silent.

This type of warfare did not appeal to Johnson's hotbloods. They began mocking the English and Provincial soldiers for tunneling like animals afraid of the daylight. The Indians grew more and more restless. Had they come to Niagara to listen only to French cannons?

The Joncaire brothers sensed the Iroquois discontent. De Chabert, in particular, knew the Iroquois, having been brought up in a Seneca village. Since some of his Seneca friends were with him in the fort, he decided to try a little diplomacy on the disgruntled Indians. So the fort drawbridge (similar to that which again spans the dry moat) creaked down and Kaendae, a skilled and respected Seneca elder, strolled out to converse with his fellows.

Johnson watched with a gnawing uneasiness, but he could only fume as the Indians spoke, for to capture Kaendae would have been such an affront to the loyal Iroquois that the entire nation might shuffle home in disgust.

Kaendae had many items in his favor. He told his tribesmen that Fort Niagara was so strong it could never be taken, that they were only wasting their time here when they should be hunting meat for their wives and children, that the English, far more than the French, coveted their land. And he whispered that de Ligneris and his host of voyageurs and Algonquins would soon repeat the blinding victory that had demolished Braddock.

Kaendae conferred for two days, then Johnson's fears seemed to be confirmed as an Onondaga chief and two Cayugas returned with the Seneca to Niagara to speak in person with the silken-tongued Joncaires. The Iroquois were led, blindfolded, through the massive entranceway, where the French had inscribed *Porte Des Cinq Nations* to win favor with the longhouse tribes, they continued across the clattering stones of the courtyard to the chateau where Pouchot and the Joncaires had their headquarters. Here, in one of the low-beamed rooms, the blindfolds were removed. The chiefs had brought a white wampum peace belt with them; and Pouchot smiled broadly, imagining his troubles were over. But as the conversation went on, the French commander realized that the three Indians had come mainly to induce their friends the Joncaire brothers to leave before the British trench wormed close enough for their bombardiers to begin dropping explosives within the fort. At this, Pouchot reblindfolded the Indians and brusquely escorted them out the gate. So far Johnson had kept his Iroquois.

After eleven days the British erected their first earthen battery. Cannons were dragged down the trench and rolled into position. As the men cheered wildly, their cannons at last roared into action. Soon rocks were splintering from the fort walls and crashes from within announced that the mortars were doing their work. Indeed, such was the accuracy of the British fire that a cannonball looped down a chateau chimney and smashed into the very room where Pouchot was sleeping.

Colonel Prideaux, pleased with the progress, stood close by the cannons praising the men for their firing ability. But suddenly one of the British shells exploded prematurely. When the smoke cleared, Prideaux was dead and Johnson was the new supreme commander.

The abrupt change made the regulars uneasy for Johnson knew nothing about siege operations. And when Amherst learned of what he regarded as a disaster, he sent General Thomas Gage (who had led Braddock's column) hotfooting it up the Iroquois Trail to take over. But events were now moving so rapidly that Gage was still on the road when the crucial fighting occurred.

At first Johnson had no thought of abandoning his predecessor's battle plan. Even while the cannons were rumbling from the first battery, the trench was extended several hundred yards closer to the fort and a second battery erected. Then, with the newly placed guns harassing the French, the trench was angled forward more than half a mile where the third, climactic battery was put into action only 140 yards from the northern end of the fort walls. This was nearly point-blank range and soon the French were desperately plugging their cracking ramparts with anything available, including even the Joncaires' valuable pelts.

Yet Johnson had growing worries. To maintain his attack, it was essential that the Iroquois Trail, now jammed with wagons and bateaux loaded with food and military supplies, be kept open. The French knew this and had sent a force to destroy the fort at Oswego. Although the French were repulsed in a fierce battle, the supply line was disrupted. This caused Johnson both to rush a letter to the fort commander in which he stated "our ammunition I fear will fall very short, also provisions, unless we can have a supply from you," and at the same time to start construction of scaling ladders for what would be a costly frontal attack in case he ran out of powder to complete a breach in the walls.

To add to Johnson's concern, reports of the advancing relief force of over sixteen hundred French and Indians now began coming in. De Ligneris, hard-drinking former commander of Fort Duquesne, had already landed near the head of Lake Erie (now Buffalo). His expert forest fighters, both red and white, were openly boasting that Johnson would soon be driven into Lake Ontario. Having little respect for British woodland battle tactics, de Ligneris's main strategy was to detach the Iroquois. Accordingly, he sent four western tribesmen brazenly to the Iroquois where, in Johnson's presence, they stated that the French and their own braves had no quarrel with the Iroquois and that, therefore, it would be advantageous if the Longhouse stood aside while the irresistible fury of de Ligneris tended to the whites.

Johnson noted signs of wavering among his Iroquois friends, since there was considerable sentiment that it was folly to kill other Indians, even though they be Algonquins, in a white man's war. However, the western diplomats departed without the Iroquois giving anything more than a vague declaration of possible neutrality.

In addition to his difficulties with the Iroquois and his dwindling stock of supplies, Johnson had to resolve his tactics concerning how to meet de Ligneris while at the same time not allowing Pouchot to sally out and destroy the weakened force he must leave around the fort. Finally he hit upon a dangerous plan. He would allow the relieving force to approach nearly to the fort. Then, still keeping most of his men deployed so that Pouchot could not lead a successful sortie, he would have 600 soldiers and 950 Iroquois attempt to ambush de Ligneris. For the scheme to succeed, Pouchot must not know what was happening until it was too late for him to aid de Ligneris and the Iroquois must not let him down in the fighting.

De Ligneris advanced with self-assurance. He and his men passed the deafening falls laughing and singing, at the same time checking their powder and sharpening their knife blades. Any slight uneasiness de Ligneris may have had came when Indian delegates he sent to the Iroquois first reported that the nation still would not commit itself to abandoning the English; then others that were sent remained themselves in Johnson's camp.

Soon de Ligneris reached the scenic bluff near Lewistown. Only six miles ahead was Fort Niagara, with smoke from the surrounding British fires smudging the horizon. If Johnson was to intercept him before he met Pouchot, he should have done it by now. Could the British be afraid to give him battle?

But now the forest settled in around them. The Algonquins shuddered. This was Iroquois country. Their fathers and grandfathers had spoken in awe of these fighters from the east. The Shawnee had once been their vassels. The Chippewa and Ottawa had been pushed out of Canada by the Iroquois. The Huron, Illini, Erie and other nations had been ushered to oblivion by the men of the Longhouse. Did they dare, then, to march into the very heartland of this ferocious tribe?

As they drew nearer to Fort Niagara, the western warriors began melting away. The voyageurs called them cowards. Why should they behave like women with victory so close?

Nonetheless, so feared were the Iroquois, that eventually only thirty of the original thousand Algonquins were left in de Ligneris's ranks.

But Johnson, too, was having trouble with his Indians. The western emissaries had had their effect, for the moody braves refused to go to war against people of their own race. Even when the French surprised a dozen English soldiers guarding some bateaux on the Niagara River and impaled their heads on poles, the Iroquois sent out to learn what the shooting was about did nothing more than grunt impassively as they watched the action, then saunter off into the woods. And when Johnson set him men constructing a half-mile V-shaped barricade cleverly disguised with freshly cut branches along the road the French were taking, the Iroquois would not help garrison the ambush. Instead only a hundred or so onlookers wandered about to relay information to the mass of braves lounging undecided in their camp a short distance north. However, Johnson had no choice except to depend on them, for he could spare no more men.

Pouchot watched, perplexed, from the battlements of Fort Niagara. He could see the activity among Johnson's troops, so close was the trap; but he could not discern precisely what was going on in the woods just beyond his vision. Although his men were on the ready, he hesitated to order an attack, since he could not be certain that Johnson was not merely trying to lure him out. Yet he knew de Ligneris was expected momentarily. Pouchot's five hundred troops could sway the tide of battle—if a battle was approaching—but at what point could he take the chance of ordering a sortie?

With the trap laid, Johnson's soldiers knelt behind the disguised barricade. Officers walked stealthily behind them, cautioning everyone to remain silent. Birds began twittering in the trees again.

Gradually the men grew restless. Their legs ached from their cramped position. Still the officers would not let them move. There must be no noise to let the French know of the ambush.

Suddenly the bird calls stopped. For a moment there was absolute silence. Then, faintly at first, came the thud of marching feet. Slowly the tramping grew louder. Johnson, waiting at camp, could feel his emotions rise. He remembered his fine promises to General Amherst. Yet now that he needed them, his Iroquois were milling undecided about their wigwams. The planning at Canajoharie, the hardships of the trail, the danger of the siege were all over now. The moment of truth was at hand.

The first French appeared down the road. Husky, bronzed men they were. Painted like the savages with whom they had spent the better part of their lives. And just as determined fighters. Their faces betrayed no strain, for they were almost within sight of the fort, and still the English had been afraid to show their faces.

Johnson's officer in charge raised his sword. Then he slashed downward. Six hundred muskets roared a most "warm reception" to Niagara—as Johnson wrote the next day.

Although the French force was now reduced from sixteen hundred to a mere six hundred, de Ligneris was not one to flinch from a fight. He ordered his men to charge the English and Colonials. The firing reverberated to the anxious ears of Commander Pouchot. Still he wavered. And the noise increased.

The fury of the battle reached the Iroquois, too. When it did, their loyalty to Johnson combined with the blood-lust nurtured by half a millenium of warfare took hold of them. As of one mind, they leaped to their feet and dashed to the scene of action. When the voyageurs saw the terrible Iroquois joining the British ranks, they tried even more frantically to pierce through to the fort. But there was no resisting the wild men of the Finger Lakes. And de Ligneris was forced to give ground.

Pouchot, in the meantime, realized that this was no diversion, that de Ligneris was heavily engaged. Accordingly he sent the drawbridge crashing earthward and his soldiers ran southward to aid the relief force. But no sooner had they emerged than Johnson ordered a thousand men out of the trenches where he had astutely hidden them. Thus surprised, Pouchot frantically fired his cannons to signal his men back into the fort.

At two in the afternoon of July 24, 1759, Johnson sent a message to Pouchot informing him that de Ligneris had been overwhelmed and demanding the surrender of Fort Niagara. Pouchot could not believe that the hardy voyageurs could have been so completely defeated as not to mount a counterattack. So he sent one of his officers into Johnson's camp where, from the lips of the wounded prisoners, many famous for their prowess on the riverways, he learned the truth. Man for man they could have whipped the British, they groaned, but once the Iroquois entered the fray, they had no chance. Even when they fled down the Lake Erie Road (Route 181 at this point), the Indians kept at their heels. De Ligneris himself had been shot, then captured, and was slowly dying. No, there would be no counterattack.

When Pouchot received the doleful news, he agreed to

Johnson's terms and the next day the British commander and the 44th Regiment, "drums beating and colors flying," marched into the citadel of French trans-Allegheny power. Pouchot invited Johnson to join him for a final banquet. And while the Iroquois, shouting with jubilation, looted the fort, the two commanders with their staffs poured brandy and mused over their tactics in the campaign now ended.

At the same table were the Joncaire brothers. They toasted Johnson, for many years their unseen adversary, then swapped stories with him about the chiefs they had known, maids they had loved, and tricks they had played on each other. But although the Joncaire's feigned good humor, Johnson knew they were ruined men, for each had lost a fortune in furs and the trade was about to pass out of their hands.

Yet there was more to it than the removal of the French, Johnson realized. The capitulation of Fort Niagara meant that the Iroquois no longer held the balance of power on the frontier. With a total population of only twenty thousand, the Five Nations could not hope to hold back the coming surge of English pioneers.

Later Johnson and Pouchot tended to the formal capitulation. British and French troops stood at attention as the Fleur-de-lis was lowered for the last time. Then the Union Jack rose to the top of the flagpole. It fluttered gently in the wind.

The era of the French—and of the Iroquois—was over.

The American Revolution, 1774–81

13.   On the Brink of a Precipice

The weather was hot and dry the autumn of 1774, and dust clung in a gray patina over the trees that drooped beside the King's Highway. But the heat did not affect the spirits of the multitude who had driven a half-dozen miles out of New Haven to await the coach from Boston. There was a strained excitement about the gathering, for many felt that these delegates to the Continental Congress held the key to the welfare of the colonies.

A shout went up as fingers jabbed at a cloud of dust rolling southward along the road. A murmur rose as the coach-and-four drew closer. Then a cheer broke out as peppery John Adams poked his head out from between the leather curtains. Quickly Adams (at age thirty-seven having the time of his life), Bob Paine, and Tom Chushing stepped down from the coach. But none of them was the luminary of the Massachusetts delegation. Although John Adams (whose diary is our main source for this monumental journey down the King's Highway) does not note the fact, certainly a hush came over the assembly as the grand architect of the patriot cause, the artful Master of the Puppets as his enemies called him, climbed out of the coach.

At first sight Sam Adams disappointed those who expected a blazing revolutionary. He was of middle age, with gray hair, a casual disregard for clothes, and hands perpetually ashake with palsy. He was a reserved individual who kept his emotions ever

181

in rein—as distinguished from his ebullient younger cousin John.
Those who valued men with sharp business minds found Sam's
acumen pitiful, and were not surprised to learn he had failed
miserably as a merchant and as a brewer, and had even so fouled
up his accounts as Boston tax collector that many felt the seventy
thousand dollar shortage verged on embezzlement—although
negligent management was a more accurate description.

Yet Adams was not a fool. Graduating fifth in his class at
Harvard, he found that his talents lay in the political, rather than
the economic field. Here he was most conscientious, as a contemporary Tory indicated: "He eats little, drinks little, sleeps
little, thinks much, and is most decisive and indefatigable in the
pursuit of his objects."

As the welcoming speeches ended and the coach set out for
New Haven with its triumphant honor guard of horsemen and
carriages, Sam Adams may well have mused on his part in the
events which led to the calling of the Continental Congress. His
initial move had been to gain predominance in the little-known
Boston Caucus—whose name was derived from the ship caulk-
ers, who, along with the artisans and shopkeepers, made up
much of its membership. Using the tightly organized caucus
voting block to control the Boston town meeting, Adams found
that he could create a political machine (America's first) by
rewarding his workers with such jobs as assessors, collectors, and
fire wardens.

Next he subtly extended his power base by bringing in the
gangs that had made Boston's waterfront a storm center for riots
and violence. Organizing them into squads under their own
officers, he used them as his own private army—and they enjoyed the ennobling experience of combining fisticuffs with patriotism. Then Adams enmeshed the wealth and influence of such
fashionable young blades as John Hancock and Joseph Warren
into his organization.

Sam Adams's ruminations may have been interrupted by his
colorful entry into New Haven. "As we came into the town,"
wrote his cousin, "all the bells in town were set to ringing, and
the people—men, women, and children—were crowding at the

doors and windows as if it was to see a coronation. At nine o'clock the cannons were fired . . ."[51]

Possibly Sam Adams smiled as he thought how he had helped mold public opinion so that such a welcome was possible. It had begun in 1767 when Champagne Charlie Townshend, witty but irrational British Chancellor of the Exchequer, routed through Parliament a repressive tax on tea—America's favorite beverage. Although the purpose of the act had been to relieve the British taxpayer, overburdened as a result of the French and Indian War, the fact that a customs commission was established to enforce collection of the duty had given Adams his opening. When customs officials boarded John Hancock's sloop *Liberty* to check its cargo for smuggled goods (of which there were many), Adams's waterfront storm troopers had pitched the officials into the harbor.

After that it was easy. The Liberty Riot led to the stationing of British redcoats in Boston. This in turn resulted in the killing of five members of an unruly mob that had been threatening some soldiers. Sam, through speeches in the Faneuil Hall town meeting and through articles in the wide-circulating *Boston Gazette* (both under his control), had magnified the self-defense shooting into a full-blown massacre. This had enabled him to gain sympathy throughout the colonies.

With events now moving along at a merry pace, Sam accomplished an even more masterful stroke. In November, 1772, he had the Boston town meeting establish what was innocently called a Committee of Correspondence whose purpose was to send letters to the other Massachusetts towns keeping them informed of British wrongs done in Boston. While Thomas Hutchinson, one of the sharpest governors in the Empire, was referring to the committee derisively as "a foolish scheme," Adams's messengers were galloping over the King's Highway and its many feeder lines seeking out the staunchest patriots, who in turn formed committees of their own. Before Hutchinson and the Torys were aware of it, crafty Adams was the head of a virtually separate government.

The idea was such a resounding success that it wasn't long

before Virginia radicals were urging the establishment of similar committees throughout the colonies. Had the King's Highway not been so well developed at this time, it is doubtful that such groups, depending on sea communication, could have had much influence. But given existing communications, once New York, Philadelphia, Williamsburg, and other important towns had strong groups, only some hostile act by the British was needed for the committees to unify the country in opposition.

Adams had been delighted to maneuver the British into such a blunder. When in 1773 the British attempted to send cheap tea from the nearly bankrupt East India Company to American ports (thereby rudely upsetting the smuggling trade so dear to Hancock and other merchants), Adams unleashed his hooligans, now called Sons of Liberty. Disguised haphazardly as Mohawks, they rampaged aboard the tea ship, heaving the entire cargo into Boston Bay. This caused the enraged Parliament to retaliate with what became known as the Intolerable Acts.

Any one of these measures would have gladdened Sam Adams; but to have them all presented at the same time—that was more than he had dreamed! First, there was the Boston Port Act which, by closing Boston to all commerce until the tea was paid for, threatened to starve her into submission. Then there was the Administration of Justice Act which would require persons accused of certain capital crimes to be packed off across the stormy Atlantic for trial in England. Next was the Quartering Act bound to irritate Americans by decreeing that British soldiers could be forced on them as lodgers (and spies). And lastly, the Quebec Act slashed off the entire Ohio-Mississippi valley— for which Colonials serving with Braddock, Forbes, and Johnson had given their lives (and for which such land speculators as Washington, Franklin and others had plunked down hard-earned money)—and incorporated it into Canada.

Now the organization Adams had inspired sprang into action. Almost immediately New York merchants advocated an intercolonial meeting to discuss their grievances. Quickly the Philadelphia Committee of Correspondence announced its approval of such a plan. Finally in Virginia a rump legislature, meeting in the smoky sanctuary of the Raleigh Tavern, issued a formal call for a congress.

With that the deed was done. In most colonies special conventions gathered at which delegates to the congress were chosen. Other delegates were selected by the colonial legislatures, such as in Massachusetts where Sam Adams gained the election of himself and his slate by bolting the assembly doors both to conservative members who opposed him and to the governor's agent, shrieking outside that the assembly was dissolved. Since in almost no case was the choice of delegates left up to the general public, the membership reflected no overwhelming endorsement by the people at large. As a nearly spontaneous coup by the committes (linked, of course, by the King's Highway) it was as much a tribute to the astuteness of Sam Adams as to the blundering of the British.

Sam Adams and the Massachusetts delegation continued on towards the congressional meeting place in Philadelphia. In New York they were taken on a merry round of parties, at one of which they enjoyed "the most splendid dinner I ever saw" (wrote John Adams) with more than fifty gentlemen of the Committee of Correspondence. Taking the ferry to New Jersey, they passed through New Brunswick, then reached Princeton, to be entertained by the college president John Witherspoon, who was "as high a Son of Liberty as any man in America." Crossing the Delaware River at Trenton, they were met five miles out of Philadelphia by a great number of persons including many delegates from other colonies.

Then the procession continued down the King's Highway into the heart of Philadelphia, which, with a population of thirty-eight thousand was second only to London in size in the British Empire! Although Adams recorded that they arrived "dirty, dusty, and fatigued," he conceded they "could not resist the opportunity to go to the [City] Tavern." There, amid another of John Adams's most elegant banquets, they were introduced to more of the delegates. Only near midnight was the last glass of Madeira clinked.

At ten the next morning, September 5, they were back in the City Tavern, some undoubtedly bleary-eyed from the previous night's festivities. From there they strolled the block and a half to their meeting room. Although Joseph Galloway, conservative Speaker of the Pennsylvania Legislature, had offered them the spacious statehouse, the radicals asserted their influence by having the fifty-six members gather in a cramped chamber of Carpenters Hall (which modern visitors see without the original partition which split it in two).

Despite this early show of strength, Sam Adams had no delusions about the weakness of his position. Only about a third of the congressmen could be classified as outright radicals, and even they lacked Sam's lust for independence. Somehow within the short space of time that the congress would meet, he must not only make the radicals realize that a permanent break with England was desirable, but must prevent the powerful conservative faction, led by able Joseph Galloway, from channeling the protest toward reconciliation.

The first day was spent in electing a chairman, Peyton Randolph of Virginia, and in discussions as to whether the voting should be by individuals or by colonies (it was later decided each colony should have a single vote). The very next day Sam Adams, wondering how to rouse the congress against Britain, had a marvelous piece of luck (or was it his own shrewd planning?). Down the King's Highway clattered a messenger from New York, announcing that the British had bombed and burned Boston! The congressmen were stunned and incensed. "This city is in the utmost confusion," delegate Silas Deane wrote to his wife in Connecticut, "all the bells toll muffled, and the most unfeigned marks of sorrow appear in every countenance." There was talk of revenge. Soon more express riders came in, reporting that the entire Massachusetts colony was in armed revolt down to and including parts of Connecticut!

While the origin of this shocking and utterly untrue story

has never been determined, Sam Adams was quick to take advantage of it. Realizing that the colonies had now been at least partially united, he used the occasion to call upon Reverend Jacob Duché to bring God in on their side. "Fight against them that fight against me," the preacher thundered from Psalms. "Take hold of shield and buckler and stand up for mine help . . ." He was so inspiring that he continued giving his warlike prayers for the entire session.

But with all the gabble of possible armed conflict the moderates were still in control. The business that had brought the congress into existence was not independence but merely the need to voice the colonies' objections to Britain's high-handed methods of coercion. Accordingly two committees were appointed: the first to state American grievances and the second to form a nonimportation agreement by which the colonies could work on the mother country in a more forceable, yet still not military, manner.

Yet while these committees met, Sam Adams was plotting new moves which would nudge the delegates toward an outright break. The King's Highway was an essential tie between Adams in Philadelphia and his revolutionary organization in Massachusetts—indeed, without the constant expresses between the two cities it is probable that Adams's plans could never have matured. "I have been waiting with great impatience for a letter from the Committee of Correspondence," he wrote to Boston on September 14. And when Paul Revere barreled into Philadelphia a few days later it was clear what Adams had been so impatient about.

"By express which arrived here yesterday from the Committee of the town of Boston to the Continental Congress," Delaware's Caesar Rodney said in a letter to one of his constituents, "we are informed the County of Suffolk, of which the town of Boston is the capital, had entered into certain resolutions, a copy of which was enclosed us. . . . The Congress met on that business this day and . . . ordered [the resolves] immediately to be printed that the people might know what they thought of the matter." [52]

The Suffolk Resolves, engineered by Adams's deft hench-
man Joseph Warren, took the daring and unprecedented step of
proclaiming that the Intolerable Acts should be disregarded, that
the Colonial Assembly should collect and withhold taxes until
their objections were met, and that preparations for hostilities
should be commenced. It was an outright act of revolution. Of
course the British could hardly be expected to tremble over such
bombastic resolves passed by a single American county, but
when Adams got the congress to recognize them, they took on a
new degree of importance.

Now, however, the Tories mustered their strength. Joseph
Galloway, who John Adams describes as "sensible and learned,"
not only found support in an important faction of the congress,
but his views of maintaining close ties with Britain was a fair
reflection of the temper of the country as a whole.

In order to thwart the radicals, Galloway, on September 28,
introduced a plan which might have led to a satisfactory solution
of the dispute. He suggested an intercolonial legislature, or
grand council, which would have a veto over any Parliamentary
law which it found unsuitable. In addition, this grand council
could initiate legislation itself, which, however, either Parliament or a royal governor appointed by the king could veto. By
putting Britain and America on a nearly equal partnership basis,
a permanent, mutually beneficial trans-Atlantic union could have
evolved.

Although the debates were kept secret, for many subjects
approached treason and were, therefore, punishable by hanging,
it is obvious that Galloway's plan occasioned warm and lengthly
discussions. "I came with the idea of getting a bill of rights and
permanent relief," roared South Carolinian Edward Rutledge
(according to John Adams's notes). "I think [Galloway's] plan
may be freed from almost every objection. I think it is almost a
perfect plan." But Patrick Henry, one of the congress's most
impassioned orators, adamantly opposed it, for he was convinced
that Parliament would purchase its way into control of the
American grand council since "bribery is a part of her system of
government."

During the fierce debate, the delegates were besieged by a stream of news from Massachusetts (most of it managed by Sam Adams and Joseph Warren). The goat was Boston-based General Thomas Gage, whom we met fifteen years earlier hurrying rather tardily down the Iroquois Trail to relieve William Johnson of command at Niagara. Gage was actually a "good natured, peaceable, and sociable man" (admitted John Adams) but, under Sam Adams's clever manipulation, he was transformed into an archmilitarist scheming toward the destruction of all Colonial liberty. Galloway later described both Adams's handling of Gage and the importance of the King's Highway in the congressional debates:

> While the two parties in Congress remained thus during three weeks on an equal balance, the republicans were calling to their assistance the aid of their factions without. Continual expresses were employed between Philadelphia and Boston. These were under the management of Samuel Adams —a man, who though by no means remarkable for brilliant abilities, yet is [unequaled] in popular intrigue and the management of a faction. . . . It was this man who by his superior application managed at once the faction in Congress at Philadelphia and the factions in New England. Whatever these patriots in Congress wished to have done by their colleagues without to induce General Gage, then at the head of his Majesty's army at Boston, to give them a pretext for violent opposition or to promote their measures in Congress, Mr. Adams advised and directed to be done; and when done, it was dispatched by express to Congress.[53]

Yet even with the untiring efforts of Sam Adams and his Sons of Liberty, voting on Galloway's plan was extremely close. As the members of each delegation caucused to determine how their colony would go, they must have heard the impassioned words of Galloway (as later recorded by John Adams); "We [need] the aid and assistance and protection of . . . our Mother Country. . . . Can we wish to become aliens to the Mother State?" Could they renounce the land which had nurtured them, which had protected them from the French and the Indians, a country with whom they had the warmest cultural ties and in which many had relatives and close friends.

After the votes were counted, the result was five colonies for Galloway and six against. Since the proceedings were all secret, we do not know what colony besides Georgia, which was not present, did not vote nor how many of the six were carried by a bare majority. Perhaps in a more tranquil era—when Adams was not heaping coals on the fire in Massachusetts—there would have been renewed debate, some compromise, maybe even a national referendum. But time would not wait. Galloway had no chance to reintroduce his plan.

Sam Adams and the other radicals now fastened their grip on the congress. One after another measures that could only antagonize the British were passed. There was a Declaration of Rights which reaffirmed the radicals' contention that Parliament could not tax Americans without their consent. There was a haughty Address to the People of Great Britain which stated that their mercantilistic policy was oppressing the Colonies beyond belief and that the Americans would "never submit to be hewers of wood or drawers of water." Even more ominous was a message to the French at Quebec urging them to refuse to bear arms for Britain should hostilities arise. And as a final culmination, a strict nonimportation agreement was passed whereby not only was all commerce with Great Britain cut off, but militant Committees of Safety were to be formed in "every county, city, or town," whose purpose was to strong-arm unpatriotic merchants who tried to trade on the sly.

On October 26 the First Continental Congress concluded its meetings by signing a petition to King George, warning him to rid himself of the designing and dangerous men who were ruining the Colonies. Several days later, the delegates were back on the King's Highway, their heads spinning with the momentous events they had been part of. All along the way they were queried by curious Americans as to the doings in Philadelphia:

at the village taverns where they paused for food, drink, and conversation, at the ferries where the boatmen and other passengers were avid for information, at the roadside inns where the punch was plentiful and the evening talk always saturated with politics.

Yet even at this juncture, with the country "on the brink of a precipice" (as the congressional secretary Charles Thomson wrote to Benjamin Franklin in London), many delegates, including those quite radical, had the feeling that the work of the congress was over. John Adams, setting out in a drenching rain, was one of these: "It is not very likely that I shall ever see this part of the world again," he wrote in his diary, "but I shall ever retain a most grateful, pleasing sense of the many civilities I have received in it."

Certainly none of the fifty-six delegates would have believed that within six months British and American blood would be flowing and the road over which they were now traveling would ring to the thump of soldiers' boots.

That is no one except old Sam Adams.

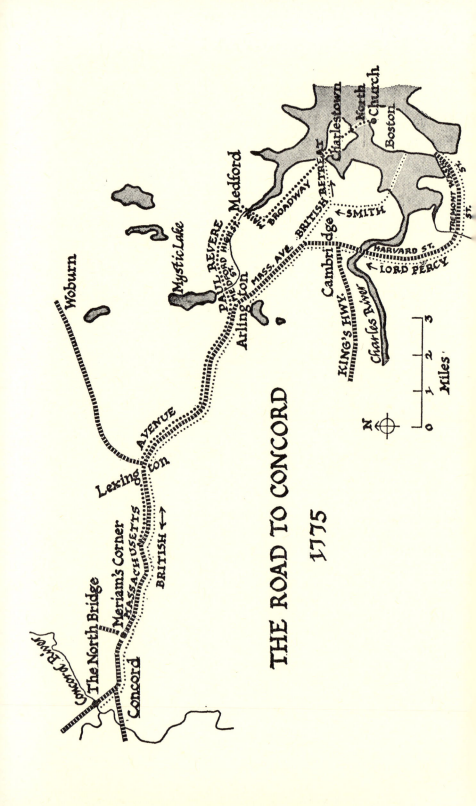

THE ROAD TO CONCORD
1775

14. If They Want to Begin a War, Let It Begin Here

Starlight played on the twin arches of Boston's town gates, catching as it did the cold steel of the sentries' bayonets. Nearby could be heard the wash of the tide on both sides of the narrow causeway which connected the semi-island city with the mainland. The air was chilly, for it was mid-April, in the year 1775. The British guards blew on their hands while they muttered oaths against their general Thomas Gage, whom they called Tommy derisively. One guard poked his finger gingerly on the shimmering bayonet point. Wouldn't he like to see how the smart-mouthed Yankees would stand up to a close-order charge by husky grenadiers! As Colonel Earl Percy had said of the Americans: they "talk much and do little. . . . Whenever we appear they are frightened out of their wits."

The sentries heard the clop, clop, clop of an approaching rider. At their challenge, a horseman reined up and the friendly face of blue-eyed, twenty-nine-year-old Billy Dawes beamed down upon them. After some sharp questioning, the sentries permitted Dawes to canter down the King's Highway toward Roxbury. Dawes took a leisurely pace, apparently enjoying the night. The sentries watched him for a while, perhaps thinking that it was odd for a gentleman to be taking a chilly ten o'clock jaunt on any night—but especially on this night. But before they could order him back, Billy Dawes had passed over a slight rise and was lost from sight.

Dawes gave a quick glance behind him, then dug into his horse. The animal gave a startled jerk and bounded ahead. Soon his horse's thundering hooves were striking sparks on the cobblestones of the King's Highway. Dawes galloped through slumbering Roxbury, clattered over the aged bridge which spanned the Charles River, and raced through Cambridge, where he left the King's Highway to take the fork which led to Lexington and Concord. And as he sped northward, each village and farmhouse heard his shrill cry: "The British are coming! The British are coming!"

An hour after Dawes eased through the guarded Boston gates, Joseph Warren, Sam Adams's number one man in the city, doubting that even smooth-talking Dawes could get past the sentries, dispatched Paul Revere in a tippy little rowboat across the bay under the nose of an unsuspecting British man-of-war. From Charlestown Sons of Liberty, already alerted by lanterns in the North Church steeple, Revere borrowed a horse and immediately set out into the slumbering countryside. And as he hurried through the calm night, now made eerie by the ghostly light of a rising moon, he, too, roused the inhabitants with the shout: "The British are coming! The British are coming!"

Indeed, the British were not only coming, but at least one patrol was already on the prowl. "After I had passed Charlestown neck," Revere wrote, "I saw two men on horseback under a tree. When I got near them, I discovered they were British officers. One tried to get ahead of me, and the other to take me. I turned my horse very quick and galloped towards Charlestown neck and then pushed for the Medford road. The one who chased me, endeavouring to cut me off, got [stuck] in a clay pond." [54]

Revere and Dawes arrived in Lexington within thirty minutes of each other. Revere, the first, raced past the triangular-shaped common to the clapboard home of Reverend Jonas Clarke (which still stands). At the door he was stopped by one of the militia guards that had been posted to protect Sam Adams and John Hancock, who were sleeping there. When the guard captain tried to keep the excited courier from making too much noise, Revere roared: "Noise! You'll have noise enough before long. The regulars are coming!" With that the two leaders were awakened, their baggage hurriedly packed, and they themselves sped off in a chaise for Woburn.

With Dawes joining him, Revere lit out for Concord, six miles farther on, whose store of guns and ammunition, they surmised, was one of the British objectives. Just out of Lexington they met up with Sam Prescott on his way home from late evening's sparking with a certain Miss Milliken. Revere and Dawes, knowing Prescott to be a "high Son of Liberty," allowed him to join them. And it was well for the patriot cause that they did, for the trio blundered into four British officers. With pistols and drawn swords they forced them off the road and into a pasture. But Prescott, familiar with the area, suddenly spurred his horse over a low stone wall and dashed on to warn Concord. At nearly the same time Billy Dawes bounded off in the opposite direction. A pair of British pursued him into the moonlit darkness, but when the clever Dawes yelled out to nobody: "Hallo, boys. I've got two of 'em," the soldiers wheeled back.

Revere, more closely guarded, wrote that a major "clapped his pistol to my head," and escorted him toward Lexington. However, when the British heard the rap of exploding muskets as the Americans began to gather, they let Revere go and melted into the night.

Once back in Lexington, Revere found a sleepy-eyed assortment of militia slouching around Buckman's Tavern (which still squats beside the village green). Captain John Parker, a large, hulking man, was staring down the Boston road. He was somewhat provoked with Revere for his scouts had either not bothered to return or had discovered no British troops. Now his men were grumbling that it was too cold a night to be routed out of their comfortable beds on a false alarm. Some were already trailing back home, while others congregated in the tavern enjoying, as best they could at this ungodly hour, John Buckman's beer and heady rum toddies.

Gradually the dark eastern horizon lightened to turquoise. Buckman tossed another log into the giant fireplace. Another wasted night, one of the men muttered. Revere and Dawes with their silly tales about the British! Damn!

But the British were even then almost on them. Mild-man-

nered Tommy Gage had received a preemptory order from the
Earl of Dartmouth (who once thought so much of the Colonials
that he donated heavily to the college afterward named after
him in gratitude). Gage should "arrest and imprison the principal actors and abettors in the Provincial Congress," Dartmouth
commanded. Since the Massachusetts legislature had just fin-
ished meeting in Concord, only twenty-one tantalizing miles
away, it was obvious to Gage that he should snatch up Sam
Adams, John Hancock, and any other lesser leaders he could
surprise. Of course there was the disquieting fact that he must
send his men through a country where numerous militia companies had been training for months. Yet Dartmouth, writing in the
cozy security of his snug little island, had stated confidently that
"any efforts of the people, unprepared to encounter with a
regular force, cannot be very formidable." So Gage decided he
really must move.

It is difficult to believe that the American leaders had not
given considerable thought to the selection of Concord as their
temporary capital. The King's Highway and the Concord fork
provided them easy communication with the rest of Massachusetts—and, as Sam Adams's letters reveal, there was a constant
exchange of communiqués, most of which concerned either the
economic mobilization of the colony to support Boston or the
formation of Minute Men companies "that upon a very short
notice . . . will be able to assemble [into] a formidable army."
In addition, since Sam realized the temper of the other colonies
would not countenance any outright attack on the redcoats, he
emphasized to his followers that they must be resolved "not to be
the aggressors in an open quarrel with the troops." With the
Minute Men in active training, Concord was then selected as the
assembly point for a large store of military supplies. Just a
six-hour march from Gage in Boston, the supplies were offered as
a juicy lure.

Gage, a far from incompetent officer, had laid his plans with
secrecy and daring. The seven hundred men of the flying detachment would not even be told of their destination until the very
night they were led down to the boats—which would then ferry

them across the bay to the deserted environs around the hamlet of Somerville. Thus, bypassing the main roads where Minute Men could spot them, the troops would stealthily quick-step down midnight lanes, striking the Concord road a mile or so below Arlington, the halfway point. While the country slept, the redcoats would pour into Lexington, where Gage's plans proba- bly called for the arrest of Adams and Hancock; and long before dawn they would descend on Concord to destroy the important arms cache. As the Minute Men started to assemble, the British would be fast-moving out of the country and soon be safely tucked away in Boston. It would be neat, clean, and decisive.

But the success of Gage's plan depended on timing.

However Gage had never been a lucky man. Revere and Dawes had managed to elude his patrols and reach Lexington to warn Adams and Hancock; and Prescott's lucky leap over a stone hedge had enabled him to bolt into Concord. In addition, Gage's seven-hundred-man detachment was making its own difficulties.

The landing at the Somerville marsh was trickier than antici- pated. Then a further wait was necessary while other boats ferried over provisions—most of which the soldiers improvi- dently tossed into the swamp as excess baggage. Finally, the overweight commander Colonel Francis Smith slowed the men to the waddling gait of his staggering steed. The detachment inched down paths that should have been flown over. Eventually Smith realized he must hurry, particularly when the patrol who had terminated Paul Revere's brief but glamorous ride informed him that Minute Men from many towns were beginning to muster. With that Smith sent Major John Pitcairn ahead with four hundred fast men.

Meanwhile Captain Parker was fidgeting at Lexington. Al- though he could hear the rattle of muskets from every direction as the countryside was awakened by the prearranged signal, he had a bare seventy-five men loitering around the green, many of them bleary from too much of John Buckman's brew. Then a scout came racing into town crying that the British were only a

quarter-mile away. Instantly Parker's drummer sounded the muster alarm and his men formed a somewhat disheveled line.
Parker shouted: "Don't fire unless fired upon; but if they want to
begin a war, let it begin here!" According to one of the Minute
Men here is what happened next:

> The British troops approached us rapidly in platoon, with a
> general officer [Major Pitcairn] at their head. The officer
> came up to within about 30 feet of the center of the company
> where I stood. . . . The officer then swung his sword and
> said, "Lay down your arms, you damned rebels, or you are all
> dead men!" [55]

Although the writer claimed that Pitcairn ordered his troops
to shoot in the same breath, there is strong evidence that an
American fired first and that Pitcairn actually tried to prevent his
men from returning the fire. But the four hundred redcoats were
momentarily out of control. They blasted at Parker's feeble seventy-five, then charged head on with their bayonets. When the
carnage was over, seventeen Americans lay dead or gasping for
life. The British gave three lusty cheers and fired off a volley in
token of their victory. As soon as they were joined by Smith, they
resumed their march toward Concord.

Yet Gage in Boston was nervous. He, more than most
Britons, knew the fighting temper of the Americans and realized
that King George (blithely boasting, "once those rebels have felt
a small blow, they will submit") was grossly deceiving himself.
Thus, at four in the morning, Gage had routed cocky Lord Percy
and a thousand men out of their beds; and by nine the relief
column was swinging down the King's Highway, fifes and drums
blatantly sounding "Yankee Doodle." This was not a sly night-
time raid like the force led by Smith and Pitcairn, but a bold,
daylight march meant to intimidate the provincials. With the
emergence of Lord Percy through the Boston gates the Revolution may be said to have begun.

And it was well for the British that Percy was dispatched,
for Smith and Pitcairn were soon to find the going hazardous.
Minute Men from miles around were shouldering their guns and

hurrying toward the scene of trouble. By the time the British were on Concord's outskirts, 150 of Sam Adams's troopers were scowling at them from the hills—and their numbers were steadily growing.

Once in Concord, Colonel Smith made his headquarters at the Wright Tavern (still standing) next door to the parish house where the provincial assembly had met, in a building much like the Unitarian church which now occupies the site. Although the people of Concord, warned by Sam Prescott, had frantically carted off much of the powder and military supplies, the British were able to spike two cannons and dump some bullets and a few barrels of flour into the millpond behind the tavern.

As the search for supplies continued, Smith sent seven companies to the north bridge. But when the soldiers reached the bridge, they saw the opposite hill crowded with Americans, whose number had leaped upward to 450. As the British hurriedly ripped up bridge planks, the Americans moved forward. Corporal Amos Barrett later wrote these impressions of the action:

> We were all ordered to load—and had strict orders not to fire until they fired first, then to fire as fast as we could. We then marched . . . Captain Davis had got, I believe within fifteen rods [247 feet] of the British when they fired three guns one after the other. I saw the balls strike the river on the right of me. . . .
> We then were all ordered to fire that could fire and not kill our own men. It is strange that there weren't no more killed, but they fired too high. Captain Davis was killed, and Mr. Hosmer and a number wounded. We soon drove them from the bridge. When I got over, there was two lay dead and another almost dead. We did not follow them. There was eight or ten that was wounded, and a-running and hobbling about looking back to see if we was after them.[56]

Even after this brief but sharp exchange, the opening valley of which Ralph Waldo Emerson (whose grandfather witnessed the affair from near the now-famous Old Manse) called "the shot heard round the world," Colonel Smith dallied two hours in Concord before beginning the long trek back to Boston. But by this time the 450 militia had swelled to 700, a number equal to the British. The redcoats had only proceeded half a mile (to a point currently marked by a boulder at Meriam's Corner) when hell descended upon them:

> We were fired on from houses and behind trees [one British soldier recalled]. . . . The country was an amazing strong one, full of hills, woods, stone walls, etc., which the rebels did not fail to take advantage of, for they were all lined with people who kept up an incessant fire upon us. . . . In this way we marched between nine and ten miles [two portions of this road still exist], their number increasing from all parts while ours was reducing by deaths, wounds, and fatigue. We were totally surrounded with such an incessant fire as it's impossible to conceive; our ammunition was likewise near expended.[57]

Stumbling into Lexington, the column was far different from the arrogant troops who had tromped off in triumph a half-day earlier. Only the fact that Lord Percy was there with cannon and a thousand men saved them from utter annihilation. But even so, Percy, who had established his headquarters in the still-standing Munroe Tavern, experienced a most difficult time pushing down the road to Boston. "King Hancock forever!" was the cry as enraged Yankee farmers blazed away. Percy was forced to revise his low opinion of American fighting ability when, upon reaching Arlington, he was met openly in vicious hand-to-hand combat. By now the hard-fighting Colonials approached in numbers the entire British force of seventeen hundred. Percy surmised that even more of the flinty-eyed New Englanders would be grimly awaiting him at Great Bridge over which he must march should he choose to return to Boston by way of Cambridge and the King's Highway. Percy, therefore, abandoned his route, to slink down a side road to Charlestown and entrench himself with great haste around Bunker Hill under the protection of the men-of-war swaying in Boston harbor.

The next day Gage sent over boats and the humbled Percy, along with his dazed compatriots Smith and Pitcairn, were ferried ignominiously back home.

Thus the war began on the Concord Road. Although it had been Revere, Dawes, and Prescott who had aroused the slumbering countryside, the real architect of the event was astute Sam Adams.

Now, at last, Adams's schemings of a decade had matured. Shots had been fired; American lives had been sacrificed; and soon New England gunners would be descending on Boston in vengeance. Could the rest of the colonies stand by while their countrymen were in arms? Sam Adams thought not.

And so it was that as he and "King" Hancock, escaping from Lexington, heard the dull popping of musketry, Sam had glanced back into the reddening dawn. "Ah, what a glorious morning is this!" legend has him exclaiming. "What a most glorious morning!"

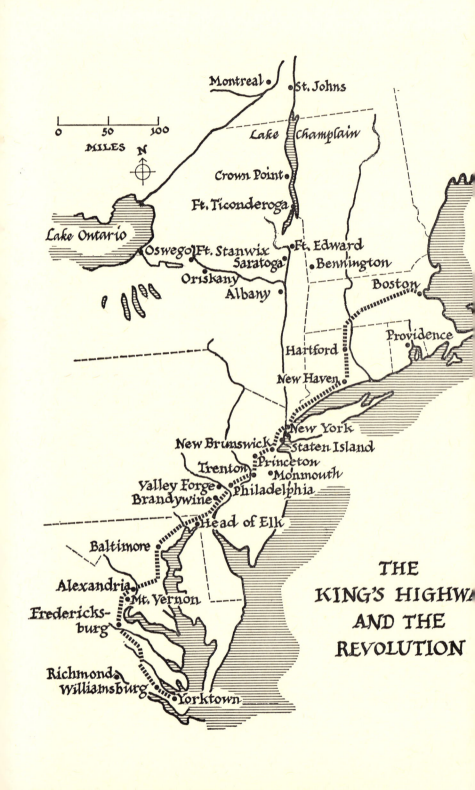

THE
KING'S HIGHWA
AND THE
REVOLUTION

15.   Our Soldiers Are in Great Distress

Never had the King's Highway seen such a splendid procession as that which set out from Philadelphia on June 23rd, 1775. All the city officials were present—their carriages glittering, their ladies dressed in their most special finery. The high militia officers trooped by in uniforms that made the road bright as a rainbow. But the position of honor was reserved for George Washington, newly appointed commander of the hodgepodge mass of armed men besieging General Gage in Boston.

As the cavalcade moved past the Pennsylvania state-house (now Independence Hall), Washington may have experienced a nagging uneasiness over the step he was taking. During his exploits along Braddock's Road and in securing the Virginia frontier from the French, he had never commanded over fifteen hundred men, which hardly made him qualified to lead ten or twenty times that number. Then, too, he was not entirely ready to renounce his allegiance to the king. His sentiments, however, were deeply hostile to the manner in which British troops had been used to coerce Boston. These mingled feelings were reflected in a letter which he mailed to George William Fairfax, then living in England, his boon companion on the surveying trip he took as a youth into the Appalachians: "Unhappy it is, though, to reflect that a brother's sword has been sheathed in a brother's breast" (ending with "affectionate compliments to Mrs. Fairfax," nee Sally Cary, Washington's first and perhaps only love).

The festive congregation filed out of Philadelphia and into farmlands where the first shoots of corn and wheat were spiking through the black earth. Near the Frankford hills the local politicians, militia bigwigs, and fat-tummied merchants gave Washington a rousing farewell. Then he, with an honor guard from the Philadelphia Light Horse, continued on toward the Trenton ferry. Once the shouting was gone and with only the thud of the horses hooves to disturb his reverie, Washington probably recalled the words he had enscribed to his brother John: "I am now to bid adieu to you and to every kind of domestic ease for a while. I am embarked on a wide ocean, boundless in its prospect, and in which, perhaps, no safe harbor is to be found."

Suddenly an express rider appeared in the distance. News from Boston! The man, caked with mud from the rain which had started falling, gasped that there had been a terrific fight at Breed's Hill across the narrow bay from Boston. Twice the British general, William Howe, had sent his men storming up at the earthworks which had been hastily dug by the Massachusetts militia. And twice the British had been met by withering volleys. On the third charge the redcoats had gained the summit, but only after the American sharpshooters had no more powder. When it was all over, the slope (which modern visitors may survey from a monumental shaft atop the rise erroneously called Bunker Hill) was covered with the wounded and dying bodies of nearly half the original British force of 2,250!

If Washington had had any doubts before this, the Battle of Bunker Hill was the ultimate act of revolution. Lexington had been spontaneous, but Bunker Hill was planned.

Washington continued on through rainy New Jersey. He spent the following night in New Brunswick. The next afternoon, rather than crossing the Hudson by way of the Elizabeth ferry, Washington and his retinue continued to Newark where members of the New York Congress assured him of a favorable welcome in their city—while admitting there was considerable pro-British sentiment. Thus around four in the afternoon Washington landed at Laight Street (near the mouth of the modern Holland Tunnel) to be met by some five hundred militiamen, resplendent in their uniforms, and "a greater number of the principal inhabitants of this city than ever appeared here on any occasion before!"—so, at least, went a contemporary newspaper account. However, the luster of the festivities was considerably dimmed when it was later learned that most of the throng gave an equally enthusiastic greeting to the new British governor William Tryon (formerly of North Carolina), who arrived only a few hours later.

That night, after Washington had conferred with men familiar with the situation around Boston, he sent an urgent dispatch to his former colleagues in the Continental Congress: "Powder is so essential an article that I cannot help again repeating the necessity of a supply. The camp at Boston from the best accounts I can get from thence, is but very poorly supplied." The New York Congress had sent a wagonload of gunpowder rumbling up the treacherous highway, but even such a small amount, Washington noted, "has left this place [New York] almost destitute."

It wasn't until late the next afternoon that Washington could break away from his hosts. Then he moved up along the King's Highway, past Kissing Bridge, through what is now Central Park, and into the heights of Harlem close to where Columbia University would one day be located. By the time he had reached the inn near the King's Bridge (which spanned the Harlem River at modern Broadway), darkness had come. While he settled down for the night, the Philadelphia Light Horse, along with that portion of the New York militia which was not feting Governor Tryon, gave Washington a final salute, then trooped off.

From Kingsbridge, Washington traveled over the rough road beyond Rye, down the dizzy precipice at Horseneck, and across the Housatonic on the rocking ferry. He and his aides eventually reached New Haven, where a smart company of Yale College students greeted them. New Haven also provided a colorful exit the following morning "by a company of young gentlemen . . . whose expertness in the military exercises gained the approbation of the Generals."

Washington bedded down the next night in Wethersfield at the home of Mrs. Silas Deane, whose husband was one of

Connecticut's representatives to the Continental Congress. After leaving the comfortable frame house (which still stands), Washington and his group rode through Hartford and on to Springfield, where they were met by Dr. Benjamin Church of the Massachusetts Provincial Congress. Church had been instructed "to make suitable provision for them in the manner following, viz.: by a number of gentlemen of this colony from Springfield to Brookfield; and by another company raised in that neighborhood from there to Worcester; and by another company, there provided, from thence to Marlborough; and, from thence, by the troop of horse of that place to the army." [58] With this series of ceremonial honor guards, Washington was escorted down the Connecticut Path to his headquarters at Cambridge. His route had been lined by cheering people, but now the days of cheering were over and the difficult job of organizing an army had to be commenced.

Once he was installed in the spacious home now identified with Henry Wadsworth Longfellow, but in Colonial days the residence of Harvard's president, Washington came to his first, and perpetually greatest, problem. It was that of supplies. On July 10, when he had been only a week at the front, he sent a courier pounding off to Philadelphia pressing John Hancock, President of the Continental Congress, to have that body immediately appoint a quartermaster who was "indispensably necessary for the survival of the army." He endorsed Thomas Mifflin and Congress quickly approved of his choice.

Mifflin rode to Cambridge posthaste. His most urgent concern was the matter of food. The militiamen who had gaily streamed to Cambridge in the weeks after Lexington, had stuffed their knapsacks with a loaf of bread, maybe some dried fruit, and perhaps a piece or two of salt pork; but they had assumed they would be provided for, although there was no supply system then in operation. Now with a population larger than Boston itself, the rebel army created an almost insupportable strain on transportation facilities, since the daily rations established by the Massachusetts Provincial Congress, sitting in nearby Watertown, called for one pound of bread, a half-pound of beef and a half-pound of pork, a quarter-pint of peas or beans, a pint of milk or a cup of rice, some butter, and, to bolster the drudgery of camp life, one full quart of beer.

At first the local farmers had been able to provide much of the produce. But, as the number of troops grew to ten thousand then fifteen thousand, and finally, with the arrival over the King's Highway of reinforcements from Pennsylvania, Maryland, and Virginia, to nearly twenty thousand, the make-shift system began to break down. Mifflin found that merely to obtain enough flour for bread he must have at least thirty large freight wagons constantly rumbling to farms along the King's Highway or to the mire-clogged feeder paths that meandered out into the country-side. And to make the going tougher, the wagons, usually drawn by four husky draft horses, had to force their way through large herds of cattle and hogs being driven to the newly-created army market near Cambridge.

And food wasn't Mifflin's only headache. Most of the soldiers had little protection from the elements, as one Isaac Bangs noted in his journal: "When we first arrived upon the hills . . . we had no cover from the weather but apple trees (a miserable shelter from storms and March winds); for the Regulars had previously set fire to almost all the houses and barns on the Neck." Bangs, as well as a large percentage of the men, soon came down with colds, flu, dysentery, and a dozen other camp ailments which had Mifflin appealing to Congress for medical supplies. At the same time he began sending out foragers to obtain lumber for barrack cabins. As a make-do remedy, he used drafty tents made of sail canvas obtained from Salem and other seaports.

As the winter of 1775 approached, Washington grew increasingly concerned over the lack of warm clothing. Many months earlier he had written President Hancock that he would require at least ten thousand hunting jackets (there was as yet no standard uniform) and Mifflin some months later reiterated the need. But the Continental Congress, struggling with the stupendous complexities of organizing a war and a nation at the same time, did not even get around to appointing a committee to investigate the matter until late September.

Blankets, too, were in precariously short stock, and after Mifflin had scoured Massachusetts and Connecticut for them, Washington was forced to write a letter to the New Hampshire Convention in which he pleaded: "Our soldiers are in great distress; and I know of no other way to remedy the evil than applying to you. Cannot some blankets be got from the different towns? Most houses could spare one; some of them many." This pathetic appeal netted an insignificant 180 blankets.

Firewood was another item of which the army was seriously short. Mifflin estimated he would need a full twenty-five hundred wagonloads for cooking and warmth to tide him over the winter. Indeed, such was the crisis that Washington reported "different regiments were upon the point of cutting each others' throats for a few standing locusts near their encampments to cook their vituals with."

Even when blankets, clothing, or lumber was available, Mifflin often lacked the horses to pull the wagons to get them. Therefore Washington wrote the Massachusetts Provincial Congress and told them flatly that "unless some expedient is adopted by your honourable body to draw more teams into the service, or the Quartermaster-General empowered to impress them, this Army, if there comes a spell of rain or cold weather, must inevitably disperse."

But the worst of Washington's troubles concerned the lack of gunpowder. Although when he had arrived in July he had a force which outnumbered Gage well over two to one, his store of powder was so low that not only was it impossible to mount an offensive, but his troops were ordered not to return British fire. Between July 1775 and February 1776 Washington's letters to the Continental Congress are filled with descriptions of his critical shortage of powder. For example, on August 4 he said: "Our situation in the article of powder is much more alarming than I had the most distant idea of"—he had only 9900 pounds, or about 114 shots per soldier. In September Ben Franklin and a concerned congressional committee made the arduous trip up the King's Highway to confer with Washington about the matter of supplies. Although powder works were frantically begun, the only immediate result of the conference was ten thousand pounds which were squeezed out of the middle colonies and rushed northward via New Brunswick and New York.

This was not nearly enough and Washington had to write in February that "a golden opportunity has been lost" when, for lack of powder, he was unable to attack the British over the rare cover of ice which extended from Roxbury to the Common.

Gradually, however, more powder trickled in. Governor Trumbull of Connecticut sent 4217 pounds and the Continental Congress was somehow able to scrounge up thirty thousand more pounds around New York. Then from Fort Ticonderoga, which had fallen to the flamboyant Green Mountain giant Ethan Allen, came fifty essential pieces of artillery, carefully sledded across the snowy Berkshires to Springfield, from where they were dragged over the King's Highway by teams of oxen to Washington anxiously waiting at Cambridge.

At last with the gunpowder and artillery Washington could move. As dusk gathered on the evening of March 4, 1776, he ordered a diversionary cannonade from Roxbury, while simultaneously three thousand picked men moved silently up darkened Dorchester Heights, an unoccupied rise south across the water from Boston. Behind them were three hundred wagons loaded with bundles of tightly bound sticks and sturdy timber frames which would form the walls of the fort they were to erect. The troops labored silently and with great rapidity throughout the night.

The next morning (according to a British deserter) General Howe, who had replaced Gage, was astonished at the battlement which had suddenly brought American guns within range of his encampment. "Good God!" Howe is said to have exclaimed,

"these fellows have done more work in one night than I could
have made my army do in three months!" When a furious storm
wrecked Howe's plans for an assault on Dorchester Heights, he
ordered an immediate evacuation of Boston. Washington's victorious troops soon streamed into the city, to be met by the huzzas
and "tender embraces" of a populace freed of British troops for
the first time since the days of the Liberty Riot of 1768.

But the victory was not what it seemed. The British had
long realized that Boston, isolated on its little peninsula and
surrounded by the most rabid rebels in the Colonies, was not a
proper military base. Thus Howe had already been instructed to
transfer his headquarters to New York, a Tory stronghold and an
ideal location from which to quarantine the New England radicals from the rest of the colonies.

No sooner had the British warships and troop transports
faded into the Atlantic mists, than Washington began hurrying
his men down the King's Highway (both the Hartford and
Providence routes) to New York City. Time was essential, for he
must prepare batteries and defense positions on Manhattan as
well as Long Island and the Bronx. Yet the process of breaking
camp and moving 250 miles was laborious. Tents must be
packed, knapsacks and canteens filled, companies formed, and
marching order established. The regimental quartermasters had
to see that the proper quantities of food, firewood, blankets,
shoes, water, etc., were constantly available. Countless wagons
had to be mustered to carry the heavier equipment as well as
provisions. Finally the shrill notes of the fifers and thud of the
drummers were heard as the columns gradually swung into
formation and started off for New York.

Farm families gathered along stone hedges to cheer the
Colonials by. It would take hours for the men to pass—a farmer
could plow his field to the thunder of tramping feet, enjoy a
noonday meal while the artillery rumbled by, and retire at dusk
to hear the passing cattle, hogs, and freight wagons. But when

he arose the next day, his enthusiasm would be gone, for he would find the road rutted beyond repair, much of his firewood vanished, and the stench of rotting manure wafting over the landscape.

Washington sent his wife, Martha, who had wintered at Cambridge with him, to New York by way of Hartford. He himself took the coastal route in order to supervise the embarcation of many of his men, whom he preferred going by packet rather than forcing their way over the treacherous and time-consuming land segment around Horseneck. He reached Providence on April 5, his first day out of Boston. The next night he was at New London. Then he passed through New Haven and arrived in New York on the thirteenth. Two days later, in a letter to the Continental Congress, he noted: "The whole of the troops may be reasonably expected here in the course of this week. The badness of the roads and difficulty of providing teams for bringing the stores and baggage have greatly prolonged their arrival." It would not be the last time he would complain about these matters.

Meanwhile the congress had been having troubles of its own. One of its main concerns was how to finance the war. Since the congress was merely a gathering of men elected by the provincial assemblies with no enumerated powers of their own, there was no way to bring funds into the congressional coffers. Yet the very first letter Washington had written from Cambridge stated: "I find myself already much embarrassed for want of a Military Chest . . . I must therefore request that money may be forwarded as soon as possible." But where could the congress get it?

Although there was talk of a loan from France, it was quickly realized that King Louis would hardly squander his money on a rebellion that not only had failed to demonstrate it could stand up against a power that France herself had seldom bested but, in addition, had not yet even renounced a peaceful reconciliation with Britain. Thus until an important battle could be won and a firm declaration of independence passed, French aid was impossible.

Therefore the congress had no recourse except to the printing press. Originally many congressmen were optimistic about the possibilities of paper dollars. James Duane, for example, wrote a cheery message to the New York Assembly in June 1775 saying: "Your great complaint of the want of money will, I hope, be soon removed. For your present satisfaction, we have obtained leave of the Congress to inform you that the General Committee of the whole body have reported a resolution to emit, in Continental paper currency, a sum not exceeding the value of two millions of Spanish dollars," adding (and here was the rub) "for the redemption of which all the Colonies are to be pledged." [59] Although there was ample evidence that none of the colonies would tax themselves to retire the Continental bills with cash, the paper money for Washington's military chest was packed into strongboxes, placed in a heavily guarded coach, and sent up the King's Highway.

Congress, however, had no comprehension of the huge amount of funds necessary for a war. By September Washington was commenting to his officers that "the expense of supporting this army will so far exceed any idea that was formed in Congress that I do not know what will be the consequences." Notwithstanding the fact that the Continental bills circulated at nearly par with hard currency early in the war, Washington required $125,000 each month to pay his troops, and another $275,000 for food and military supplies. Thus, even with constant caravans of money moving from Philadelphia to army headquarters, Washington soon was writing that, because his war chest was empty, he had to send some of his militia home without pay —to which he added the gross understatement: "This occasioned great uneasiness among them."

It wasn't the lack of cash alone which caused "great uneasiness" among the troops gathering at New York. Although the roads were clogged with wagons, carts, packhorses, and cattle, supplies were so inadequate that many soldiers did not even have guns. It was a most "distressful situation," Washington fretted, but one about which the Continental Congress could do little, since Britain's policy prohibiting Colonial manufacture had left them with virtually no ironworks. Such was the dearth of weapons that New York militia orders ran: "Each man who shall not have arms shall bring with him a shovel, spade, pickaxe, or scythe straightened and fixed on a pole." Ben Franklin even advocated the use of bows and arrows!

Lead for bullets, too, was lacking—and only by ruthlessly stripping New York homes of their piping and roofing and by melting down a huge, equestrian statue of George III, which stood on the Bowling Green, was Washington able to approach the minimum stock deemed necessary to meet Howe.

Eventually morale started cracking and discipline became a problem. Intercolonial squabbling, rampant even in the Continental Congress itself, became much more serious when instigated by rough men with knives and pistols close at hand. Washington's orderly book warned on August 1, 1776: "the General understands that jealousies etc. are arisen among the troops from the different Provinces," and that persons who indulge in these hostilities "shall be severely punished and dismissed from the service with disgrace." However a persistent rumour, probably growing from a kernel of fact, circulated as far as amused circles in London that New Englanders, New Yorkers, and Pennsylvanians had partaken in a "most dreadful fray," leaving Washington's army seriously split.

In truth the discipline problem was nearly of crisis proportions. The army, virtually stranded on Manhattan Island, was utterly dependent on the neighboring farmers for fresh produce. Yet the unruly troopers would insult the farmers and sometimes make off with their goods. Thus the orderly book states: "Complaints have been made that some of the soldiers ill treat the country people who come to market. The General most positively forbids such behavior and hopes the officers will exert themselves to prevent it. Good policy as well as justice demands that they should have all possible encouragement, as the health of the soldiers much depends upon supplies of vegetables." [60]

The physical condition of his troops was another concern to Washington, whose ten thousand sketchily trained, poorly equipped men were in shaky condition to combat the thirty thousand iron-disciplined, well-supplied fighters that Howe was then mustering on Staten Island. Yet, worse still, was the fact that thirty-seven hundred of the American were sick and out of action.

Proper military tactics demanded that Washington abandon New York, since he obviously could not hold it. But Washington not only had an unreasonably stubborn streak, as demonstrated by his foolhardy stand at Fort Necessity twenty-two years earlier, but he was misled by the concept that it was the possession of cities rather than the destruction of armies which would decide the fate of America. The occupation of New York City by the British would be a "fatal stab" to American interests he thought; although when it did happen the effect was minimal. Thus Washington prepared to risk the very existence of his army on the defense of New York.

With the important battle shaping up, the Continental Congress finally decided it should tackle the matter of supplies in a more businesslike manner. Therefore early in the summer of 1776 a special Board of War and Ordnance was appointed. This vital five-man group, headed by the dynamic workhorse John Adams, was one of the most important committees ever created by the congress. Washington could not have kept the field without the board, whose functions were to furnish him "all the artillery, arms, ammunition, and warlike stores belonging to the United Colonies" (as Adams recorded in his autobiography), to establish warehouses for these stores, to recruit the express riders who established communication over the King's Highway with the front, to transmit, under proper guard, all monies needed for military use, and to "superintend the raising, fitting out, and dispatching of all such Land Forces as may be ordered for the service of the United Colonies."

John Adams threw himself into the job with such characteristic energy that "it [was] necessary for me to spend almost my whole time in it: mornings till Congress met and evenings till late at night." His autobiography is filled with the endless matters that came under his careful attention, for nearly all of Washington's letters were referred to the board for action—from the urgent appeals for gunpowder and clothing (searched out by the board's special purchasing agents) to the demand for more troops (the board ordered the states to send certain militia companies and endorsed plans for the raising of Continental regulars.)

At the same time that Adams was trying to bring some sort of order into the chaos that was threatening Washington's army, the congress was arguing over a score of important items. There were money matters, always pressing; Indian affairs (particularly among the British-leaning Iroquois); arrangements for beginning a navy; plans for laying out a postal system to replace the old British one; the possibilities of a French alliance; and the delicate choosing of high military officers from the bevy of political bigwigs, vociferous merchants, and local caesars. Yet superseding all else, for the moment, was the question of declaring for independence.

This last issue was supposedly resolved, though not without considerable and heated arguments, on July 4, 1776, with the formal adoption of the declaration written by young Tom Jefferson. Yet even so, that September when Admiral Richard Howe, older brother of the general and commander of the largest fleet which had ever gathered off American shores, invited representatives of the congress to consider reconciliation, the peace party was strong enough to force the acceptance of this offer. Accordingly Ben Franklin, John Adams, and Edward Rutledge (one of Adams's war board associates) set out for British headquarters on Staten Island.

Franklin and Adams drove down the King's Highway in chaises, while Rutledge trotted beside them on horseback. They had to push through large masses of American soldiers on their way to reinforce Washington, and the disorganization and rowdyism filled Adams's neat New England mind with dismay:

> On the Road and at all the public houses, we saw such numbers of officers and soldiers, straggling and loitering, as gave me at least but a poor opinion of the discipline of our

forces and excited as much indignation as anxiety. Such thoughtless dissipation at a time so critical was not calculated to inspire very sanguine hopes . . .[61]

So great was the traffic that not even such personages as Franklin and Adams, two of the foremost men in the Colonies, could obtain proper lodging. Adams tells the delightful tale of how he and Franklin had to bed together in a New Brunswick inn. Two men with such different temperaments were bound to have disagreements. Genial, outdoor-loving Franklin flung open the window to let in the chilly autumn air. Adams marched over and slammed the window down. When Franklin argued (according to Adams) "Come open the window," Adams reluctantly shoved it up and leaped beneath the covers. Franklin then began explaining in detail his theory concerning the power of fresh air over colds, "with which," Adams wryly notes, "I was so much amused that I soon fell asleep, and left him and his Philosophy together."

They continued to Amboy the next day, where a barge took them across to Staten Island. There they were escorted through "lines of guards of Grenadiers looking as fierce as ten furies" to meet with Admiral Howe in the "romantically elegant" Conference House which still stands. However the interview was fruitless. The Americans returned to Philadelphia; and General Howe prepared for action.

General Howe had already mauled Washington at a battle around the hamlet of Brooklyn; and only the miraculous appearance of a dense fog enabled Colonel John Glover and his Marblehead fishermen to ferry the Americans secretly to Manhattan. Now three weeks later, as Washington watched the British massing on Long Island, he at last realized his danger of being hemmed in by a flank attack up the East River. Therefore on September 14, Washington ordered his wagons packed and the hurried removal of his supplies—although, as he admitted in a letter he sent winging down the King's Highway to a worried congress, the disorganized condition of his troops and the probability of a momentary attack presented almost insuperable diffi-culties. The supply trains ground ponderously through the heights of Harlem, then over the ancient span at Kingsbridge. It was painfully slow. If he could have just a little longer, he could get away. But he was trying to accomplish now what should have been completed at leisure several weeks earlier. The next day General Howe struck.

Americans in the trenches along the East River knew some-thing was astir, according to one of the soldiers, when, as dawn broke, "we saw boats coming out of a creek or cove on the Long Island side of the water filled with British soldiers. When they came to the edge of the tide, they formed their boats in line. They continued to augment their forces from the island until they appeared like a large clover field in full bloom." [62] Then cannons from British warships blasted at the American onlookers and they scampered blindly down the King's Highway toward Harlem Heights, where Washington had providently erected secondary fortifications.

It was a disgraceful rout. Washington, coming on his men in the midst of a large cornfield (near the site of the public library at Fifth Avenue and 42nd Street), bellowed for them to rally. But they flooded, panic-crazed, past him. When even the officers ignored his preemptory orders, Washington became so angry he threw his hat on the ground and struck some of the offenders with the flat of his sword. The British advance guard was almost upon him when some of his aides managed to lead him to safety. "Have I got such troops as those!" an eyewitness heard him roar.

Howe had the war in the bag—should he move with the slightest amount of speed. But as he and his entourage were on their way to the front, they paused at charming Mrs. Murray's country home (then standing near the King's Highway and modern 38th Street). Here, so tradition has it, the agreeable Quaker lady treated them to cakes and an inordinate amount of wine. The afternoon was torrid, and the respite was most re-warding—yet while Howe and Governor Tyron whiled away two precious hours, the Americans slipped out of range.

Still the war was all but over. The disheveled American

army dug in at Harlem Heights and Washington established his headquarters in the still-standing Jumel Mansion. When Howe managed to rouse himself nearly a month later, he sent a strong flanking force far up the East River to Throg's Neck with the intention of snipping off Washington's retreat route over King's Bridge. Washington, out-maneuvered again, quickly broke camp and managed to scoot across the exposed bridge while Howe was temporarily delayed by the heroic action of a well-entrenched detachment under dependable John Glover. During this retreat, Washington, realizing his utter dependence on wagons, issued an order expressly forbidding the use of the vehicles by other than the quartermasters or other authorized personnel, since "upon the due regulation and management of the wagons, the health and safety of the army entirely depends."

Although Washington regrouped at White Plains, Howe cracked the American front and took Chatterton's Hill which dominated the field; Washington was licked once more.

Another retreat. Tents and provisions were hastily dumped onto the wagons. The soldiers shuffled off for New Jersey—no money in their pockets, no powder for their guns, no shoes to protect their feet, and no hope to avoid further punishment by the perpetually victorious British. Militia deserted in droves—the King's Highway through Connecticut was filled with them. They brought the sad news to the farm families who queried them on their way and grumbled in the taverns where they paused for beer and a crust of bread. Even Washington, encamped at Fort Lee across the Hudson from Manhattan, confessed to the Continental Congress that he was so crucially short of supplies, particularly artillery, that the lack must make him operate "without the probability of success."

Two days after Washington mailed this pessimistic estimation of the situation, the Hessians gave him a defeat even more resounding than any suffered thus far. Allowing himself to be swayed by General Nathanael Greene, an otherwise perceptive young Rhode Islander, he left a garrison of twenty-eight hundred atop an upjutting block of stone that is now called Fort Tryon but then Fort Washington. Blue-coated Hessians (mercenaries mainly from Hesse, Germany) scaled the precipitous slopes and soon the defenders were forced to surrender to the nearly eight thousand men who surrounded them. The British soldiers laughed at the dirty militia in their tattered hunting jackets; and the Germans brazenly stripped them of all articles of value. It had been ridiculously easy, joked the Hessians. Who had said the Americans were fighters?

Washington then abandoned Fort Lee with such haste that the British found his fires still smoldering. He had not only been beaten, but had been humiliated in five successive battles. With only three thousand broken and demoralized men to oppose Howe with thirty thousand, it was apparently only a matter of weeks, if not days, before the short-lived revolution would reach its ignoble conclusion.

16.   Like an Eagle upon a Hen

The people of Trenton muttered discontentedly as the rebel soldiers came down the King's Highway. The troops did not inspire confidence. Their cheeks were sunken with hunger. Their feet were bloody or swathed in mud-caked burlap. Few had coats even though the bitter weather whistled about them. Their beards were scraggly and they smelled of sweat and grime and campfire soot. They marched in such disorganization and utter confusion that Washington himself did not know how many men he actually had, although he estimated a little over three thousand.

Washington set up a temporary camp near the important ferry crossing while he sent patrols hurrying up and down the Delaware River to collect all boats, no matter how small, that might be used by the British to reach the Pennsylvania side and the road to Philadelphia. Meanwhile nervous scouts on the King's Highway reported the surprisingly leisurely British pursuit. Howe eventually arrived at Elizabeth. Then his advance guards passed through New Brunswick. After a while they reached Princeton, and finally approached Trenton. With the most advanced British and Hessian units within cannon shot, the Americans, having successfully denuded the shore of boats, paddled furiously across to Pennsylvania. Trenton Tories watched them depart with undisguised pleasure. Few had any doubts that they had seen the last of Mr. Washington and his disreputable, ragtag mob.

Economics and the King's Highway determined the forth-coming series of almost unbelievable events.

On December 20, 1776, Washington wrote a pessimistic letter to President Hancock and his anxious congressmen in which he stated quite bluntly that "ten days more will put an end to the existence of our army"—referring to the fact that many enlistments would be over by January 1 and recruiting was not providing needed replacements because the potential sol-diers, whose families must have money while they were in the army, had no faith in the Continental currency. Truly, the money had begun to depreciate at such an alarming rate that some members of congress were having doubts that it would ever be redeemed.

Thus with disaster looming, Washington decided he must make a most difficult maneuver. Although he was outnumbered and facing vastly superior firepower, he would attack!

The configuration of the massive force opposing him was not entirely unfavorable, however. Such numbers required wide-spread foraging. In order to shorten each unit's supply lines, Howe had strung his army out along the King's Highway, with each group expected to live largely off the surrounding farms. Thus, Howe himself was at New York, while other units were at New Brunswick, Amboy, Princeton, and, the farthest, at Trenton—which was to serve as the springboard for the spring campaign. These were hardened German troops under lean Colonel Rall, who had grown contemptuous of American fight-ing abilities after his easy conquest of Fort Washington.

On December 23 the American cooks were given orders to prepare rations for three days—some of the bread being baked in the grist mill which is now part of Pennsylvania's Washington Crossing State Park. As word went out to the troops, a new spirit took hold of them. Was it really so? Their retreat was over? Men who had turned tail at Manhattan, who had experienced the humiliation of White Plains, who had winced at the jibes as they passed through Loyalist sections of New Jersey suddenly found new strength. Washington had faith in them. Perhaps they weren't the good-for-nothing rabble their enemies called them!

From mouth to mouth the password was whispered. "Victory or Death!" Yes, it was true. Once they recrossed the Delaware into the British lair there would be no turning back. It would certainly be victory or death—or, what was worse, an indefinite confinement in one of the dank prison ships whose evil reputations were daily growing.

On Christmas morning the quartermasters distributed new flints and ammunition. Colonel Glover's fishermen readied the boats which had been hidden from spies. One of Washington's aides, probably Colonel John Fitzgerald, described the scene in well-chosen, staccato phrases:

> 6 P.M.—It is fearfully cold and raw and a snowstorm is setting in. The wind is northeast and beats in the faces of the men. It will be a terrible night for the soldiers who have no shoes. Some of them have tied old rags around their feet; others are barefoot, but I have not heard a man complain. They are ready to suffer any hardship . . .[63]

It took nine hours to ferry the twenty-four hundred troops and twenty pieces of heavy artillery across the treacherous river. Back and forth Glover and his fishermen went, ugly cakes of ice gouging dangerous grooves on the sides of their boats. But by 3 A.M. Colonel Fitzgerald, resting with Washington at the still-standing McKonkey Ferry house, scribbled in his journal: "I am writing in the ferry house. The troops are all over. . . . We are three hours behind the set time. . . . I never have seen Washington so determined as he is now. He stands on the bank of the river, wrapped in his cloak, superintending the landing . . ."[64]

Three hours late—three precious hours. Washington had planned to reach Trenton, eight miles south, before dawn, while the Hessians were sleeping off the effects of a rollicking German Christmas. Now he would not arrive until clear daylight, a fact which he later admitted "made me despair of surprising the town." Should he go on? There was no hesitation. Down a narrow road (now known as Continental Lane) the army marched. When Bear Tavern was reached (a marker indicates the site), Washington had his men split: the left wing, which would travel over Pennington Road, was under General Greene and the right wing, moving down River Road, under General John Sullivan.

The swirling snow changed to sleet. Soon the men's clothing was glazed with slush and their faces bruised from wind-blown ice pellets. Worse, yet, the snow was dampening the gunpowder. Sullivan, fearful that his men would not be able to maintain an effective fire, sent a messenger hurrying to Washington (riding with Greene) who was then at West Trenton. Washington, with magnificent confidence, would not let Sullivan call off the attack. "Tell General Sullivan," Washington roared (according to Fitzgerald), "to use the bayonet. I am resolved to take Trenton!" The march continued.

Colonel Rall and his fourteen hundred Hessians had had a most pleasant Christmas. Trained from childhood to the rigors of warfare, they were enjoying this romp through New York and New Jersey. Howe, recognizing their bellicose qualities, had given them the position of honor at the head of his string of encampments along the King's Highway. Rall had done little to strengthen himself. Deriding the Americans as country clowns, he placed two of his six cannons decoratively in front of his headquarters and, despite urgent warnings by Tories that Washington was planning something, dismissed the thought of a counterattack. Even as Washington was actually on the move, when Rall—in the midst of cards and wine—was handed a note by a farmer describing in detail the American advance, he stuffed the paper into his pocket without bothering to read it. Later he sauntered off to bed.

Rall and many of his men were still drunk or asleep (or both) when the night turned into gray dawn. But suddenly the troops stationed at an outpost a half-mile out of town were jarred by the sight of more than a thousand Americans appearing out of nowhere. "The enemy! The enemy!" they shouted frantically. "Turn out!" Greene's soldiers opened fire and the Hessians retreated rapidly across the fields to Trenton. Quickly Greene posted his cannons at the point where the Pennington road met the King's Highway, the current site of an impressive battle monument.

About this time Rall staggered out of his quarters. He could scarcely believe the confusion and outright terror which had taken hold of his men. Seeing them retreat toward the Assunpink, a creek which bordered the town on the south, Rall bellowed "Advance, my brave troopers. Advance!" But Washington's battle plan was working too well. Before the Germans could unlimber their cannons, an American company, led by a young lieutenant named James Monroe (later to become president), surrounded and captured them. The Hessians tried to rally around the sturdy old barracks building, but soon booming cannons announced that the second American army, led by Sullivan, had arrived. Then Colonel Rall, still whining for his men to charge, went down with a fatal bullet in his side.

The leaderless Hessians, realizing that resistance was useless, surrendered. Of the original fourteen hundred nearly a thousand were either killed or captured. American losses were only two killed and three wounded. Washington "pounced upon the Hessians like an eagle upon a hen," wrote an elated Colonel Fitzgerald. Confidence in Washington soared—not only among the soldiers, but throughout the United Colonies. The Continental currency was, at least temporarily, given a new lease on life and recruiting would soon proceed at such a pace that the American army was no longer in danger of breaking up.

But this amazing episode was not yet over. As soon as the British in Princeton, only eleven miles away, learned of the disaster, they relayed the word to the beefy Charles, Lord Cornwallis, in New Brunswick. Instantly the hard-fighting general mustered eight thousand men and sloshed down the King's Highway knee deep in mud and snow. At Trenton he came upon Washington whose force had been augmented to five thousand by some Pennsylvania militia. The Americans fell back across the Assunpink; and Cornwallis, in true British fashion, settled down for a leisurely evening before crushing them on the morrow.

Yet when dawn came, the entire American army had vanished! Left were only the several hundred smoldering campfires which had fooled the British all night.

Cornwallis was even more thunderstruck when he learned that Washington had not fled across the Delaware, but had moved against Princeton. Cornwallis immediately ordered his men up the King's Highway still sure he could catch the Old Fox, as Washington was beginning to be called.

The American drive on Princeton had two main purposes. The first was to gain an additional victory prior to retiring before the overwhelming numbers of redcoats. The second, and certainly just as important, was the hope of capturing some of the stores accumulated there. Taking a back road via Clarksville, by sunrise Washington was on a hill in view of his objective. Detaching General Hugh Mercer to destroy the King's Highway bridge over Stony Brook in order to delay Cornwallis, Washington pounced on Princeton.

The British fought stubbornly. The American detachment at Stony Brook was routed—but not before the important bridge was destroyed and General Mercer was brought, dying, into the Clark house (now part of Princeton Battlefield State Park). Within the town itself many British holed up in Nassau Hall. Young Alexander Hamilton sent a cannonball crashing through one window; and, after a few more such blasts, the defenders surrendered.

An odd situation now presented itself. With Cornwallis closing in fast, the American army was still in most serious danger. However only twenty-five miles up the King's Highway lay New Brunswick with mountains of supplies and virtually all the funds with which Howe was to conduct the war. If Washington could zip up the highway, snatch the money and materiel, and hit the hills around Morristown, he could actually "put an end to the war"—or so he indicated in a letter to the Continental Congress.

How tantalizing it was! Then Washington surveyed his troops. Many of them had no shoes—and this in early January. Food was scarce and the men had not slept for over thirty hours. With eight hundred fresh troops he could have taken New Brunswick. Only eight hundred! But without them he was forced to give up his daring plan. Turning off the King's Highway, the Americans filed into the mountains, where they went into winter quarters at Morristown.

One of the most important and amazing campaigns in military history was over.

17. A Gathering Storm on My Left

The French Canadians wandered around the bustling British encampment at St. John's with more curiosity than patriotism. Although they had been British subjects ever since Amherst had driven them from Ticonderoga and Wolfe had scaled the heights of Quebec, they felt a particular lack of enthusiasm at the mustering of Johnny Burgoyne's army. There had been a day when General Montcalm's white-coated legions had excited them, for the lily banner still snapped over New France and the *coureurs* were proud and independent spirits, not mere hirelings of the two big, impersonal fur companies that now dominated the trade.

English officers, their scarlet jackets ashine in the June sun, spurred past the French onlookers. Sergeants shouted at their men to form into lines and prepare to board the transports tugging at their lines in the Richelieu River. Other soldiers, stripped to the waist, hustled to get the last supplies and equipment aboard the long, flat-bottomed barges. In the near distance could be heard neighing horses and bellowing cattle being herded together prior to setting out on the rugged land route to rejoin the army above Ticonderoga 115 miles south.

How the English boasted. Even though Burgoyne, a bouncy optimist with a flair for play-writing, gambling, and carousing, as well as the military, had witnessed the amazingly accurate American fire that had leveled a thousand British regulars at Bunker Hill, he had a low opinion of American staying power. Now, with ninety-four hundred well-trained men—healthy and as confident as their leader—Burgoyne anticipated smashing through Ticonderoga, plowing down the Hudson Valley (where he would be reinforced by two thousand Indians and Britons under Barry St. Leger coming along the Mohawk River), and eventually linking up with General Howe, sweeping up from New York City. This whirlwind campaign would completely isolate the obstreperous New England colonies. Once this was accomplished, the war could be brought to a speedy conclusion.

The French stood by quietly while the British—along with their blue-coated Hessian, green-clad American Loyalist, and vermilion-painted Indian allies—put out into the river. A few *coureurs* and voyageurs were with them—including vigorous old Charles Langlade, in his twilight years as incorrigible a warrior as when he had led his Wisconsin savages against Croghan's Pickawillany post. But this was not essentially a French war. And though the Americans had just last year sent an army up the much-used Lake Champlain-Richelieu River route against Quebec, the fierce northern winter, lack of supplies, and a fortunate British reinforcement, rather than resistance from the Canadian population, had ultimately defeated the invaders.

And so the French shrugged as the great army faded down the river. Soon they directed their carriages back to Montreal twenty miles away. It had been a pleasant excursion; now there was nothing to look forward to before the trade fair in the fall. Even that was only a sad shadow of yesteryear when French birchbarks were found on every beaver-rich river, stream, and creek west of the Alleghenies. Today the beaver were vanishing, the Indians declining, and the French empire no more.

Let the British and Americans battle for the continent. The Canadians didn't care any longer. *"Je me souviens"* ("I remember") the French murmured; and the nostalgic phrase became the official motto of Quebec Province. The tide of history had passed them by.

It was otherwise with Gentleman Johnny Burgoyne, who was certain his superbly outfitted army would re-establish Britain forever in North America. Down the ancient invasion waterway he and his magnificent force sailed. Soon they came to the lake which had enchanted Samuel de Champlain 168 years earlier. Seventeen to twenty miles a day they advanced—with American spy boats carrying word of their progress to the inadequate garrison entrenching itself at Ticonderoga. One encampment was made at Crown Point, where old French battlements still stood, gaunt and deserted against the summer sky. Continuing down the lake, the army presented "one of the most pleasing spectacles I ever beheld"—so wrote Thomas Anburey of the 24th Regiment in his journal *With Burgoyne from Quebec*. He continued:

> In front, the Indians went with their birch canoes, containing twenty or thirty in each; then the advanced corps in a regular line with the gunboats. Then followed the "Royal George" and "Inflexible" . . . with the other brigs and sloops following. After them the first brigade in a regular line. Then the Generals Burgoyne, Phillips, and Riedesel in the pinnaces. Next to them was the second brigade, followed by the German brigades, and the rear was brought up with the sutlers and followers of the army. Upon the appearance of so formidable a fleet, you may imagine they were not a little dismayed at Ticonderoga . . .[65]

But this impressive force depended on the grubby little scows plying back and forth from St. John's with supplies. They were not enough; and even from the first food had to be conserved. Additional care had to be taken with the horses; for should any number die, the army would have trouble moving once it left Lake Champlain. Nonetheless, Burgoyne's weakness was not apparent as he drew up before Ticonderoga. Although rumor had it that upwards of twelve thousand American troops manned the rambling outworks, General Arthur St. Clair had only twenty-three hundred.

On July 1, 1777, Burgoyne paused in his battle plans to issue a bombastic proclamation designed to throw the garrison (already frightened enough) and the bordering countryside into panic. If, in spite of his royal master's clemency, the population continued in the state of rebellion, he and his men, whom he called the messengers of justice and wrath, would spread "devastation, famine, and every concomitant horror that a reluctant but indispensable prosecution of military duty must occasion."

The proclamation, along with the British occupation of Mt. Defiance from which their siege guns could play on the fort, convinced St. Clair, who knew Ticonderoga's weaknesses from having served with Amherst during the French and Indian War, that it would be well for him to seek a more salubrious clime. Thus on the night of the fifth, the Americans slunk out of the key fortress controlling the Lake Champlain supply line, leaving only four hardy fellows and a loaded cannon aimed at the gates to surprise the British as they entered in triumph. "Had these men obeyed their instructions," Anburey confessed, "they would . . . have done great mischief. But, allured by the sweets of plunder and liquor, instead of obeying their orders, we found them dead drunk by a case of Madeira."

Exhilarated by the easy victory (which Washington admitted "has given a very disagreeable turn to our affairs"), Burgoyne scorned the usual, and far quicker, invasion trail down Lake George to take out after St. Clair over a rough road which led far eastward (via modern Vermont 73 and 30). It was through "an excessive woody and bad country," complained Anburey, who admitted that the "exertions of the day had so far wearied me that, drinking heartily of rum and water, I lay down in my bearskin and blanket and did not awake till twelve the next day."

The Americans fled before them, setting fire to Fort Edward, the northernmost post on the Hudson River. By August 6 Burgoyne was gathering supplies for the attack on Albany, just forty-nine miles south. With good reason Gentleman Johnny viewed the campaign as almost won—and even Washington thought Burgoyne "will find little difficulty in penetrating to Albany." In England bells were rung and King George roared in delight "I have beat all the Americans!" Indeed, it seemed as if the rebellion was tottering. One more push—one major battle— and . . .

But Howe, unpredictable as usual, had picked this precise moment for a sea voyage—his ultimate destination not Albany but Philadelphia. And Colonel St. Leger, who was supposed to be rumbling along the Mohawk, was having certain problems . . .

His part in the joint operations had begun propitiously enough. Joseph Brant—a Mohawk protégé of William Johnson (now dead) and his wife Molly (who was Brant's sister)—had rounded up a thousand warriors and met St. Leger at Oswego with around eight hundred American Tories and British regulars. Then on July 26 the army ascended the Oswego River, fifes shrilling, tom-toms thumping, cannon wheels creaking, and hopes soaring.

The only major obstruction barring their way was Fort Stanwix garrisoned by only 750 men. With much boasting and bluster, St. Leger surrounded the star-shaped fort that guarded the Great Carrying Place on the Iroquois Trail. Then, according to the defenders' second-in-command Marius Willet, the enemy "sent in a flag, who told us of their great power, strength, and determination." But the garrison's banner—which, though it was merely the red and white strips from soldiers' shirts and blue from a woman's petticoat, was the first American flag to be hoisted in battle—continued to flutter proudly. Thus while the Indians pegged away from behind trees, St. Leger was forced to commence the laborious siege operations. Slowly his trenches snaked toward the fort until they were only 150 yards away.

But the settlements to the east had been aroused. Led by Nicholas Herkimer, around a thousand militia rendezvoused at German Flats (since renamed Mohawk) and, accompanied by four hundred wagons stacked high with supplies and ammunition, squeaked up the Iroquois Trail to relieve the garrison. However spies quickly brought Brant news of Herkimer's advance so that by the time the Americans began filing into the forested Oriskany gulch, the Iroquois were there to greet them with a well-planned ambush.

However Nicholas Herkimer was not a Braddock, and his men were too wise in frontier fighting to stand in the open.

Diving for cover behind trees, boulders, or wagons, they returned Brant's fire bullet for bullet. Herkimer, waving his sword,
shouted orders and encouragements—continuing to do so even
after a vicious wound in the leg (which caused his death ten
days later) forced him to direct the battle propped against a
stump.

Seldom has there been a fight as fierce as that in Oriskany
ravine (now marked by a tall, stone shaft). But prolonged
warfare was not the Indian style. Gradually an enraged Brant
saw his braves drift back to the main British camp. And although
the Americans lost two hundred men and were in no condition to
relieve Fort Stanwix, the Mohawks had suffered far more heavily
in proportion to their total population.

That night the Indian death chant moaned through the still
air. In the days that followed Brant had increasing difficulty
holding his warriors to the siege. Then, when it was confirmed
that one of Washington's best generals, fiery Benedict Arnold,
had organized another relief force, the Indians deserted en
masse. Without them, St. Leger had no choice except to break
camp and return to Oswego, leaving his tents, stores, and cannons to the astonished defenders who knew nothing of Arnold's
approach.

Meanwhile Burgoyne, awaiting supplies before the descent
on Albany, suddenly found himself in the midst of a hornets'
nest. His slow progress had allowed the countryside to mobilize;
and on August 20 he sent a worried letter to Lord Germaine
explaining his difficulties:

> The great bulk of the country is undoubtedly with the Conti-
> nental Congress . . . and their measures are executed with a
> secrecy and dispatch that are not to be equalled . . . militia,
> to the amount of three or four thousand, assemble in twenty-
> four hours; they bring with them their subsistence, etc., and,
> the alarm over, they return to their farms. The Hampshire
> Grants in particular, a country unpeopled and almost un-
> known in the last war, now abounds in the most active and

most rebellious race of the continent and hangs like a gathering storm upon my left.[66]

The gathering storm that Burgoyne referred to had already crushed a once-proud Hessian detachment which he had dispatched into the Hampshire Grants (i.e., Vermont). Colonel Baume, a blunt German who spoke no English, had orders to confiscate at least one thousand horses, all the wagons he could find, any cattle fit for slaughter, and the valuable cache of supplies at Bennington. Baume had expected only light resistance on this essential foraging venture. Instead he had run into a large force led by John Stark, an experienced warhorse who helped Washington blast the Hessians at Trenton. The sharp engagement seesawed back and forth. But with nearly twenty-five hundred Americans pouring a devastating fire on fifteen hundred Germans, the issue was finally settled by weight of numbers. Baume was killed and the Hessians limped back minus the much needed supplies and half their comrades. Upon learning of the disaster, Thomas Anburey remarked laconically: "This no doubt will be a matter of great exultation to the Americans."

Gentleman Johnny was so shaken by the repulse at Bennington that he abandoned his wine and newly acquired mistress to push on down the Hudson. But the American force, swelled to nine thousand by victory-scenting volunteers, had stopped retreating. At the site of the modern Saratoga National Park thirty miles above Albany, Burgoyne bumped into them. Their strong earthen entrenchments blocked the road and the dense forest and gulley-scarred highlands made it impossible for Burgoyne to bypass them. Thus he had no choice except to blast his way through the American position. And so on September 19, 1777, began the first of a pair of major contests known collectively as the Battle of Saratoga.

Burgoyne had no idea how many American opposed him nor exactly where they were entrenched, for his Indians, dismayed by the defeat at Bennington and the dour news from Fort

Stanwix, had taken this moment to head for their homelands in the west. Burgoyne split his army into three columns: with the Germans taking the river road, the British right wing shoving through the forest, and Burgoyne directing the center. It was the center which made the first contact—this with the elite Virginia riflemen of Daniel Morgan.

As the thunder of battle reached General Horatio Gates, the American commander, he rushed a few reinforcements to Morgan—hesitating to dispatch more in fear that the action was merely a feint. Yet under the insistent urgings of Benedict Arnold, the hotblood who had frightened St. Leger, more and more troops were flung into action.

The fighting continued at a furious pace until darkness forced the Americans to retire to their fortifications. Technically Burgoyne had won the battle for he was left in possession of the field. But he knew better; he had not been able to push on to Albany and replenish his supplies. Quickly he had his troops dig entrenchments. Then for the next three weeks he waited—praying help would arrive from Howe, whom he still did not know was at sea. Meanwhile food ran low. Simultaneously there was the growing fear that perhaps the British would not be able to break through. As Anburey put it: "the courage and obstinancy with which the Americans fought were the astonishment of everyone, and we now became fully convinced they were not that contemptible enemy we had hitherto imagined them . . ."

September turned to chill October. The British had to sleep on the damp, cold ground, constantly tense because American raiders popped away at their pickets. The rugged condition of the country made foraging difficult; and any party that sallied too far from camp was in grave danger of being captured by Morgan's stealthy riflemen. Just as hard on their morale was the ugly snarling of wolves attracted by the battlefield carnage. "When they approached a corpse," Anburey exclaimed in disgust, "their noise was hideous till they had scratched it up."

At last Burgoyne realized he could wait no longer. He had only two choices: either risk an all-out attack against the Americans, whose numbers, although he did not realize it, had soared to twenty thousand, or retreat in disgrace—if, indeed, retreat was still possible. Burgoyne chose to attack. Thus on October 7th, his fifes and drums sounded and the weary troops, now reduced to less than six thousand effectives, were given orders to advance.

Upon learning of Burgoyne's movement, Gates motioned to an aide. "Order on Morgan to begin the game," he grunted. Gliding through the woods, the Virginia riflemen suddenly emerged on Burgoyne's right flank. At nearly the same moment other Americans engaged his front. Sharpshooters, whom the British had always feared, picked off the officers. Burgoyne retreated to prepared positions; but when one of the strongest of them, Balcarres Redoubt, was taken by Arnold, always in the thick of the fight, Burgoyne knew he had lost.

Hurriedly he moved his broken army back north, hoping to shake loose and make it to Canada. But Gates and Arnold were on him, and Burgoyne realized another fight would result in the needless deaths of hundreds of his men. So on October 17, he agreed to Gates's surprisingly lenient terms of surrender.

Although Anburey, proud even to the end, wrote that "we yielded with becoming dignity," another member of the British army, Lieutenant William Digby, was more explicit. Burgoyne, he remarked, was so choked up he could not speak. As for the troops themselves: "at about 10 o'clock we marched out, according to the treaty, with drums beating and the honours of war. But the drums seemed to have lost their former inspiriting sounds. . . . As to my own feelings, I cannot express them. Tears (though unmanly) forced their way, and if alone, I should have burst to give myself vent." [67]

They passed through lines of grizzled Americans, who though they were silent in respect for the fallen, were exuberant with the knowledge that they had whipped one of the best armies Britain could field.

Yet as important in the victory as the heroism of the raw militia, most of whom were facing musketry for the first time, was the implacable Champlain Trail. It was too long—that glimmering, island-studded waterway of deluding tranquility—

and the lack of supplies from Canada was the ultimate fact which impelled Burgoyne's surrender.

Saratoga was one of the most important successes of the Revolution because it determined the vacillating French to enter the war. Soon French supplies and money were pumping new life into the American cause. And eventually French troops and a powerful French fleet would appear with more muscle. The way was now open for the climactic battle—Yorktown.

18.   The World Turned Upside Down

Gates's success at Saratoga could not have come at a more opportune moment, for Washington was experiencing a series of defeats which would have wrecked a man of lesser fortitude. When Howe sailed out of New York, Washington was certain he was going to attack Philadelphia by sea. Therefore he moved rapidly down the King's Highway to post himself between Philadelphia and Howe's landing at the head of the Chesapeake.

As the Patriots paraded through the capital on their way to the encampment at Wilmington, Delaware, John Adams, soon to leave his important job as head of the Board of War for a troubleshooting spot in Europe, gave an optimistic description: "Four grand divisions of the army and artillery. . . . marched twelve deep and yet took up about two hours in passing . . . we have now an army well appointed between us and Mr. Howe . . . so that I feel as secure as if I were at Braintree [his home town]."

Yet Howe outmaneuvered Washington, as was his habit, at Brandywine Creek by sending his hard-fighting ace Lord Cornwallis on Washington's flank by way of the Birmingham meetinghouse (which still is part of the Brandywine Battlefield Park). Within a matter of a few hours the well-appointed army was in headlong flight toward Chester, and only the stubborn rearguard action of Nathanael Greene's men prevented the retreat from becoming a rout.

With Washington, battered but still formidable, between him and Philadelphia, Howe made a few artistic jabs toward the west to send the Americans scurrying up the Schuylkill to protect the fords, then simply slipped downriver to unguarded Philadelphia. On the morning of September 26, 1777, Cornwallis, accompanied by an I-told-you-so Joseph Galloway, strutted into America's greatest city. There, according to a Tory account, "the fine appearance of the soldiery, the strictness of their discipline, the politeness of the officers, and the orderly behavior of the whole body immediately dispelled every apprehension of the inhabitants."

Washington counterattacked furiously a week later at Germantown on the hills above the city; but a misguided delay caused by a few British troops ensconced in the sturdy Chew Mansion (still standing) allowed the British to regroup and led to another American defeat. Washington then went into winter quarters at Valley Forge, only twenty-five miles up the Schuylkill from Philadelphia permitting him to keep an eye on his adversary. However, the neighborhood had been stripped of food and other supplies; and the Board of War, no longer under Adams's firm hand, failed to bring in a sufficient quantity from other parts of the country. Thus Washington (headquartering in the small stone house now an attraction in the modern state park) spent some of his darkest months in this snow-driven valley. His men lived in nine hundred miserable log cabins (many of which are reconstructed) with the icy wind slicing between the crude daubings and with food to maintain them barely above the starvation level. One discouraged trooper wrote:

> I am sick, discontented, and out of humor. Poor food. Hard lodging. Cold weather. Fatigue. Nasty clothes. Nasty cookery. Vomit half my time . . . I can't endure it. Why are we sent here to starve and freeze? [68]

With up to 3,000 men dead and those 11,800 who remained weak, ill-outfitted, and gloomy, another of the many crises in the Revolution was clearly at hand. Then in February, 1778, the treaty of alliance with France, Europe's greatest land power, was signed. With this hats were tossed in the air at Valley Forge— and the war took on a completely new aspect.

The British ministry and the king himself were severely shaken by the French entry into hostilities. Since a powerful French fleet was already massing in the West Indies, the British realized they could no longer count on control of the sea—either for their supplies or to move their troops. Therefore they made the agonizing decision to write off the war in the north, where the resistance was so determined, and concentrate on the south, which they would detach and continue to occupy as a beachhead for operations at a later time.

This new policy aimed at abandoning Philadelphia and concentrating a strong garrison in New York. Thus in June Henry Clinton, the lackluster officer who had replaced genial Howe, marched his troops, together with three thousand nervous American Tories, out of Philadelphia toward New York. To avoid ambush from one of the forested ridges which paralleled the King's Highway through Jersey, Clinton decided to take a more southeasterly route. Crossing the Delaware at Philadelphia, the British moved to Allentown (along a line of march generally followed by the New Jersey Turnpike) then turned east toward Monmouth courthouse.

This little traveled road was pure drudgery: so sandy that the horses could gain little footing. The fifteen hundred wagons, carriages, and carts moved less than six miles per day. There was no relief from the blistering sun. Hundreds of men were felled by heat exhaustion, and hundreds more deserted to seek the cooler clime along the tree-shaded King's Highway. Washington, smelling victory, shifted his troops toward the British.

But Washington's hard luck held. As General Charles Lee, once in British service, brought his men up before a line of redcoat rear guards, he lost heart, probably as much in his own generalship as in the ragged soldiers he commanded. Declining to launch an attack, which most observers agree would have succeeded, Lee ordered his men to fall back. The retrograde movement quickly became a general retreat. When Washington appeared (in a most violent temper), Lee whined, "these troops are not able to meet British Grenadiers." To which Washington roared: "Sir, they are and by God they shall do it!" The retreat was halted and the line held against an attack. But the spirit was gone and Clinton's sweaty horde was allowed to reach Sandy Hook from where the fleet ferried it to New York.

Monmouth was the last major battle in the north. For the rest of 1778 and most of 1779, Clinton fortified himself in New York. His main wall reached westward across most of the island from the foot of the modern Williamsburg Bridge along Houston Street to the hillocks around Broadway. Strong gun emplacements were also concentrated at the Battery (now part of a spacious bay-front park) and around the entrance to the modern Brooklyn Bridge.

With New York thus battened down, Clinton extended his fist into the South. The key was Charleston with its magnificent harbor and linkup with the interior via the King's Highway, the Augusta traders' path, and a road which ran nearly due north through Camden, S.C. to the Upper Road. The Upper Road (now Interstate 85) in turn followed the edge of the Appalachian highlands to Fredericksburg, Virginia, and was already supplanting the swampy, mosquito-infested King's Highway as the South's main immigration trail.

Late in 1779 Clinton with seventy-six hundred troops sailed for Charleston. He landed thirty miles south of the rebel-held city; and while he waited to gather in forces made available from the capture of Savannah, South Carolinians under General Benjamin Lincoln frantically threw up an earthen rampart which spanned the Charleston peninsula at modern Cannon Street, then just outside the city. By the time Clinton crossed the Ashley River and marched down the southernmost segment of the King's Highway, the Charleston wall bristled with artillery and was of such a height and thickness that it obviously could not be taken by direct assault. Clinton, therefore, was obliged to open siege operations—while the defenders' cannons gave him a smart fire (to the delight of the Charleston ladies who took excursions from the city to watch the display).

Gradually, however, Clinton's zigzags were only 250 yards

from the American rampart. There were no ladies on the walls when the British artillery began systematically to blast them away. With the British fleet blockading the harbor, it was only a matter of time until Lincoln was forced to surrender. On May 12, 1780, the garrison filed out, their colors cased due to Clinton's humiliating stipulation. Five thousand soldiers and armed civilians were lost to the American cause that day. It was the severest defeat of the entire war.

With Charleston safely tucked away, Clinton, putting the next phase of the Southern conquest plans into operation, sent his legions fanning out to secure the countryside. One, under a splashy daredevil by the name of Banastre Tarleton, sped up the King's Highway to roar into Georgetown, which had no choice except to capitulate. Another column took the path that had once heard little except jingling traders' bells to subjugate Augusta. The third, and most important, moved deep into the interior on the linkup route to the Upper Road. Led by Lord Cornwallis, Briton's most skilled troubleshooter, this army of twenty-five hundred easily took Camden, the last center of South Carolinian resistance.

Although Clinton, believing the whirlwind campaign over, appointed Cornwallis as administrator of the conquered province and set sail for New York, the Continental Congress had not yet abandoned the South. Horatio Gates, hero of Saratoga, was appointed commander of a motley force which marched blindly down on Camden from the north—where it was promptly pounced upon by Cornwallis. The British victory was so complete that a jubilant Tory newspaper printed a bantering want ad which ran:

REWARD! Strayed, deserted, or stolen from the Subscriber on the 16th of August, last near Camden, in the State of South Carolina, a whole army, consisting of Horse, Foot, and Dragoons, to the amount of near ten thousand. . . . Any person or persons civil or military, who will give information either to the Subscriber, or to Charles Thompson, Esq., Secretary to the Continental Congress, where the said Army is, so that they may be recovered and rallied again, shall be entitled to demand from the Treasurer of the United States, the sum of Three Millions of Paper Dollars as soon as they can be spared . . .[69]

Cornwallis, much more aggressive than Clinton his unimaginitive superior, found dreams for the resubjugation of Virginia —and Maryland too—now prancing through his brain. A big, fearless man in the prime of life, the general had sublime faith in his abilities. As the dazed Colonials reassembled at Hillsboro, recently replacing swamp-bound, semi-isolated New Bern as the North Carolina capital, Cornwallis led his troops through Charlotte and north on the Upper Road toward the American position. But his plans were momentarily disrupted on October 7 when a conglomerate force of frontiersmen and North Carolina and Virginia militia defeated his left wing at King's Mountain (now a national park) thirty miles west of Charlotte. With the winter rainy season threatening to wreck the muddy road to Hillsboro and Cornwallis himself twisting with fever aboard a hospital wagon, the British army took post at Winnsboro, where it could protect the garrisons at Camden and Augusta.

Although he had been temporarily stopped, Cornwallis felt he could still batter down resistance in the South and push over the Upper Road to retake Virginia. Thus in January, when Nathanael Greene, reshaping the American army which had moved down to Charlotte, sent a detachment under Daniel Morgan moving along the Upper Road toward the quaint little pasture called Hannah's Cowpens, Tarleton was ordered to make the big-boned Virginian pay for his part in Burgoyne's demise. But though Morgan was crippled with arthritis, he knew his battle tactics. Tarleton, brash as always, flung his troops against skillfully prepared positions without the support of his cavalry, which he held in reserve. Morgan's men, inspired by their leader, crushed the British advance. Then, before the astonished Tarleton could shoot his horsemen forward, an American bayonet charge pricked the entire British force into an uncontrollable retreat.

The setback at Cowpens left Cornwallis in a rage. Determined to capture the wily Morgan and at the same time move on Richmond, Cornwallis stripped his army for pursuit—setting an example by burning all his own personal belongings that might slow him down. Soon he was hot after Morgan—and Greene who had taken charge of the detachment in person. Brushing aside the American rear guard at Cowan's Ford on the Catawba (near the Eufola interchange of Interstate 85), Cornwallis hurried toward Salisbury—reaching the town just in time to see the last panting Americans ferried over the rising Yadkin. For two days Cornwallis cooled his heels waiting for the water to recede. Then he was off again—on the trail, although he did not know it, which would eventually lead to Yorktown.

Greene had not wasted his reprieve. Leaving the Upper Road, he had plunged westward into the rugged piedmont. Cornwallis, hoping to cut off the Americans before they crossed the Dan at the Virginia border, was led farther and farther from his supply base, then centered at Wilmington, N.C. On the fourteenth of February Green dove across the Dan taking all the available boats with him, just as Cornwallis, late again, appeared on the southern shore.

With the American army thus driven out of North Carolina, Cornwallis marched his gaunt, exhausted men to Hillsboro on the Upper Road, where his commissary stalked from house to house requisitioning food. The sparsely settled countryside could furnish him little, however; and when Greene, greatly reinforced with Virginians, recrossed the Dan, Cornwallis had no choice except to set out once again to destroy him. This time Greene did not give way before him. Taking a strong position at Guilford Courthouse (now a national park) he arranged his men in three lines. The front, composed of quavering, untrained North Carolina militia, fired a few rounds as the redcoats approached then scampered off—as Greene knew they would. Then Cornwallis, leading his twenty-two hundred troops in person, found himself facing the second line, militia too, but seasoned Virginians. The firing became sharper now, with the deadly aim of the Americans taking a gruesome toll. But at last the Virginians were forced to fall back.

Victory seemed assured, for the British had put nearly twenty-six hundred militia to flight. But then Cornwallis butted up against Greene's third line: sixteen hundred elite Continentals. Cannons and musketry roared as neither side gave. Tarleton, in the thick of the fighting, later wrote: "at this period the event of action was doubtful and victory alternately presided over each army." Finally, as the British began to turn Greene's left flank, he drew off—leaving the field and claims of victory with the British; but leaving, in addition, Cornwallis with more than five hundred casualties and a delay in his timetable which would spell his ultimate doom.

In order to recover from the dubious triumph (Horace Walpole in London commented dryly that a few more such conquests would leave Cornwallis fresh out of troops), the nearly starving British had to retreat to their supply base at Wilmington.

Once the army was revictualed and back in shape, Cornwallis turned again to rebellious Virginia. Although Henry Clinton in New York had made it clear that he did not regard Virginia as a subject for a major effort, Cornwallis was doggedly convinced that he could take the Old Dominion and with it end all resistance in the South.

Therefore on April 25, 1781, Cornwallis set out cross-country for Virginia, the fateful decision which would determine the future of the continent made without the approval of any higher authority. Entering the state at Emporia nearly three weeks later, he reached Petersburg on May 20, there to combine with another British force under hero-turned-traitor Benedict Arnold. Having now seventy-two hundred tested troops, Cornwallis drove upon the Marquis de Lafayette, a thin-faced twenty-three-year-old French nobleman to whom Washington had entrusted the defense of the province. Lafayette, with only thirty-two hundred men, did not dare to make a stand at Richmond. "I am not strong enough even to get beaten," he confessed.

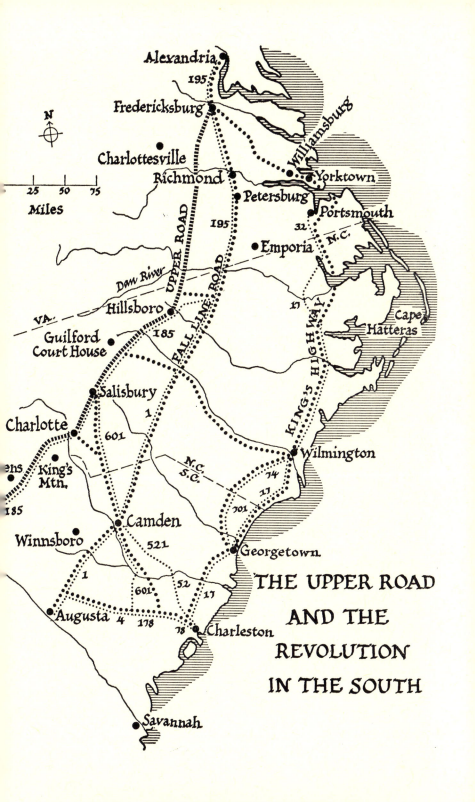

THE UPPER ROAD
AND THE
REVOLUTION
IN THE SOUTH

Nevertheless Lafayette harassed Cornwallis with great effect; and when the British moved against him in force, he faded away. In frustration Cornwallis sent Banastre Tarleton and his fast-riding legion dashing to Charlottesville in an attempt to capture the Virginia legislature meeting there temporarily and at the same time scoop up Governor Thomas Jefferson at Monticello, his beautiful mansion nearby. But at the last possible moment, Jefferson and the legislators received word; and in this raid, too, Cornwallis was unsuccessful.

Soon Lafayette began receiving sizable reinforcements. Although Nathanael Greene had dropped down into South Carolina where he was methodically snuffing out one British fort after another, General Anthony Wayne, a ferocious campaigner, with a thousand Pennsylvanians united with Lafayette—as did Von Steuben and also William Campbell with some of the buckskinned giants who had seen service at King's Mountain. So when Cornwallis moved against Williamsburg, Lafayette set out to prevent his taking that important town. On June 23, the British marched through New Kent on the King's Highway. Three days later they were at Spencer's Ordinary, an old tavern stop seven miles from the Virginia capital. Here some of Lafayette's troops made a stand, but Cornwallis was still too strong and he pushed into Williamsburg—where he spent the next few days in the house of the president of William and Mary College (now part of Williamsburg's extensive restorations).

However Cornwallis's relaxations were rather quickly terminated by a communique from Henry Clinton who had been artfully misled by Washington, reinforced by French troops, into believing he was about to be attacked. Ordered to ship a large portion of his army to New York, Cornwallis reluctantly moved out of Williamsburg and crossed over the James River at Jamestown to the harbor at Portsmouth.

As Cornwallis prepared to embark his men for New York, he received another dispatch from his confused superior informing him that he had changed his mind and Cornwallis should now entrench himself somewhere on the James or York rivers until the situation clarified. The exasperated general, who took little pains to disguise his irritation at Clinton's interference, chose Yorktown for his temporary encampment—his main reason being that Yorktown's sheltered harbor, used for decades by planters and shippers going to Williamsburg, afforded him ideal communication with the British fleet.

Yes, it was an excellent selection, chosen with Cornwallis's usual care. But there was one thing wrong. The British fleet no longer had uncontested superiority on the American coastline. Even as the general confidently threw up the customary earthworks, a powerful French armada was unfurling its sails in the Caribbean.

Washington had long prayed for just such a stroke of luck. Earlier in the spring he had conferred with the Comte de Rochambeau, suave, handsome commander of the French expeditionary army. Huddling in a neat little house which still stands in Wethersfield, Connecticut, the two generals could arrive at no conclusive plan of operation until the French fleet made its appearance. During the summer the French and American armies conducted desultory actions around King's Bridge. But they lacked the manpower to do anything more than rattle their swords at Clinton behind his strong battlements.

Then on August 14, a week after Cornwallis had settled down at Yorktown, Washington was handed a secret message containing the electrifying news that the Comte de Grasse with twenty-eight warships and thirty-two hundred troops was sailing northward. He could remain away from the important sugar islands only a short time; so if Washington was to take advantage of the situation, he must act immediately.

Instantly Washington sent a courier speeding down the King's Highway to Lafayette, whose increasingly augmented army was keeping a watchful eye on Cornwallis. Since Washington hoped to snare the general and all his men in the trap Cornwallis himself had made, Washington ordered that Lafayette "immediately take such a position as will best enable you to prevent their sudden retreat through North Carolina." In addition, he cautioned the young Frenchman to keep the news of de Grasse's destination absolutely secret so that Cornwallis would have no reason to attempt a breakthrough—given the inferior size of Lafayette's army, a worrisome possibility.

Now began the greatest drama ever to unfold on the King's Highway. Wagons were loaded, artillery limbered up, horses hitched, and companies mustered. Soon eight thousand French and American soldiers were streaming down the plain west of Newark Bay. In order to keep Clinton from guessing their destination and warning Cornwallis, the line of march seemed to be heading for Staten Island. Next the force fanned out in three widely spaced columns. "By these maneuvers," gloated Washington's secretary, "our own army no less than the enemy are completely deceived. No movement perhaps was ever attended with more conjectures . . . not one I believe penetrated the real design."

But once the French and Americans struck southward through New Brunswick, it was a mystery no longer. The race was on.

At the same moment that Washington was dashing south, a potent British fleet was likewise headed for the Chesapeake to repel de Grasse, whose blockade of Cornwallis was the most essential part of the allied operations. On August 25 British units entered the bay; but, finding the waters deserted, cruised back to New York. Five days later de Grasse slipped through the capes unmolested. Soon he was disembarking troops on Jamestown Island; and the cordon around Cornwallis was begun.

De Grasse, however, was impatient to return to the Caribbean. Not caring to wait for Washington and Rochambeau to make their way over the rutted, ponderously difficult highway, de Grasse urged Lafayette to open the attack. But the cautious marquis wisely kept putting the seadog off.

Slowly the northern army trudged through Jersey, passing Princeton with memories of a day when Washington was fleeing from, not rushing toward, Lord Cornwallis. On the twenty-ninth the seemingly endless task of ferrying the army over the Delaware at Trenton was begun. Leaving the job to his subordinates,

Washington, accompanied by Rochambeau and a brilliant retinue, proceeded down the King's Highway through Bristol and Frankford, where they were met by an honor guard of Philadelphia horsemen. Entering the capital amid the wild acclamation of the joyous citizens, Washington went directly to the City Tavern, where he received the best wishes of the most influential citizens. Then he rode to the South Front Street home of Robert Morris, who as Superintendent of Finance had taken on most of the duties of the malfunctioning Board of War. Washington banqueted there to the roar of riverboats firing salutes. That evening the city was illuminated and (according to a newspaper account) "his Excellency walked through some of the principal streets, attended by a numerous concourse of people eagerly pressing to see their beloved General."

Washington had hoped Morris and his agents could round up enough boats at Philadelphia to ship the army to the York Peninsula, thus avoiding many days of marching. This was impossible. So Washington ordered his army on down the King's Highway toward the Head of Elk, where Morris was frantically trying to collect more transport vessels. But time was slipping by; and on September 2 Washington, upon learning that the British fleet was again heading southward from New York, wrote to Lafayette that he was "distressed beyond expression."

And well might Washington fret, for even as he rode through Chester to the great camp rising at the Head of Elk, the Chesapeake capes were suddenly studded with the sails of nineteen British warships, a sight which so shook de Grasse that he put out to sea with more than eighteen hundred of his sailors still ashore. As de Grasse and his twenty-four vessels, canvas billowing, disappeared over the horizon, the fate of Yorktown hung in balance.

While the fleets were at sea, Washington struggled with the almost insurmountable difficulties of supplying and outfitting such a large body of men over the thin pipeline known as the King's Highway. In a communique to Lafayette, Washington stated that heavy cannon, ordnance stores, ammunition, and entrenching tools were gradually being accumulated. However he admitted "having also from the first moment been extremely anxious respecting the supplies of the army (in which I comprehend not only provisions of the bread and meat kind, etc., but also forage and the means of transportation)" he was beseeching the surrounding states to fulfill their quotas, "as we have no other resources to rely upon for the support of the army." [70]

With news of the sea fight still lacking, Washington began putting his goods and artillery aboard the oyster boats and other scows that had been assembled at the Head of Elk, then marched the main body of his troops down the King's Highway to Baltimore and Annapolis, where they would await more shipping. Washington spent the night of September 8 in Baltimore, having been escorted to the Fountain Inn by a troop of the city's light dragoons.

The next morning he left his troops to resume his southward journey accompanied by a single member of his staff. At each town and hamlet along his way he found the people aroused and expectant. Soon he was across the Potomac at Alexandria and riding through the drought-stricken Virginia countryside. By evening he was at Mount Vernon. It had been sixty rugged miles from Baltimore, but he was in his beloved home for the first time in over six years.

The general was served a sumptuous dinner—and quarters were prepared for Rochambeau and his aides, who arrived dusty and tired later the same evening. Washington sent word to Lafayette in Williamsburg to assemble a military escort at New Kent for the growing number of high officers gathering at Mount Vernon. Then he dispatched an express to the Governor of Maryland appealing for food for the hungry troops now beginning to land around Jamestown.

On the twelfth of September Washington, Rochambeau, and their staffs were back in the saddle. Near Dumfries on the way to Fredericksburg, they met a rider hurrying northward who revealed that no word had yet been heard of either the French or British fleets. The uncertainty caused Washington to order all boats transporting troops down the Chesapeake to put ashore until the battle outcome was learned. The cavalcade rode on to

Fredericksburg in gloom, where they spent a tense night, perhaps at the Rising Sun tavern built by Washington's brother.

Early the next morning they were off once more—on the same tedious road that Washington had taken so many times before as a young legislator traveling to the House of Burgesses. They passed through New Kent and around four o'clock of the fourteenth rode into Williamsburg to the tumultuous blasts of twenty-one cannons.

Lafayette, rising from a sickbed, rushed to greet Washington; and such was the young man's enthusiasm that he "caught the General round his body, hugged him as close as it was possible, and absolutely kissed him from ear to ear"—so wrote an astonished bystander. Excitement was high as Washington and Rochambeau reviewed the troops. Yet behind it all was the disquieting lack of news concerning de Grasse.

Late that very night a dispatch smelling of salt water was shoved into Washington's hand. He learned that de Grasse was back in the Chesapeake; and soon the rest of the drama was told. On September 5 the two fleets had locked in a thunderous battle; the results were inconclusive and for three days they had lain within sight of one another, each undecided whether to risk a continuation of the fight. Winds blew them ever farther southward, and the British were off Cape Hatteras when de Grasse lost sight of them. Then it took de Grasse several days to make it back.

This was the news Washington had been awaiting. Troop movements from the north were resumed; and by the twenty-eighth the army—composed of fifty-two hundred Continentals, three thousand American militia, and seventy-five hundred French--marched out of the Williamsburg encampment and down the segment of the King's Highway which led to Yorktown. The formal siege of Cornwallis and his once-omnipotent army was begun.

With his supplies cut off and confronted by an army twice his size, Cornwallis's situation was desperate. His only hope was to hold out until the British fleet, soon to be reinforced, could once again challenge de Grasse. But time was not on his side. At

dusk on October 6 an entrenching party of fifteen hundred
began constructing the first siege line, which ran like an arc from
the deep gully of Yorktown Creek to the bluffs overlooking the
York River. Three days later the batteries were completed and
the cannonading was started.

This was the culmination of all the days of hardship, all the
frustrations of the march, all the pleading for supplies and
ammunition. The artillery devastated Cornwallis's position. "One
could . . . not avoid the horribly many cannon balls either inside
or outside the city," complained a British soldier, ". . . many
[men] were badly injured and mortally wounded by the frag-
ments of bombs which exploded partly in the air and partly on
the ground, their arms and legs severed or themselves struck
dead . . . One saw men lying nearly everywhere . . ." [71]

Soon the trenches wormed closer to Yorktown and preparations for the second siege line were commenced. But before this
line could be completed a pair of fortified British outposts had to
be stormed. The honor of taking Redoubt Number 9 was given to
the French, and Redoubt Number 10 to an American detachment of four hundred led by a slim West Indian lad named
Alexander Hamilton. The night action at this bunker (now reconstructed) was short but violent, as the account of one of
Hamilton's men, Sargeant Joseph Martin, reveals:

> Just as we arrived at the abatis [an entanglement of sharp-
> ened branches which encircled the earthwork], the enemy
> discovered us and . . . opened a sharp fire upon us. . . . As
> soon as the firing began our people began to cry . . . "Rush
> on, boys!" The sappers and miners soon cleared a passage for
> the infantry who entered it rapidly. . . . While passing, a
> man at my side received a ball in his head and fell under my
> feet, crying out bitterly . . . [72]

Shortly after the redoubts were taken, the American and
French artillery bombarded Yorktown from point-blank range.
Cornwallis, desperately praying for the return of the British fleet,
was barely able to return the fire. His ammunition was nearly
exhausted, and those of his men who were not wounded or dead

were so fatigued by the constant cannonade that their will to fight had been worn almost away. But the tough old campaigner was not through. On the evening of October 15 he sent a portion of his army charging out of his entrenchments and into the second siege line. Although the British temporarily drove back the besiegers and spiked some cannons, Cornwallis lacked the manpower to hold his position and soon the allied guns were firing once more.

The next night Cornwallis attempted to ferry his army across the York River to Gloucester Point, held by Tarleton, for a sprint for New York. But when a storm broke up this effort, he realized he had no choice except surrender. The parley was held at Augustine Moore's farmhouse (currently restored). Once the terms were settled, Washington and Rochambeau signed the document, probably at their command position in Redoubt Number 10.

On the afternoon of October 19, the British army, clad in bright new uniforms, filed out of the crumbling fortress while their band intoned the droll military march aptly entitled "The World Turned Upside Down." Cornwallis, sick at heart if not in body, remained in smoldering Yorktown while General O'Hara gave his sword, the symbol of defeat, first to Rochambeau who referred him to Washington, then to General Lincoln when Washington refused to deal with a subordinate in command.

Although the war would continue officially until the final peace was concluded in Paris two years later, this capitulation of the second British army in the field brought an end to hostilities east of the Appalachians. And it had been the King's Highway which had played an indispensable part in the victory at Yorktown, since without the facility to move his long train of cumbersome supply wagons and heavy artillery, as well as his soldiers, Washington could never have reached the York Peninsula in time to breach Cornwallis's stout ramparts before the British fleet returned—which it did, forty-four ships strong, only nine days after the surrender.

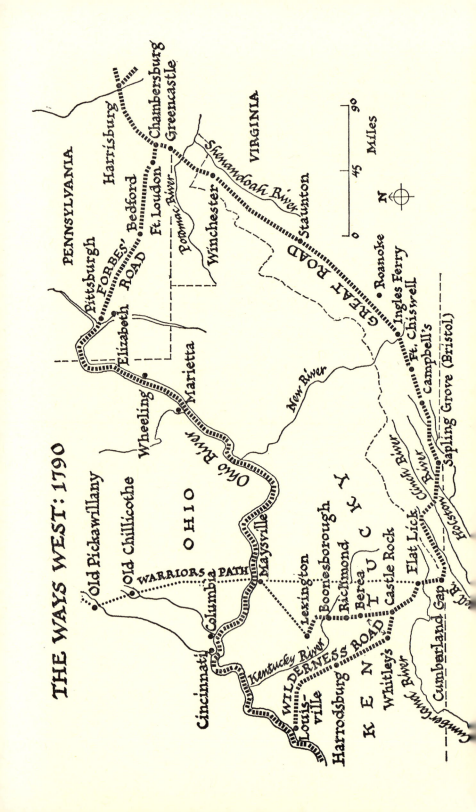

THE WAYS WEST: 1790

The Conquest of the Mississippi Valley, 1775–1850

19.   The Worst on the Continent

The German craftsmen at Lancaster and other towns in the Conestoga Valley were proud of their work. They had designed their huge wagons with bodies shaped like lazy, inverted rainbows to carry their produce to market in Philadelphia. Although the rigs were so heavy that six husky horses were required to pull them, they couldn't be constructed any other way, for it took the toughest oak to keep the vehicles from being shaken apart—as many less-well-made wagons were. Then, too, the hickory-spoked wheels, lofty as a man's shoulder, were especially built not only to withstand the most jarring boulder, but to carry the wagon above the tree stumps which studded all but the most frequented roads.

Sturdiness was not the only quality that brought the thrifty Pennsylvania Dutch an ever-increasing bounty in wagon sales. A Conestoga's body was fully sixteen feet long—big enough to accommodate most of the personal belongings pioneer families wished to take to their otherwise barren log cabins. In addition, the upward-tilting body ends kept the baggage from spilling out on the many steep grades. And the high-riding canvas top—supported by eight hoops and rising six feet above the wagon panels—virtually doubled the total storage space.

Even before the French and Indian War lumbering Conestogas were carrying pioneers down the road which began at

Philadelphia—landing point for thousands of land-hungry Germans and Scotch-Irish—passed through Lancaster and Harrisburg, and then turned leftward to funnel down the trough between North and South mountains. Whereas the traders' path that would soon become a monument to John Forbes veered off into the mountains at Chambersburg, most early pioneers preferred to continue in a more southerly direction along the relatively level and fertile valley that stretched out before them for half a thousand miles.

Beyond the ferry which crossed the Potomac near Hagerstown, the Great Road, as it was generally called, entered the lovely valley of the Shenandoah. Following a route later taken by Interstate 81, the Conestogas rumbled through Winchester, founded in 1744, and continued south by southwest—with the impenetrable Appalachians looming on the right and the haze-drenched Blue Ridge on the left. As the farms thinned out, the children, who usually insisted on running beside the wagon rather than endure the constant, skull-rattling bumping, would come upon numerous discarded tomahawks, arrow shafts, and bits of feathers to remind them that they were using a highway that had once been the main invasion path between the far-ranging Iroquois and the trembling tribes of the south.

Year after year the procession of new settlers moved farther down the Great Valley. A majority were Scotch-Irish who, renouncing the rocky soil of their adopted Northern Ireland as well as family ties with their native Scotland, outnumbered even the Germans in this backwoods paradise. And for a while at least, the long trail to their settlements was alternately known as the Irish Road. Soon a village called Big Lick (later renamed the more dignified Roanoke) was laid out on an intermountain tableland around a large salt deposit long favored by buffalo and other wild animals. From there the pioneer tide moved on, by packhorse now, around the crumpled foothills of Walker Mountain, which protruded far into the Great Valley, to fill the rolling basin of the Holston.

When Braddock's disaster at Fort Duquesne opened the Virginia frontier to the onslaught of Indians, Colonel William

Byrd III, helping Washington maintain Virginia's tenuous hold in the west, widened the Great Road to wagons as far as the exposed hamlets on the newly settled Holston. Important in the defense system was Fort Chiswell, guarding the crossroads where a trunk route (now U.S. 52) crossed over the New River, and the Blue Ridge beyond, to Winston-Salem and the Upper Road.

After Forbes's victory, immigration increased down the Great Road as countless Conestogas—their red wheels, white tops, and blue bodies making a colorfully patriotic picture—clattered southward. By 1762 George Ingles, a hard-working Irishman, had built a ferry at what is now Radford to help the wagoners cross the New River. But hostile Cherokees and other tribesmen still lurked in the dark forest; so Arthur Campbell, a red-tousled Scotch-Irishman, constructed a fortresslike home beside the road (near modern Marion) from which he guided the defense of the frontier below Fort Chiswell. For thirty years Campbell's Royal Oak remained a comforting landmark along the dangerous highway.

Beyond Royal Oak was a Scotch-Irish settlement named Wolf Hills (now Abingdon) for the packs of wolves which howled menacingly near. At Sapling Grove (Bristol) the southwesterly Great Road met a faint Indian trace which meandered off due west into the foreboding hulk of Clinch Mountain, thirty-five miles distant, a rugged outrider of the main Appalachian barrier. Clinch Mountain, so the rumor went, was notched by a lofty pass known as Moccasin Gap by the warriors who used it during their excursions against white settlers in the Holston and against other tribes farther south. On the other side of Clinch Mountain were two more ranges and another gap, then Kentucky, fabled for its fertility yet occupied by no tribe due to its location between the constantly warring northern Indians led by the ferocious Shawnees and the southern ones led by the quick-witted Cherokees. Although the Indians called the area the "dark and bloody ground," this *kentucky* had a growing allure to the callused pioneer farmers scraping a living from the less desirable soil on the uplands beside the Great Road.

Could the way through the mountain wilderness be accurately marked, a horde of pioneers would pour into the lush land —so, at least, were the thoughts of Judge Richard Henderson and his Transylvania Company. Despatching a caravan of wagons crammed with ten thousand pounds of gifts southward along the Great Road, Henderson invited the Cherokees to a conference at Sycamore Shoals (now Elizabethton, Tennessee) just down the valley from Sapling Grove. Even while the Cherokees were gleefully pawning off Kentucky to which their Shawnee enemies had better title, Henderson sent Daniel Boone with thirty heavily armed men "to mark out a road [as Boone wrote in his all-too-brief memoirs] in the best passage from the settlement through the wilderness to Kentucke." Although Boone in his matter-of-fact style omits all but the meagerest details, the establishment of the Wilderness Trail was one of the most important events in American history. It was due mainly to the early Kentucky pioneers, rooted so tenaciously in the midst of the hostile Indian-held West, that Great Britain ceded the entire vast region between the Appalachians and the Mississippi to the United States at the close of the Revolutionary War.

But in March of 1775 Boone had little inkling of the trail's vital function as he emblazoned the way, already fuzzily outlined from the sporadic passage of Indian war parties and a few white hunters. Following a route now taken by U.S. 58, he and his men ascended Moccasin Gap, forded the Clinch River, then struggled up formidable Powell Mountain, the pass over which was six hundred feet higher than the Cumberland Gap farther on. Once on the summit Boone had unpleasant memories, for it was here that his son James, age seventeen, had been murdered by Shawnees only a year and a half back.

But the thirty trailblazers fingered their guns and descended into the Powell Valley. The way was momentarily easy, for the valley floor was flat. Twenty-five miles up the valley, with the Appalachians (here called the Cumberlands) rising in gray splendor on their right, they came upon Joseph Martin building a station at what is now Rose Hill, Virginia. Martin, whose settlement would eventually become one of the main stopping

places on the Wilderness Road, was informed that he was tres-
passing on land purchased by the Transylvania Company (Henderson later made him his agent); then Boone and his crew
resumed their march.

Soon they noted the White Rocks, light-colored capstone on
the Cumberlands, which announced they were approaching the
hidden gap which would take them through the mountains. A
few hours later they spied the J-shaped dent through which
Thomas Walker, the gap's discoveror, had traveled twenty-five
years earlier, and over which Boone had passed twice previously.
The ascent was gentle, for the Cumberland Gap had been created by a since-vanished river whose bed had been smoothed by
eons of wind and rain. Gradually the towering projection which
Walker referred to as the Steep Ridge (but which modern
tourists admiring the far-reaching view from its crest call the
Pinnacle) rose ever larger. Almost imperceptably they passed
over the divide and into Kentucky.

They soon came upon the headwaters of westward-flowing
Yellow Creek, so called from the amber tint gathered from the
sulphurous coal over which it tumbled. Yellow Creek had cut a
narrow arroyo where only a slender buffalo and Indian trace
edged through a thick barrier of canes. Boone and his men
struggled down the rocky canyon for about twenty-five miles
before coming to the pleasant vale at modern Barbourville,
where Thomas Walker and his party of five had once erected a
cabin and planted a token patch of corn.

Although Walker had failed to penetrate the rocky Cumberland upland far enough to reach that section of the country later
to be famous for its rich pastures of European-imported bluegrass, Boone pushed on. The going was tough for the Warrior's
Path, which had tramped down the original buffalo trace, turned
off at Flat Lick toward Shawnee country. So the men forced
their way through thickets, weeds, and forests. At intervals they
would pause to chop away logs, overhanging branches, and
other obstructions which would hinder the pioneer pack trains
that would follow. When their horses, weak from the arduous
journey, started balking, switches snapped against their flanks

and the party plodded on down the dreary path now taken by
high-speed Interstate 75. Just south of modern Berea the rough
hills came to an abrupt end, and the men gazed out over the
Kentucky heartland.

Here they certainly stopped to drink in the scene. They
were the vanguards of civilization. The crude trail they were
blazing would soon become an entryway for thousands of settlers. A scene such as they beheld at this instant would soon be
gone. The forest and the countless wild animals who made it
their home would give way to farms and cows. Towns and
villages would dot the landscape and the smoke from countless
hearth fires would smudge the sky that had known only the
delicate curl of Indian campfires. This precious moment must
have been like that of which Daniel Boone wrote upon his first
visit to the area:

> From the top of an eminence [I] saw with pleasure the
> beautiful level of Kentucke. . . . We found everywhere abun-
> dance of wild beasts of all sorts through this vast forest. The
> buffaloes were more frequent than I have seen cattle in
> the settlements . . . we practiced hunting with great
> success . . .[73]

On March 24, exactly two weeks after setting out from the
Holston, they bedded down about three miles south of modern
Richmond. Since they were only a short distance from their goal
the Kentucky River, and had safely passed the rugged mountain
portion of their journey, they slept deeply and contentedly.

Suddenly the night was shattered by the fearsome Shawnee
war cry. Tomahawks glinted in the starlight. Boone and his men,
taken completely by surprise, scattered into the forest, yet not
before two of their number were wounded and two more
sprawled dead on the ground. But the Americans rallied, with-
stood the attack, and the next morning threw together a log
barricade. Nevertheless, three days later the Indians struck
again, killing two more men and wounding three others. After
waiting over a week for the Shawnee to leave, the trailblazers

stumbled to the Kentucky River, where they immediately began constructing a large, rectangular stockade called Fort Boonesborough—Kentucky's unofficial first capital.

Boone's grim experience with the Indians proved a forecast of the hazardous conditions long to prevail on the Wilderness Road. Yet even though it was known that the Shawnees, as well as a numerous contingent of the Cherokees known as the Chickamaugas, were determined to resist the white occupation of Kentucky, scores of families loaded up their Conestogas and headed down the Great Valley for the Widlerness Road which cut off at what is now Bristol, Virginia. But disillusionment came early—even before reaching the road itself. At Fort Chiswell, the last major populated area east of the mountains, pioneers learned the disheartening truth: the Wilderness Road was not a road at all, merely the crudest of trails suitable only for packhorses. Thus their wagons and most of their belongings had to be disposed of at a loss to the sharp dealers at Fort Chiswell. Then the families tugged their scrawny horses toward the chill passes and Indian-haunted timberlands that stood between them and the Kentucky River.

Slowly the landmarks passed: rugged Moccasin Gap, the ofttimes perilous Clinch River ford, and the seemingly endless Powell Valley. Finally the White Rocks would appear and soon the famed Cumberland Gap. Then they would plow through the difficult Yellow Creek arroyo. With straining eyes they would scan the horizon for Castle Rock, the prominent outcropping which can still be seen beside U.S. 25 eight miles south of Livingston.

At Castle Rock the worst part of the journey was over. Here the Wilderness Road split. The older trail cut due north along Boone's original blazings. The other and eventually more popular fork looped more westward to Harrodsburg, a little stockaded village (now partially restored) founded a month earlier than Boonesborough by adventurers who had reached the location by the shorter, but even more dangerous, Ohio River route.

The Revolutionary era was hard on the Kentucky settlements, placed as they were nearly four hundred mountainous miles west of the ocean. The Indians, abundantly supplied by the British at Detroit, made virtually continuous attacks. Not even the efforts of William Whitley, who led retaliatory sallies from his sturdy brick mansion Sportsman Hill (still standing near Crab Orchard), could prevent murders and massacres along the Wilderness Road. Possibly the low ebb of Kentucky's fortunes occurred on February 7, 1778, when Daniel Boone with twenty-six gun-toting companions was captured by the stealthy Shawnee and marched up the Warrior's Path to their chief village Old Chillicothe (sixteen miles east of present Dayton, Ohio). Although Boone later escaped, his capture sent a chill throughout the Kentucky frontier.

Nonetheless, immigration over the Wilderness Road continued. By 1780 upwards of twelve thousand pioneers had run the hazardous gauntlet. And by the time the United States and Britain had signed the Treaty of 1783, close to ten thousand more men, women, and children had taken the trail to Kentucky. Since it was now obvious that the road had united Kentucky to the United States and that other routes would soon carry a similar influx of Americans throughout the entire trans-Appalachian region (Kentucky-based George Rogers Clark had already conquered Vincennes and Kaskaskia far to the west), British statesmen ceded the whole area to the United States rather than withhold part and thereby make certain of another war within a decade or so.

The next eleven years were the heyday of the Wilderness Road. With the Shawnees deprived of their British allies and confined north of the Ohio and the Cherokees weakened by smallpox and the effects of the constant border wars, thousands upon thousands of pioneers prodded their overburdened packhorses over the Cumberland Gap, past Castle Rock, and into the countryside where bluegrass and thoroughbred horses were beginning to make their appearance. Soon Lexington replaced Boonesborough, which crumbled away until nothing was left except a weather-worn marker in the modern state park. Lexington, however, became the largest city in the West—boasting sixteen hundred inhabitants.

During the 1780's the Wilderness Road was jammed with immigrants. As Kentucky's population rose to eighty thousand, inns and taverns sprang up all along the immigration route. One of the most popular was that of pleasure-loving Mrs. Davis at the Cumberland Gap. And it wasn't all one-way travel. There soon developed a huge back-traffic of cattle, pigs, sheep, and horses being driven to Eastern markets. Every inn had large animal pens nearby.

Still the influx continued. In 1792 Kentucky became the first state west of the Appalachians; and by the turn of the century close to a hundred thousand more persons had traveled the over-crowded, manure-packed way to Kentucky.

Yet the Wilderness Road throughout its sixty-year existence remained a makeshift concoction. Its awkward, seven hundred mile U shape from Harrisburg and the Cumberland Gap to Lexington made it fully one hundred and fifty grueling miles longer than Lexington reached by way of Forbes's Road, the Ohio River, and the short highway from Maysville, Kentucky. In addition, the rock-slide-prone mountainous terrain made the trail dangerous as well as tedious. Even after 1796 when the cramped roadbed was finally widened to accommodate wagons, a bruised, frustrated traveler denounced the road as "the worst on the whole continent."

Clearly, once the Indians were removed from their strangle-hold of the Ohio River, the twilight of the Wilderness Road would begin. And already the first hardy pioneers were making plans to invade the Shawnee homeland.

Rufus Putnam and ten associates huddled over their toddies in Boston's Bunch of Grapes Tavern. Despite the smoke and the din, Putnam managed to convey his enthusiasm. He had a marvelous plan. Did they want to become rich men? Then listen. They would pool their energies in the name of the New Ohio Company to sell stock to Revolutionary veterans in return for the supposedly worthless Certificates of Indebtedness with which the nearly bankrupt Continental Congress had paid them for risking their lives.

Now Putnam leaned closer and lowered his voice. Congress would accept these certificates at par value for Ohio lands, but few persons wanted to go there since it was an inhospitable region with no lawful government and no protection from the Shawnee, Miami, Wyandot, and Mingo tribes. But what if Congress could be induced to pass an ordinance which would place law enforcement under a federal governor and bring in federal troops to control the Indians. Ah, then wouldn't the price of the lands represented by the certificates rise!

Rum cups clinked and the New Ohio Company was formed. And Putnam was as good as his boast. His agent helped push through Congress (aided by generous land bribes) the Ordinance of 1787 establishing stable government in the newly created Northwest Territory (encompassing what would one day be Ohio, Indiana, Illinois, Michigan, Wisconsin, and part of Minnesota). Protection was guaranteed by the United States army; and provision was made for orderly progression to statehood when the population reached sixty thousand. With this law the New

Ohio Company was on its way to becoming the most successful land speculation venture in the history of the frontier.

Part of the company's success lay in the fact that the managers were sincerely interested in making Ohio fit for settlement—far different from Henderson and his quickly defunct Transylvanians, who dreamed of private empires in Kentucky. To encourage immigration, in April of 1788 Putnam and a crew of forty-eight New Englanders flatboated down the Ohio to the Muskingum, where they began building a fortified town called Marietta—the first permanent American settlement in the Northwest. A month later Colonel John May, another of the eleven charter members, arrived by flatboat with more recruits and supplies. It is through his remarkable journal that we gain a glimpse of the trails that played so essential a part in the opening of the West.

Colonel May, a blunt Yankee of proud stock dating back to the Plymouth Bay Colony, had been in the siege of Boston and later served in Rhode Island with Count Rochambeau—from whom he adopted the stiff European military bearing upon which he prided himself. Tasting the excitement of war, May was discontented with the staid Eastern world and yearned for the more fluid life of the frontier—a common motive for emigration. Thus he joined Putnam's company and soon found himself, with two companions, on the way to Marietta.

May's journey to Ohio foretold the westward movement of much of New England. Leaving Boston on April 14, 1788, he rode through Connecticut over the same "tremendous hilly country" that had confronted his Puritan ancestors. The Connecticut River at Hartford was swollen and dangerous, causing the impatient travelers to consume an entire hour in its crossing. The next day they were off to New Haven, then on through a maze of crossroads to their lodging in Fairfield, still darkened by the charred shells of eighty burnt-out houses that were souvenirs of the British. Continuing westward on the King's Highway—now called the Boston Post Road—they came to the steep ridge at Horseneck, even more difficult than usual with the frigid April rain muddying the slope and Colonel May's horse hobbling on a lame leg. They spent the night in Knapp's fine inn; but the cantankerous colonel had difficulty sleeping due to the "insufferable noise of the family."

The three riders were back on the road before sunup. However May's horse was now so lame that, after dining at Kingsbridge, he had his friends lead his horse while he continued to New York by stagecoach—a luxury the thousands of New Englanders who were eventually to take this road to the West would be unable to enjoy. After spending a few days attending to business and sightseeing (there were a "pile of new buildings nearly completed. . . . in one of [which] I traveled up five flights of stairs!") he and his rejuvinated nag made a rough crossing on the Jersey City ferry. Then they rode on to within ten miles of Princeton. The next day he crossed the Delaware near Trenton, dined at Bristol, and lodged in Philadelphia at the sign of the Conestoga Wagon.

The starchy New Englander was horrified at the cosmopolitan city, particularly at the worldly women. "I have seen a headdress in this city at least three feet across," he grumbled, adding with obvious disdain, "I stayed here only one night."

Although the main migration route would proceed over the Lancaster and Forbes's roads (now lumped together as the Pittsburgh Pike), May had business in Baltimore. Thus he continued south, soon reaching the old Swedish village of Christiana, where his horse impishly threw him just as he was making a polite bow to a lady sitting on a tavern porch. May and his friends crossed the Susquehanna at the Head of Elk, quiet after the brief flurry during Washington's race to Yorktown. The next day they entered Baltimore in the midst of a drenching rainstorm. May found the city to be a large, handsome place; the muddy, garbage-filled streets which had annoyed John Adams ten years earlier were evidently gone. He enjoyed his stay at the "high style" Indian Queen Tavern. But Marietta called; and on the twenty-ninth, fifteen days after trotting through the venerable Boston gates, he nosed his horse out of Baltimore, "then stood for the wilderness of the Western World."

The route he followed ran northwest to South Mountain, the

first of the Appalachian ridges. Although the mountain had a
"terrible appearance to a stranger tired and worn down by
constant fatigue," May, still accompanied by his companions,
slipped up a narrow river canyon emerging near the Great Road
just east of Greencastle, Pennsylvania. A German tavernkeeper
gave May a bed in a low-roofed garret where the air was so
stuffy that the colonel had an asthma attack. By 3 A.M. he had
had enough. Stomping out of bed, he routed his companions
from the barroom, where they were asleep on the floor, and
herded them onto their horses. They clattered through still-slum-
bering Greencastle, took refreshment at Mercersburg, then set
their sights on the hunched masses of the North and Tuscarora
mountains—probably joining the Pittsburgh Pike near the ruins
of old Fort Loudon. May's description of the climb over the
Tuscarora (steep even today on U.S. 30) most certainly embod-
ies the feelings of the thousands of pioneers in years to come:

> The mountain is ten miles over. It took us three hours and a
> half to cross it. It is, I can truly say, the hardest to climb we
> have yet attempted, and makes one of the four capital ranges
> of mountains which belong to the family of Alleghana, and
> the sight of which generally strikes such terror into travel-
> ers.[74]

The following day they encountered Sideling Hill which
was nearly as difficult as Tuscarora. Resting that night a little
beyond Bedford, where they had left the pike to take a lesser
road that followed a portion of what would become the modern
Pennsylvania Turnpike, by midmorning they had ascended Allegheny Mountain. There they paused to admire the expansive
panorama of blue ridges and green valleys. Now they were on
the gusty "backbone of the continent," so the colonel wrote. It
was along here that the disputed Proclamation of 1763 ran; and
even though the Proclamation was dead, May noted that he felt
as if he were passing out of the old world and into the new at
this point. Here the West truly began.

They slept that night in a comfortable farmhouse at the foot
of the mountain, where the colonel said he had "good entertain-

ment"—a statement open to various interpretations had not
May's character been of New England granite. The morning was
rainy, giving the travelers an excuse to tarry over breakfast with
the previous evenings entertainers. Reluctantly, they set out into
the mud over a road "as bad as could be," sloshing up Laurel
Hill and then Chestnut Ridge, their horses constantly skidding
over the perilous switchbacks. Men and beasts were completely
frazzled by the time the last of the Appalachian chain was
crossed.

On May 5, a week after leaving Baltimore, the colonel
reached Elizabeth on the Monongahela. The village had been
laid out only the previous year, yet it was rapidly becoming an
important center for the manufacture of flatboats, ranking not
too far behind Pittsburgh. After purchasing a goodly stock of
flour and a barrel of whiskey, which he sent by way of a
Kentucky boat (as the flats at this time were often called) to
Pittsburgh, he rode on horseback the rest of the way to the forks,
where he lodged in a tavern which was to stand for more than
fifty years across the Monongahela from the foot of Liberty
Street.

At Pittsburgh May intended to confer with other company
directors; but they were momentarily absent so he was forced to
idle away four days. It was dull in Pittsburgh. The town consisted merely of one hundred and fifty houses, most of them
crude log cabins. The nights, too, were long. There were at least
two dogs for every human and every dog spent most of the dark
hours yowling madly. One day, however, was enlivened when
General Josiah Harmar, commander of Fort Pitt, had some of his
soldiers row them to the site of Braddock's defeat. The field of
battle had become a tourist attraction where the ground glittered
with bleached bones and staring skulls. "I picked up one of
them," May wrote, "which did not seem much decayed, although
it is above thirty years since this battle."

But the colonel's main activity was concerned with the
Kentucky boats. The Pittsburgh docks bristled with them; and
the river itself was hardly ever without one or more heaving into
view. They were clumsy, unlovely creations: square-nosed,

walled up and roofed over from stem to stern, with frequent gun holes to repel Indian attacks. There were stinking pens for cattle and horses in the rear portion, baggage was strewn amidships, and the living quarters in the bow swarmed with men, women, and bawling children. Although they were theoretically steered by a helmsman standing atop the cabin pushing an unwieldy rudder pole and propelled by four men tugging at oars, they usually rotated lazily out of control down the wide Ohio, sometimes becoming marks for Indians as they stranded on sandbars, smashed on rocks, or became entangled in driftwood. In addition to these considerable dangers, the Kentucky boats cost forty dollars or more—high enough to convince the less affluent pioneers to take the low-expense Wilderness Road.

Nevertheless the boats were popular and Colonel May was astonished at the numbers on the river. Writing to his wife, he exclaimed: "the man where I lodge says he had kept account of two hundred and fifty boats . . . gone down the river this spring —and he has not been at home but a part of the time. It is also allowed there are as many go down in the night as in the day. In fact the immigration is immense." [75]

At last the company officials returned. May got his instructions and, with twenty-seven recruits, launched his twelve-by-forty-two-foot ship. "At 12½ o'clock cast off our fasts and commited ourselves to the current of the Ohio," he recorded in his journal. "The scene was beautiful. Without wind or waves we, insensibly almost, make more than five miles an hour. In eight hours we arrived at Little Beaver, a distance of forty-three miles." May was captivated by the easy glide down the majestic river, particularly when he remembered the struggle over the Pittsburgh Pike.

They continued on by moonlight. Even though May felt cramped—in addition to the men there were two cows, two calves, seven hogs, nine dogs, and eight tons of seed corn, potatoes, and baggage on board—he found this evening "one of the grandest nights in all my experience":

The scene was so grand and the sounds and echoes so various, that I could not go in but kept up five hours minding the helm the most of the time—with one lookout forwards and four to row, whilst all the rest slept. We moved on still as night. In the thick forest on either hand was to be heard the howling of savage beasts, the whooping of one kind of owl and the screaming of another, while every now and then would come a burst of thunder.[76]

The next day the Kentucky boat reached Wheeling where the colonel was entertained by Mrs. Ebenezer Zane, whose husband was a dominant figure in this thriving, though still only two-street, town which rivaled Pittsburgh as a center for flatboat disembarcation. More cows and calves were jammed aboard, then they set out in the midst of menacing rumbles from a thunderstorm. The rain did not come, however, and the colonel spent another night sharing the helm while the moon-tinted riverscape drifted by. The following afternoon they reached the Muskingum, where General Rufus Putnam had for a month been directing work on building Marietta.

Since the town was in Indian territory, the first order of business had been the construction of a strong stockade. What finally evolved was a unique structure known rather ostentatiously as the Campus Martius: a hundred-and-eighty-foot square fortification with two-story blockhouses guarding each end. There were three sets of walls: an inner one composed of the backs of the settlers' homes which faced the interior square, a barricade of sharpened pickets pointing outward just beyond, and finally a sturdy, upright palisade a few feet farther on. This quite impressive bastion was located on what became Second and Washington streets; and the original wooden Putnam home of 1788, once part of the inner walls, has been enclosed in the Campus Martius Museum, certainly one of the most important preservations in the Midwest.

The Indian menace was not idle chatter. In Pittsburgh John May had found the garrison in constant readiness. Scores of warriors often strutted insolently down the streets and during the colonel's brief stay they had killed one white man on Pitts-

burgh's outskirts. A short time later word was received that three
Kentucky boats had been captured off the shores of what would
become Cincinnati—one of the murdered men being a prominent citizen of Baltimore and an acquaintance of May's.

Nonetheless new towns began to dot the Indian side of the
Ohio. On November 18, 1788, Columbia (first of the pair of
towns that would become Cincinnati) was founded; and by
1792, there were upwards of two thousand pioneers tilling the
soil or erecting the stores and warehouses which the growing
population of Cincinnati demanded. To protect the inhabitants,
the United States government sent out a small force of soldiers
who constructed Fort Washington (mainly of lumber gathered
from beached Kentucky boats) at what was later Third and
Broadway.

Yet even with the presence of soldiers, the environs of
Cincinnati were far from safe, as Oliver Spencer, a lad of eleven,
was to find out.

Oliver had a young boy's love for adventure and was elated
when his father announced the move from New Jersey to Columbia. He could not understand his mother's tearful reluctance to
make the distant and dangerous trek. As Spencer was to remember forty-five years later: "Neither my father's description of the
Miami Country, nor the most glowing representations almost
daily published of 'the land flowing with milk and honey' could
have prevailed with my mother to abandon the home of her
fathers; . . . her faithful and long-tried friends; and above all,
some of her own daughters, who had married and settled around
her." [77] But at last she realized that her husband's losses due to
British foraging raids and the collapse of the Continental currency with which he had been paid for his services at Brandywine, Germantown, and Monmouth, left them no choice. Thus
"on a pleasant day in October of the year 1790" the family
packed up a pair of one-horse farm wagons looped over with
canvas and started out for what was then called the Far West.

Crossing the Delaware River at Easton, they chose a route

that was growing in popularity with the Northern pioneers who did not wish to take the more lengthly dogleg down to Philadelphia. They passed through Bethlehem, then Reading, then more rolling Pennsylvania Dutch country until the Pittsburgh Pike was picked up at Harrisburg—where a ferry transported them over the Susquehanna.

Ever so slowly the landmarks passed: Blue Mountain and the Tuscarora, the humming little town of Bedford, then the formidable Allegheny—bugbear of Forbes's engineers, and finally Laurel Hill which Oliver, riding ahead of the groaning wagons, found precipitous and unnerving. When in later years he took the newer pike, he "occasionally caught a glimpse of the ancient narrow road winding among the trees, now rising, now descending abruptly by steep steps of solid rock. I thought it scarcely possible that any vehicle had ever passed over it. It was travelled at the risk of limbs and even life" [78]—this last probably written as he recalled a near-disastrous overset of one of the family wagons.

At the approaches to Pittsburgh, the Spencers turned off the pike to purchase a flatboat at one of the little towns along the Youghiogheny where prices were cheaper. But there were disadvantages, too; for Pittsburgh, at the head of the Ohio, enjoyed higher water than the towns upstream. Thus the Spencers had to wait for more than a month until a late-autumn freshet gave them sufficient current to get over the rocks and half-submerged driftwood. At last in the midst of a driving rain, the Spencers, along with another family whom they met at the landing and with whom they agreed to share expenses, launched their flatboat into the swirling stream.

The trip proved to be an eerie experience for the young boy. The riverbanks were fringed with willows moaning like spirits in the wind. Higher up on the hills he imagined Indians watched in the glowering elms, in the gracefully grotesque oaks, and in the sycamores with their glinting, somehow menacing, silver bark. Panthers screamed in the distance; and at night the hills shivered to the howling of wolf packs on the prowl. The shadows seemed alive with lurking evil, and several men constantly scanned the gloomy forest from their posts atop the cabin. Guns were kept handy. "There was with us a feeling of apprehension, which after we left Pittsburgh was interrupted only as we passed by Wheeling, Marietta, Kanawha, Galliopolis, Limestone [now Maysville], and a few other intermediate settlements." And so it was with great relief that they saw the scimitar-shaped water-front of Cincinnati appear down the river.

Yet even after the Spencers moved into the tiny, two-win-dowed log cabin studded with gun holes that Oliver's father had constructed on a reconnaissance trip the previous year, the dan-ger of Indian attack was not over. Just a few weeks before they arrived General Harmar, attempting to destroy an important Miami town at the strategic Wabash-Maumee portage, had suf-fered a serious defeat. This had encouraged the Indians to attack white settlements near the Ohio. Several hundred savages, for example, had descended on Dunlap's Station just fifteen miles from the Spencers. Although Columbian frontiersmen, along with units from neighboring Losantiville, rushed to aid the sta-tion, they were not in time to prevent the gruesome bit-by-bit burning to death of Abner Hunt in full view of the helpless garrison.

Soon the danger came even closer. One night one of Oliver's sisters was terrified to see the door latch slowly rising. Leaping to her feet, she wrenched the latch down until her father threw the bar across. Lights were instantly snuffed and the gun ports manned. The Indians, seeing the element of surprise gone here, attacked another cabin—where a woman was wounded.

The danger on the Ohio frontier attracted the attention of President Washington, who, fearful that the West would re-nounce its allegiance to an ineffectual government in the East, ordered Governor Arthur St. Clair (whom we last met fleeing Burgoyne) to take the field. St. Clair and twenty-six hundred men pushed up the Miami River on September 17, 1791, laying out a road (now U.S. 127) which would become an important migration route to the interior of Ohio and Indiana. His advance seemed irresistible. Yet he was plagued by a serious lack of supplies and by such a high rate of desertion that his army had dwindled to fourteen hundred by the time Chief Little Turtle with fifteen hundred Shawnees, Miamis, and Wyandots, aided by scores of English and French traders, decided to attack. The result was one of the most serious defeats in American military history—more men lost than by Braddock!

During the spring of 1792 the garrison at Fort Washington ranged the forest trying to cut off the Indian war parties that buzzed about. Oliver's father and the other farmers went to their fields only in large groups, with some standing guard and all having their guns within hopping distance. Due to these precautions the neighborhood was relatively quiet. Thus in the summer Oliver was allowed to take a barge with eight soldiers and their giggling dates to the Fourth of July celebration at Fort Washington, a short row away.

Young Oliver enjoyed the firing of the cannons, the military parade, the fireworks at dusk, and the ball that followed. He remained in town for several days; but then unknown to the soldiers, he hitched a ride with two men and a woman canoeing upriver toward his father's cabin. They had not proceeded far when the air reverberated to the crash of two Indian rifles. The man in the bow toppled into the river, blood oozing from his right arm. The canoe tipped over. The woman was carried off in the current; and the second man, swimming to shore, was tomahawked and scalped. Then Oliver was seized and carried off into the forest. The whole episode had taken only about thirty seconds.

For a while the two Indians and their prisoner took a time-honored path that led from the Ohio River through ancient Pickawillany to the Maumee River and Detroit beyond (a route now paralleled by Interstate 75). But near modern Sidney they turned slightly to the west to pick up another trail which ran down the Auglaize, named long ago by French voyageurs for the clayish soil through which it meandered.

Of the two Indians, one was a Shawnee, surly and vicious, and the other a displaced Mohawk, intelligent and friendly (although it was he who had scalped the white man). Fortunately, Oliver was purchased by the Mohawk, who in turn gave

him temporarily to his widowed mother living in an important
village at the confluence of the Auglaize and Maumee rivers. The
elderly woman, seeing the white boy weak from dysentery and
the terrible fatigue of trudging a hundred and eighty miles in six
days through swamp, underbrush, and bramble, treated him
kindly. In a few days, under her artful concoctions of red-oak
bark, wild-cherry bark, and dewberry root (which he drank as
well as used to soak his blistered feet), he was completely
healed.

Oliver spent nine months with the Indians. He learned their
dances, their songs, and their animal calls. He went on hunts
with them, shared their food, dressed in their clothing. He was
informally engaged to Sotonegoo, a sprightly girl "with bright,
laughing eyes." He saw war parties strutting about with the
blood-stained uniforms they had taken from St. Clair's fallen.
And he learned to scoff at the new army of white misfits which
was being marched over the mountains by Mad Anthony Wayne
to be trained at a camp across from old Logstown, nineteen miles
downstream from Pittsburgh. The smirking increased that spring
when scouts reported that Wayne was preparing to ship the
motley force he pompously called the Legion of the United
States to Cincinnati in order to put it within striking distance of
the Maumee towns.

Oliver became friends with George Ironside, one of the
many English and French traders who maintained posts along
the Maumee, and with William Wells a Kentuckian captured at
the age of twelve who had not only chosen to remain with the
Miami but had married Chief Little Turtle's daughter. Through
Wells, word of Oliver's captivity reached Cincinnati and ultimately President Washington, who persuaded the British to
order Oliver's release. This was done through the agency of
George Ironside and on the last day of February, 1793, the
eleven year old boy was free.

His departure was not all happiness. His Indian godmother
"was affected even to tears," he remembered. "Taking my hands
in both of hers and cordially pressing them she bade me adieu."
And as for his bethrothed: "poor Sotonegoo sobbed loudly."

Then he was off down the Maumee, laughing, whistling, and shouting as awareness of his freedom grew. Accompanying him was the British Indian agent Matt Elliot, a dark-complected scoundrel, who was supposed to see him safely to Detroit. But Elliot pawned him off on a small group of Wyandots encamped near what would become Toledo for a gallon of rum.

Once Elliot was gone, the Indians became drunk and a fourteen-year-old bully taunted Oliver into a fight. It was a vicious battle with punching, clawing, and hair pulling. Amazingly, Oliver won. But as he walked away, the Wyandot youth drew a knife and stabbed him in the back. As the blood gushed out, one of the braves stuffed the wound with a large quid of tobacco, then bandaged it with a dirty rag.

The next morning a pair of squaws paddled the wounded boy to Detroit, where he was nursed back to health by a lieutenant and his concerned wife. After four pleasant weeks rummaging about the important British fort and the small, though active, palisaded town, he boarded a sloop (one of four ships waiting for the ice to break) and set out for Fort Niagara. The weather was good as far as Put-in-Bay on South Bass Island. But from there they met contrary winds, which once caved in the cabin windows and forced them back to Put-in-Bay three times. It wasn't for two weeks that the arrival of favorable weather enabled them to make the two-day run to the foot of the lake.

Because there was little commerce between Fort Niagara and the American portion of New York, Oliver had to wait for a trader to escort him. He passed a week watching the redcoated garrison doing precision drills (which he thought quite astonishing) and enjoying the bluff-top scenery (which he called romantic, grand, and sublime). He eventually joined one Thomas Morris heading eastward along the narrow weed-strewn path that is now the New York Thruway.

Morris's destination was the forty-house hamlet of Canandaigua seventy-five miles away. This was New York's farthermost settlement, founded just a few years earlier in the center of the diminished and humbled Seneca tribe. Here Oliver latched onto another trader who made a place for him in his flat-bottomed bateau. They paddled down the Seneca River, considerably slowed by the need to hack away the trees that had fallen across it. After four days they reached Oneida Lake, once deep in the Iroquois heartland but now virtually deserted. Portaging to the Mohawk, they skirted the ruins of Fort Stanwix, which had not been garrisoned after the Iroquois had been decimated during the Revolutionary War. The trip down the Mohawk was uneventful; and at Schenectady the fur cargo was placed in wagons which Oliver and the trader followed to Albany.

The trader took a sloop with Oliver down the Hudson to New York City where Oliver boarded a ferry for Elizabeth. Here he was joyously welcomed by a married sister and other relatives. But his trip back to Cincinnati was delayed, for the Ohio frontier had again exploded into violence.

Mad Anthony Wayne was on the march.

21. The Drivers Are Fearless

The September morning throbbed to the cadence of soldiers' heavy boots. The road leading northward from the weathered palisades of Fort Washington was thronged with spectators— possibly including the father of Oliver Spencer. The Cincinnatians had seen other armies marching confidently toward Indian country and their cheering was subdued as they remembered the bloody defeats of Harmar and of St. Clair, defeats which unleashed scores of savage war parties on the frontier. Was Mad Anthony Wayne heading into another of Chief Little Turtle's death traps?

Soon the hamlet of Cincinnati was behind them, and the legionaires were tramping up the trail haunted by a thousand dead men. As the gloomy forest hulked around them, the twenty-five hundred soldiers looked at each other uneasily. They had seemed so numerous when encamped beside the Ohio. Now they were so few—so pitifully few. Dry leaves rasped in the wind. Unseen beasts snarled from the depths of the forbidding woodland. Birds screamed in alarm as something frightened them—Shawnee scouts, no doubt, who were keeping close track of the legion's progress.

But there was no slackening in their pace for these were not the slovenly, shifty-eyed rabble that had slouched about the Logstown training ground. Wayne had drilled them for three-quarters of a year. His discipline was rigid. The men might grumble; but slowly their bearing became military, their faces bronzed, their muscles hardened. They learned the fine art of the deadly bayonet. They shrieked the fearsome battle cry Wayne

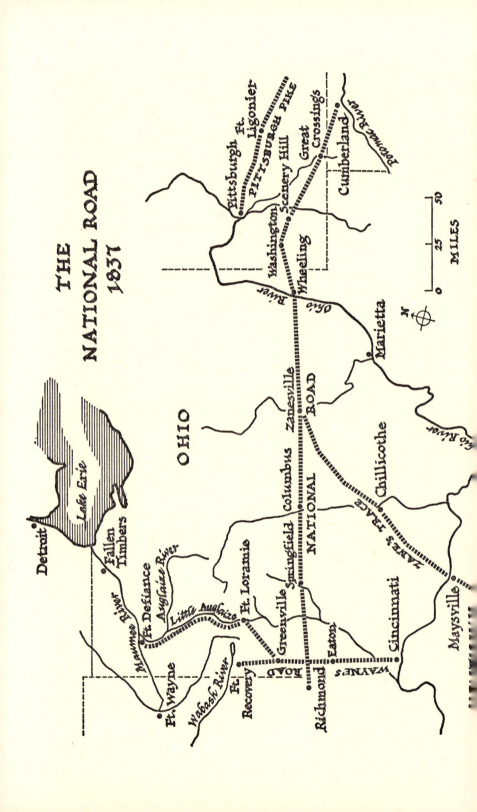

THE
NATIONAL ROAD
1831

had taught them. They were fierce. And they were proud. Thus by the time Wayne was finally given his orders to march, the Legion of the United States had become one of the finest fighting machines the nation was ever to forge.

The Indians were not smirking on the Maumee now. Little Turtle sent runners scouring the Midwest for reinforcements. Gradually they gathered at a gigantic war council at the Auglaize junction—the very location from which Oliver Spencer had fortunately departed that spring. Little Turtle warned his braves they could not expect to surprise Wayne as they had St. Clair, for "the Americans are now led by a chief who never sleeps," the Miami chief grunted.

Wayne moved ever northward—throwing up stout forts at Hamilton, Eaton, and Greenville to guard his supply line. Wintering at Greenville, he sent a flying column to construct Fort Recovery (now partially rebuilt) at the site of St. Clair's defeat. When the Indians attempted to erase this insult to their prowess, the tough legionaires bloodied their noses. Then all thought of further attacks on Recovery had to be given up as Wayne led his main body toward the Maumee River heartland.

He advanced slowly and methodically, ever ready for an ambush. So it wasn't until August, 1794, that he reached the Auglaize junction. Because the Indians had shifted their headquarters forty-eight miles downriver where the British had ominously built a fort, Wayne chose the abandoned site for a post of his own. "I defy the English, the Indians, and all the devils in hell to take it!" he thundered. Then he moved out of Fort Defiance to do battle.

The Indian army awaited him behind a formidable barrier of trees recently uprooted by a tornado. It was an ideal impediment to hinder the legionnaires' vaunted bayonet charge. And in the near distance were the British at Fort Miami. Would they come pouring out on Wayne's flank once he was engaged with the Indians?

Amid the taunts of the confident warriors, Wayne lined his soldiers up: the river at their backs and the fallen timbers before them. For a moment there was a hush. Men on both sides gripped their weapons a little more tightly. Then, at Wayne's signal, bugles sounded and the cavalry spurred forward. Red musketry roared, emptying more than a dozen saddles. Nevertheless discipline held. The charge continued. With a violent crash the horses hurdled into the intertwined branches. Sword blades sizzled through the air. Bones cracked and blood flowed.

Another signal from Wayne. The first of his two infantry waves bolted forward. They trailed their gunstocks in the grass, calling out challenges to the Indians to meet them in the open if they dared. The plan worked. Those of the Indians who were not fighting the calvalry left their sanctuary and leapt, howling with fury, into the river plain.

With a terrific clatter, the two armies jarred into one another. For a moment there was a chaotic mass of knives, tomahawks, lances, and pistol butts. The air was shattered by angry shrieks and the ugly sound of metal crunching into skulls. Yet, slowly at first, then more rapidly, the Indians gave ground. They had never known the vicious artistry of the bayonet. Panic flickered in their eyes. Little Turtle and other chiefs shouted for them to regroup, screaming that the fate of the entire Indian race depended on them—as, indeed, it did. But before any counterattack could be mustered, the American cavalry, which had regrouped in their rear, plowed into them.

With Wayne's second wave of infantry now preparing for action, Indian morale cracked. Throwing down their weapons, the warriors dashed for the British fort. Yet the commander, under orders not to precipitate war by firing at American troops on American soil, slammed the gates in the Indians' faces. The red men dispersed into the wilderness. Their defeat had been complete.

After his fine job at Fallen Timbers was over, Anthony Wayne, a sick man with less than two years to live, built a major fort named after himself at the Maumee-Wabash portage, then marched back to Greenville. There, in June, 1795, the disheartened chiefs signed a treaty which—by giving up most of Ohio as well as the keys to Midwestern transportation: Detroit and the site of Chicago—permanently cemented the entire Ohio-Mississippi basin to the United States.

The Treaty of Greenville opened a new era in American expansion. With the Indian menace removed, the stream of immigrants became a torrent. By 1800 nearly forty-five thousand persons had either stumbled over the rutted road to Pittsburgh, where they plunked down their meager resources for a flatboat (somewhat cheaper now that it was no longer necessary to wall it over for protection), or taken the cutoff to Wheeling from whence they proceeded westward by land, dodging stumps on the crude trail opened by Ebenezer Zane in 1796.

For many years Zane's Trace was vital to the communication between the interior of Ohio and the East—since the Ohio River was useless in the winter when ice often closed it and difficult in the autumn when low water uncovered boulders and other obstructions. The trace ran west from Wheeling over what is now Interstate 70 to the town of Zanesville, at the important Muskingum ford. From there it cut southward through a dense forest, passing through Lancaster (another of Zane's creations) and Chillicothe before reaching Maysville, Kentucky, where a road led to the bluegrass country or a boat could be floated down to Cincinnati.

Zane's makeshift road was the main land route of early Ohio. Chillicothe's location on it enabled the town to become the capital of the entire Northwest Territory in 1800—the building used by Governor Arthur St. Clair still stands. Three years later, when more than fifteen thousand new settlers brought Ohio's population to sixty thousand—the limit set by the Northwest Ordinance for statehood—Chillicothe became the first state capital. Rich and influential men found the town, located on the Indians' old Scioto River trail, to their liking. Many fine mansions were built; and splendid Adena, one of these, has been superbly restored.

But a bustling state required more than a quagmire path as

its main thoroughfare. Agitation for a better highway made its
way into the sequestered halls of the national capitol, since by
1810 nearly two hundred thousand additional disgruntled potential voters had elbowed through the obstacles to reach Ohio.
Thus on April 16, 1811, Congress let the first contracts for what
was called the National Road.

The plan was thrilling: to create an eighty-foot-wide paved
highway which, joining with an already existing road from Baltimore to Cumberland, Maryland, would vault the Appalachians, leap the Ohio River at Wheeling on a gigantic wooden
bridge, then unravel through the thick forests of Ohio and
Indiana, ultimately to cross the wind-blistered prairies of distant
Illinois and end on the Mississippi opposite St. Louis—a near
legendary city still more French than American (although it had
been purchased with the Louisiana Territory eight years earlier). From the Atlantic to the Mississippi—a thousand breath-
taking miles! Only Imperial Rome could boast such a feat.

Slowly the grand highway snaked westward. From Cumberland it took the same route as Braddock's Road, but rarely the
identical meandering roadbed. The way was broadened. Low
rises were smoothed out, and the grade up the higher hills was
maintained at a moderate pitch. Rivers and creeks were spanned
by sturdy bridges, some of which (such as the eighty-foot arch
just east of Grantsville, Maryland, and the graceful S bridge
seven miles west of Washington, Pennsylvania) impress modern
travelers as much as they did the pioneers. The road surface was
covered with a layer of crushed stone three inches thick. This,
after a sufficient number of wagons had packed it down, was
gradually increased to six, and even nine, inches where the
conditions required it. By 1817 the road had crept by the grassy
mound that had once been Fort Necessity, had climbed Chestnut
Ridge (where wayfarers gasped at the widest vista on the
route), and by the following year had merged with Wheeling's
dusty streets.

Once the Ohio was reached, the traffic became almost unbelievable. "Old America seems to be breaking up and moving
westward," wrote as astonished Englishman. "We are seldom out

of sight, as we travel on this grand track towards the Ohio, of family groups before and behind us." The inns, such as those still found at the Great Crossings, Scenery Hill, and Washington were always bulging with patrons. And it wasn't only migrating families who thronged the National Road. Soon merchants and pot-rattling peddlers began hauling in the manufactured goods that were suddenly demanded by the otherwise isolated farmers. A commission house at Wheeling recorded the unloading of 1,081 freight wagons in 1822—and the house was only one of five in the active city whose springtime traffic jams taxed the cussing ingenuity of even the most vociferous frontiersman.

By 1825 the first milestones (many yet stand) were being planted along opening sections in Ohio. And as the Conestoga caravans crunched into the virgin land, eastern newspapers sent out correspondents to describe for their curious readers what it was like to be part of this gigantic and momentous westward procession. One of these newspapermen was Charles Fenno Hoffman, who wrote two superlative volumes on his experiences in the Midwestern dawn. Here is how he pictured the average wagoning pioneer family:

> Unless it be raining very hard [you will] rarely see anyone in the wagon, except perhaps some child overtaken by sickness or a mother nursing a young infant. The head of the family walks by the horse, cheering and encouraging him on his way. The good woman, when not engaged as hinted above, either trudges along with her husband, or, leading some weary little traveller by the hand far behind, endeavours to keep the rest of her charge from loitering by the wayside. The old house dog—if not chained beneath the wagon to prevent the half-starved brute from foraging too freely in a friendly country—brings up the rear.[79]

But it was not all pastoral pleasantries. Hoffman discovered that "in companies so numerous, sickness must frequently overtake some of the members." The trek was particularly difficult for the women, many of whom were in various stages of pregnancy. Everyone, however, had their share of colds and flu, since the most popular time to migrate was in the early spring in order to arrive by planting time. Thus it was common to encounter day after day of frigid rain, which not only left one permanently soaked but turned the road into such a morass that one's energy was sapped by periodic struggles to assist the horses dragging the wagon out of mud holes.

Many fundless families spent the dreary nights in their wagon, with rain oozing through the worn canvas top. But the fortunate few who could afford a room would find a welcome, if all too brief, respite at one of the inns that were sprouting up along the way. After a jarring day on the National Road, what an indescribable delight to come upon one of those establishments—many of which, such as the Colonial Inn at Old Washington—can today be seen along the Ohio portion of U.S. 40, the modern National Road.

Year by year the road advanced across Ohio, its construction paid for by a portion of the money received from the quicksilver sales of federal land. Soon it entered Columbus, where the Agricultural and Mechanical College (now Ohio State University) was about to be founded. Then it continued west along the ancient path to Springfield once used by George Croghan and his traders. By 1837, twelve years after entering Ohio, the Indiana border was at last crossed.

The road ran straight as a plowed furrow through the forested Indiana flatlands, causing some wayfarers to complain of the monotony as hour after hour their horses clopped out the miles—yet still the road stretched out before them until it was "diminished to a thread-like tenuity" (a phenomenon likewise noted by motorists on Interstate 70). Nevertheless Richmond, then Indianapolis, and finally Terre Haute on the threshhold of the Illinois prairies were reached. As the way was opened, pioneers swarmed into the area with such rapidity that soon hitherto unknown Indianapolis became the seat of government; and by 1840 the fine Parthenon-inspired first capitol was a much-heralded landmark to the eight hundred thousand Indianans—most of whom had either arrived over the National Road or been born of parents who had.

Despite the thousands of wagons, stagecoaches, and riding horses using the highway, the Indiana portion seemed always to be in the process of being built—and actually the federal government eventually left it to private contractors to complete. A genial Englishman, William Oliver, writing for the thousands of his compatriots who dreamed of immigrating, left them—and us —some vivid descriptions of the Indiana road as it was when he took a coach over it in 1841:

> The National Road was still, in many places, no more than a track winding its way among boulders and the stumps of the trees which had been cut on surveying the line. But the horses are good and the drivers are fearless, and dash on through thick and thin, very much at the expense of the poor passengers' bones.[80]

Oliver found that some of the streams presented terrifying impediments. At Centerville, eight miles beyond the Ohio line, he and his coach approached a fork of the Whitewater River down a bluff where the road barely clung to the side. And at a smaller stream just outside Indianapolis they had to use a frighteningly flimsy bridge, then continue across the marshy bottomland over a corduroy road that nearly rattled the stagecoach to pieces and made the passengers more than glad to walk—particularly when they came to a wagon which had tumbled off the causeway into the mud.

Yet work was being done constantly to improve the road. At Centerville Oliver noted that "numerous workmen were blasting and splitting [rocks] and a score of carts . . . were leading away the earth and stones." Farther west he found that "numbers of workmen were busy on the National Road, raising it above the surface level . . . and covering it with a thick layer of well-broken limestone."

The way was considerably brightened by oases in the forested wilderness:

> Inns and villages . . . occur at no great distance from one another, so that the traveller on horseback or on foot has it in

his power to halt and get rest and food when he requires them. . . . The houses standing back from the line of the road, of course, cannot be seen until one is close upon them, but the owners of the inns take care to intimate their whereabouts by erecting within view huge signs which can be discerned a long way. Washington, mostly in some questionable shape . . . figures largely on those "chef d'oeuvres." [81]

However after one passed Terre Haute's famous Prairie House (the site of which is now occupied by its lineal descendant the Terre Haute House), the inns were of a deteriorating quality. One reason was that by the time the National Road reached Illinois, increasing competition from the newly emerging rail lines were giving federal legislators second thoughts about putting funds into a project that might soon be obsolete. Therefore, although bridges and grading operations were extended half way across the state to the rustic capital at Vandalia, a hard surface was never laid. Mud in the spring and deep hard ruts in the summer and fall made the Illinois portion of the National Road such a nightmare that few innkeepers bothered to erect hostelries for the misery-maddened travelers. And even the Vandalia hotels, which clustered around the capitol (now a refurbished showplace) were "notorious for their poor accommodations and high prices"—so wrote William Herndon, the friend of Abraham Lincoln who as a state legislator was instrumental in removing the capital to Springfield.

All in all, Vandalia was a dismal termination for the project which had been launched with such fanfare so many years earlier.

The Northwest Territory was not the only area to experience the fantastic in-rush of pioneers. Planned at about the same time as the National Road, but far to the south, was a second government project called the Federal Road. As early as 1805 the Creek tribe gave reluctant approval to the scheme to open a road through their lands. But little was done to broaden the old traders' path so long as savage hotbloods twanged their bowstrings. Nonetheless General John Floyd and his army plunged into Creek country during the war which ended in 1814 with the complete breakup of the tribe at the vicious Battle of Horseshoe Bend (the site, where Andrew Jackson began his rise to fame, has become a spacious, well-kept national park).

With the Creek nation joining the vanished Natchez and Arkansas in some red man's Valhalla, the way to the sunbaked cotton lands was opened. On gullied farms in Virginia and North and South Carolina, white plantation owners herded up their Negroes, clamped tight their chains, and started the sweaty hike to the gulf plains. Some took the Upper Road through the piedmont to pick up the Federal Road at Athens, Georgia. Others perferred the somewhat easier fall line route which met the Federal Road at Columbus, which was laid out in 1828. Farther on, after passing within a few miles of the long-decayed French Fort Toulouse, the Federal Road came to Montgomery, during the early days merely a pair of little villages squatting in the midst of Indian ruins. Beyond Montgomery was Selma, begun before the Creek War. It was older and more important than Montgomery—although for several years it labored under the indignity of being called High Soapstone Bluff.

The Federal Road ended at a then-important crossroads known as St. Stephens—although little now remains except a state monument. From St. Stephens a person had three choices: take a boat or the parallel river road to Mobile, Alabama's active seaport; continue west to Natchez, gateway to the fertile Mississippi bottomlands; or go southwest to New Orleans, far-and-away the grandest city beyond the Appalachians.

Activity along the Federal Road was considerable. Whereas before the Creek defeat, the non-Indian population of Alabama and Mississippi had consisted mainly of scattered traders and their half-breed families and the Spanish-French inhabitants of Mobile and Pensacola; by 1820, two hundred and thirty thousand immigrants, both black and white, were busy raising cotton, the only really dependable cash crop, or erecting the stores, warehouses, and homes that soon became growing towns sprinkled over the pinetopped countryside. Although some of these settlers had come by boat, most made the tedious trip over the Federal Road.

The journey through Georgia, Alabama, and Mississippi was a dreary one. Slave gangs chanted doleful songs while on swollen feet they padded toward a new and, as they correctly surmised, harsher environment. Inns were far less frequent than farther north. The slaves and overseers simply camped beside the road, the borders of which eventually became darkened with the soot of a thousand fires.

It was different for the male plantation owner—particularly those with funds available. They could continue on to Natchez-under-the-Hill, a town which according to a finger-wagging New Englander "extended its fame throughout the United States in wretched rhyme and viler story." Although this same observer, writing in 1835, called the row of gambling emporiums and bawdy parlors "the nucleus of vice upon the Mississippi," members of the sporting set were not so harsh with their condemnation.

Meanwhile up on the brow of the bluff, another Natchez, composed of the finest array of Greek Revival mansions anywhere in the world, luxuriated in the booming cotton production which was bringing untold wealth into the city. Roads webbed out over the countryside, accommodating endless wagons heaped high with cotton. This activity, however, did not exist on the old Natchez Trace—which, by providing flatboaters on their way home from New Orleans a shortcut to Nashville and points north, had been one of Natchez's earliest bonanzas. The trace was, by this time, being rapidly displaced by the fast-moving steamboats that came into general use by the 1830's. Eventually the trace was all but forgotten—until a more heritage-conscious generation built the Natchez Trace Parkway (a fine, paved road restricted to automobiles and free of billboards) along the route of the former trailway.

New Orleans was on the other prong of the Federal Road. Boasting a hundred thousand persons in 1840, the Crescent City was more than twice as large as her nearest Western competitor Cincinnati. Her waterfront was packed with flatboats and steamers from the upper Mississippi and Ohio country. Crowding in upon them were the larger, barnacle-encrusted ocean ships whose holds were filled with silks, wines, brandies, cutlery, coffee, and other exotic goods that upriver farmers craved in exchange for their grain and pork. The Mississippi made New Orleans an integral part of the transmountain area. Indeed, as a commercial route the Mississippi was more important than any easternheading road. In 1825, for example, the Old Northwest sent forty-five thousand tons of wheat by flatboat and paddle-wheeler to New Orleans while only forty thousand tons were freighted eastward by wagon over the National Road.

New Orleans outdid even Natchez as far as entertaining the boatmen, roustabouts, and gallants who made the Creole city their temporary headquarters. Combining French and Spanish grandees with an odd mixture of Southern blades, Yankee salts, Ohio stump-busters, and drum-pounding, compellingly rhythmic Africans, New Orleans was a uniquely hybrid city. Although a visiting Frenchman wrote: "I could almost think myself back home in the French quarter," the wildness of the Mardi Gras, just then coming into fashion, was something not found on the other side of the Atlantic. Then, too, there were the exciting quadroon balls where rich white men cavorted with their part-Negro mistresses. "Most of the girls danced very well," titillated a German duke, quickly adding, "I could not remain very long for fear of spoiling my reputation."

Yes, at both ends of the Federal Road—New Orleans and Natchez—untold pleasures awaited the traveler wealthy and dissolute enough to enjoy them.

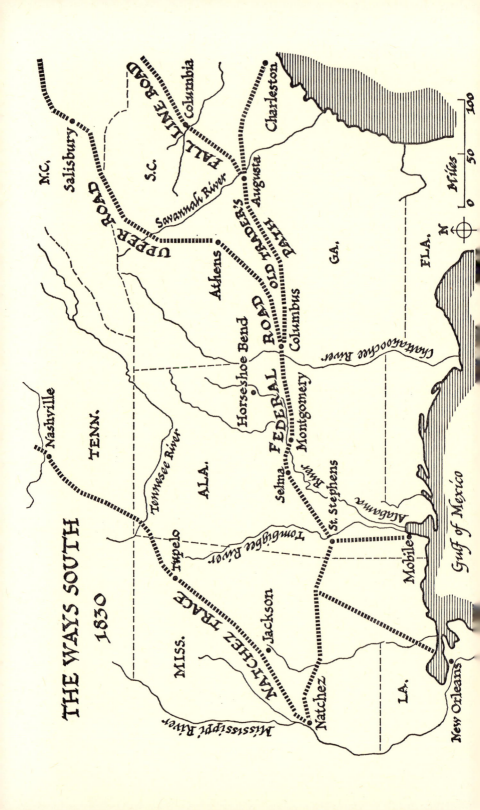

THE WAYS SOUTH
1830

N.C.

Nashville
TENN.
Salisbury

Columbia
S.C.

FALL LINE ROAD

UPPER ROAD

Charleston

Savannah River

Augusta

Athens

OLD TRADER'S PATH

Horseshoe Bend

GA.

Columbus

FEDERAL ROAD

Tennessee River

ALA.

Montgomery

Selma

Chattahoochee River

FLA.

N

Miles
0   50   100

Tupelo

Jackson

NATCHEZ TRACE

MISS.

Tombigbee River

St. Stephens

Alabama River

Mobile

Gulf of Mexico

Natchez

LA.

Mississippi River

New Orleans

22.   Finale on the Prairies

While wagons creaked over the National Road, slave chains clanked on the Federal Road, and paddlewheels churned up the Ohio-Mississippi system, an entirely new route opened farther north. It had begun in October 1825 when New York's energetic governor, DeWitt Clinton, made a junket from Buffalo to Albany. This had been done many times before, of course, by Iroquois, white traders, and even an eleven-year-old Oliver Spencer. But what made this trip unique was that Clinton went the entire way by canal—with no arduous portages, no pauses to hack away obstructing timber, not even any effort paddling, since a team of mules towed his boat.

The Erie Canal, as the new waterway was christened, was a stupendous feat. Eighty-three locks, each ninety feet long, were needed to raise a canalboat from the level of the Hudson to Lake Erie. A stone aqueduct 802 feet long arched the Genesee River and two others, one nearly a quarter-mile long, crossed and recrossed the Mohawk. The malarial Montezuma marshes west of Syracuse (now a national wildlife refuge seen from the Thruway) felled many of the predominantly Irish laborers. And at Lockport, where the seventy-five-foot Niagara escarpment had to be surmounted, special blasting powder gouged out the hard limestone for a step ladder of locks.

Abruptly New York City was linked to Detroit by way of the Great Lakes—and even more distantly to a tiny collection of traders' huts and Potawatomi wigwams flung carelessly beside the Chicago River. This was at the rim of the fantastically fertile, but until now virtually inaccessible, Illinois prairies. Suddenly a new land craze exploded into national consciousness.

One of the farmers who decided to shuck his unprofitable
plot and try his luck in the West was John Nowlin, whose son
William later wrote a description of their experiences. William
remembered with distressing clarity his frail mother's reluctance
to trade the stability of New York for the rigors of the frontier.
"Many of her friends," William wrote, "said she would not live to
get to Michigan if she started. She thought . . . that if she did
[go], herself and family would be killed by the Indians, perish in
the wilderness, or starve to death." And there were the usual
tearful farewells to neighbors and relatives they might never see
again. "We left our friends weeping, for, as they expressed it,
they thought we were going 'out of the world.' " [82]

John Nowlin was a determined man, however, and on a
rugged eight-week trip a year earlier had already purchased
eighty acres just outside the village of Dearborn, then a forested
solitude but now vibrating to the clangor of one of the Ford
Motor Company's mightiest plants. So in the early spring of
1834, husband and wife and five children, of whom William, age
twelve, was the eldest, boarded a sleek seventy-foot canalboat
and set off on their dangerous argosy to Michigan.

At first there was a deceptive tranquility to the trip on the
Erie Canal. A pair of mules towed the packet along at three or
four miles an hour, presenting a leisurely panorama to the passengers reclining on the rooftop. The Mohawk Valley was peaceful with the Iroquois gone, and neat towns, such as Herkimer
and Utica, nestled beneath the rounded bluffs. The canal skirted
Oneida Lake and flowed through Syracuse, rapidly becoming a
major port. In the day, the men would make the easy leap to
shore, to stroll along the towpath or gather wild fruit that grew
nearby. And at night the passengers would sleep on board, lulled
into sweet dreams by the rustle of the water as the boat continued on its course.

But there was peril, nonetheless. The canal passed under
some three hundred bridges, for most of which it was necessary
to bow one's head (if sitting on the rooftop, as was customary).
And once in a while when the helmsman shouted very low
bridge, everyone had to sprawl flat on their backs. One man told

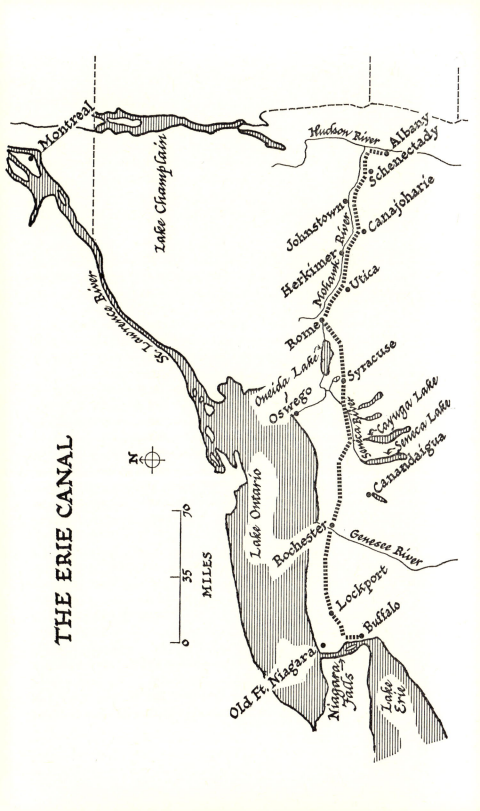

THE ERIE CANAL

N

MILES

0   35   70

Montreal

Lake Champlain

St. Lawrence River

Hudson River   Albany
                Schenectady
        Johnstown   Canajoharie
        Herkimer River
                Mohawk River   Utica
        Rome
Oneida Lake   Syracuse
Oswego   Cayuga Lake
        Seneca River   Seneca Lake
                        Canandaigua

Lake Ontario

Rochester   Genesee River

                Lockport
Old Ft. Niagara   Niagara Falls   Buffalo

Lake Erie

of a young English woman, asleep with her head on a box, who had her skull crushed by a low bridge when she did not waken in time. Then, too, there was the grave possibility of children falling into the water. This actually happened to a Nowlin boy. Only quick action by a passenger saved the four-year-old from drowning. And others had to take care. William himself once missed his jump to shore, fell into the four feet of water (the canal's usual depth), and barely escaped being crushed between the boat and steep canal bank as his father yanked him up.

Finally the Nowlins reached Buffalo on Lake Erie. Buffalo was a roaring frontier town, chartered as a city only two years earlier but boasting a population of more than ten thousand. Its zooming growth came from its position where the canalboats met the Great Lakes steamers. A brand-new lighthouse had just been completed at the harbor entrance—where it stands today as a monument to the past. But for all its nascent civic pride, Buffalo was the habitation of some of the most persistent crooks on the continent, as the Nowlins were to discover.

Since they carried their life savings of five hundred dollars in silver with them, the Nowlins were wary. Spending the night in a dingy hotel room with no windows, they suddenly found a man with a candle in their sleeping quarters. William's father lunged at the intruder, but succeeded only in ripping off a sleeve as he squirmed off into the darkness. Several hours later, the stealthy pad of stockinged feet was heard outside their door. Mrs. Nowlin, trembling with fear, cried out: "Have your pistols ready, John"—although her husband's only weapon was an upraised chair. The shuffling moved away, only to return two more times during the long, sleepless night. On each occasion the Nowlins frightened him, or them, away with references to the arsenal of bloody weapons they supposedly carried.

When they knew by the street noise that daylight had come, the bleary-eyed family staggered down the three flights of stairs and boarded the steamer *Michigan,* which, with its decks jammed with six hundred passengers, was already fired up.

As the ship nosed past Buffalo's vaunted lighthouse, the wind whipped up and a storm descended upon it. Here is how

William remembered the shattering events that were to happen many times to pioneers on the Great Lakes run:

> We were violently tempest-tossed. Many of the passengers despaired of getting through. Their lamentations were piteous and all had gloomy forebodings of impending ruin. The dark, blue, cold waves, pressed hard by the wind, rolled and tumbled our vessel frightfully. . . . I was miserably sick, as were nearly all the passengers. . . . It seemed as if the steamer could not withstand the furious powers that were upon her. The front part of the boat would seem to settle down—down—lower—and lower, if possible, than it had been before. It looked to me, often, as though we were going to plunge head-foremost—boat and all—into the deep. . . . The most awful terror marked nearly every face. Some wept, some prayed, some swore, and a few looked calm and resigned. . . . Our clothes and bedding were all drenched, and to make our condition still more perilous, the boat was discovered to be on fire!

A frantic bucket brigade, in which John Nowlin was active, extinguished the fire; and eventually the battered steamer made landfall at Detroit. The staunch patriarch led his bedraggled family to Woodward Avenue, where the Old City Hall now stands, but which then was merely a grazing common speckled with some small wooden buildings. Then they set out southwest through the forest on the Chicago Road, of which Nowlin was to recall: "I could just see a streak ahead four or five miles, with the trees standing thick and dark on either side."

In a few miles when the Nowlins reached Dearborn, they stopped. For them the fearsome migration was over.

Others, however, heard the beguiling call of Chicago and the superlative prairie lands to the west. For those enchanted souls the often-horrendous steamship passage across Lake Erie was a fitting introduction to the Chicago Road. The Chicago Road had been surveyed by the federal government the same

year that the Erie Canal was completed; and by 1833 the first
mud-splattered stagecoaches had made the run from Detroit. But
it was not a ramble to be looked forward to. "Never in all life
before did I see such roads!" complained young John Went-
worth, one day to become Chicago's mayor. His coach kept
breaking down, necessitating the travelers to squirm through
mud that oozed to their very boot tops. They drove from 3 A.M.
until far into the night, but the trip still took six days along a
route that speeding cars on U.S. 12 (or better yet on Interstate
94 a few miles north) cover in six hours. Even Indians on the
original Great Sauk Trail (which could be seen winding back
and forth along the road like a thin snake) made better time—
but, of course, they had a minimum of baggage.

However, it was not all drudgery. Soon some fine hostelries
rose beside the road. One of these was at Clinton, generally the
first night's stopping point. The Clinton Inn (since moved by
Henry Ford to Greenfield Village, his interesting montage of
nineteenth century buildings in Dearborn) was a handsome
structure, two stories high with a long colonnade supporting the
front roof. Slightly further down the Chicago Road, after passing
through the green moraine called the Irish Hills after its early
settlers, one came to the Walker Tavern which still stands in its
original location in Cambridge Junction. Here, amid a group of
English pioneers who periodically enjoyed a bit of fisticuffs with
their Irish neighbors, a traveler could ease into a rocking chair
on the spacious porch or enjoy a good night's sleep in one of the
sixteen rooms, perhaps even that used by James Fenimore
Cooper or Daniel Webster.

Farther on one came to reminders of the Indians. Near the
St. Joseph River was a large conical rock containing indentions
which were supposedly the footprints of the Great Spirit. A lady
traveler passing this holy site in 1830 found Indian offerings of
tobacco around it. Close by was the village of White Pigeon,
named in gratitude for the chieftain who had saved the settlers
from an Indian uprising.

An early tourist on the Chicago Road was Charles Fenno
Hoffman, the newspaperman we last met on the National Road

near Wheeling. Hoffman journeyed in a four-horse wagon which he found most comfortable. At Niles he was ferried over the St. Joseph's River in a low-sided scow whose boatman was kept busy chopping through the ice and dodging floes—for it was winter. On the other side Hoffman saw a long white building, the Carey Mission, surrounded by about four hundred Potawatomi wigwams. Although these Indians were being instructed by Baptists in civilized methods of farming and handicrafts, they would soon fall victim to President Jackson's Indian removal program and would be carted off to the far West and oblivion.

Hoffman spotted Lake Michigan the next day at sunset. On horseback now (he had left his luggage on a slower-moving coach) he was thrilled by the "broad bosom" of water which stretched far away in crimson splendor. Plowing through the deserted Gary dunes, with the sand reaching his horse's fetlocks, he and a friend finally emerged on the lakeshore where the semifrozen sand was packed as hard as rock. They spurred their horses down the beach, guided only by a heaven bursting with stars. Silver waves crashed on their right, dune hills rolled away on the left, an invigorating breeze sang in their ears, and their horses' hooves struck sparks from the beach pebbles. It was an experience the New Yorker would always remember.

Hoffman spent that night in a crude inn (probably just west of U.S. Steel's huge blast furnaces) wrapped in a buffalo robe with his saddle for a pillow. He slept well, however, and the next morning resumed his exhilerating shore ride. "We galloped at full speed, every man choosing his own route along the beach, our horses' hoofs ringing the while as if it were a pavement of flint beneath them." The riders continued until they came to the Calumet River (at the precise point where Interstate 94 now soars over the Chicago Skyway Bridge). Although now the location is spiked with the sooty smokestacks of another U.S. Steel plant, then there was only a solitary ferry house on the riverbank.

After warming themselves in the cabin, they crossed the "fine stream" (alas, today irretrievably polluted) and trotted through prairie grasslands to reach the tiny cluster of shacks and

shanties in which were housed the two hundred and fifty optimistic persons who made up all there was of Chicago. Hoffman,
undoubtedly viewed as a celebrity, was invited to a ball that
same night. Dancing was done to a sketchy band consisting of "a
dandy Negro with his violin, a fine military-looking bass drummer from the fort [old Fort Dearborn still squatted on the south
bank of the river at the modern Michigan Avenue bridge] and a
volunteer citizen who alternately played an accompaniment
upon the flute and triangle." It wasn't much, but it was respect-
able enough for a village that didn't even exist eighteen months
earlier.

Hoffman visited Chicago in 1834 at the very beginning of
the most astounding population surge ever experienced by a
major American city. Just four years later four thousand persons
(part arriving over the Chicago Road and part on the storm-
ruffled Great Lakes route) were furiously buying and selling
land in a dizzying speculation. But this was only the beginning.
Within seven years the population had doubled; and by 1848,
when one John Peyton left us the following exposé of Chicago
streets, more than twenty thousand rambunctious new citizens
were attempting to buy, bellow, or bamboozle their way to
wealth:

> There was no pavement, no macadamized streets, no drain-
> age. . . . To render the streets and side walks passable, they
> were covered with deal boards from house to house, the
> boards resting upon cross sills of heavy timber. This kind of
> track is called "the plank road." Under these planks the water
> was standing on the surface over three-fourths of the city,
> and as the sewers from the houses were emptied under them,
> a frightful odour was emitted in summer, causing fevers and
> other diseases. . . . It not unfrequently happened that from
> the settling or rolling of a sleeper, that a loose plank would
> give way under the weight of a passing cab, when the foul
> water would spurt into the air high as the windows.[83]

One of the main reasons for Chicago's wild growth was its situation at the head of a newly emerging road system that was fanning out into the black loam prairies just beyond. Due south ran Hubbard's Trace, following a route now taken by Illinois 1, through Danville from whence it bent westward to meet the National Road at Effingham. Soon a wagon line began operating on Hubbard's Trace between Chicago and the Kankakee River, at which point flatboats drifted along a current once taken by La Salle until they made connection with steamboats around Peoria on the Illinois River.

A second road accommodated coaches (including that of our friend Charles Hoffman) as well as mail wagons down the Illinois River, past Starved Rock (then, as now, a major tourist attraction) to St. Louis. And a third road ran northward from Chicago along what would soon be called Milwaukee Avenue until it reached the upper prairies and Wisconsin.

But the most important route, called the State Road, unraveled due west through Rockford (originally called Midway) to Galena near the Mississippi. Galena had been the center of considerable lead mining activity ever since the days when Father Hennepin had drawn the Indian diggings on his map of 1687. The rollicking town of fifteen thousand had been, until this time, connected to the rest of the nation solely by the Mississippi.

As settlers streamed off the bevy of boats which made berth in the Chicago harbor (there were more than four hundred and fifty docking there in 1836) as well as from the wagons, coaches, and horses which had transported them over the Chicago Road, they set their sights mainly to the prairies due west on the State Road.

Up to this time pioneers had avoided the prairies, where the grass grew taller than a man's head in late summer. For this was a land completely alien to the American experience. Whether on the Old Connecticut Path, the Wilderness Trail, the National Road, or the Ohio River, the pioneers' tradition concerned the forest. Here they found wood for their log cabins, for cooking fires and winter warmth, for split-rail fences to keep their animals from wandering off. The forest sheltered them from January blasts, cooled and shaded them in August, provided home for game animals and song birds.

But it was different with the awesome Illinois grasslands. There was a desolation here that gnawed at one's soul. Charles Dickens, viewing the prairie in 1842, called it lovely and wild, and oppressive at the same time—"not a scene to be forgotten." And even such an uncomplaining traveler as Hoffman, who found himself crossing Illinois during the winter, described it in nervous tones:

> The . . . prairie, for the first six miles, was high and level, with not a stick of timber—one broad snowcovered plain, where you could see the dark figure of a wolf for miles off as it stood in relief against the white unbroken surface. A prospect more bleak and lonely, when night is closing in and you press towards some distant grove whose tree-tops cannot yet be discovered above the monotonous plains, is inconceivable.[84]

But pioneers did brave the bleak and lonely prairie. Between 1835 and 1837 an estimated five hundred new farm towns were laid out amid the stupendous grasslands. This bespoke of actual farms in the tens of thousands—a quite considerable feat when it is realized it took four to six straining oxen to drag a massive, hundred-pound plow through sod that had clutched the land since the Glacial Age. Then three more years were required for the rotting roots to release the rich loam. Usually it cost more to break the land than it did to purchase it from the crowded Chicago Land Office. The farmer, his wife, and bewildered children often had to live in a miserable clay shanty while planks for their home were being freighted down the State Road via Chicago or Galena from the just-opening timberlands of upper Wisconsin.

Nonetheless the land was tamed and the wolves killed. By the 1840's the State Road no longer edged between threatening waves of coarse-leaved prairie grass; but, instead, sauntered along neat fields of corn and golden-topped wheat. Inns ap-

peared at frequent intervals, such as the Tisdell Inn five miles
west of Freeport and the Buckhorn Inn at Lena just beyond—
both of which still stand. Frink and Walker stagecoaches made
the regular two-day run from Chicago to Galena, where visitors,
then as now, luxuriated in the DeSoto Hotel favored by Abraham Lincoln and Ulysses Grant. Soon the State Road was filled
with other travelers: peddlers, merchants, freighters, politicians,
ministers, and con artists, who roamed through the smiling countryside carrying the necessities, luxuries, and perils of civilization
to the trusting, Gothic-faced pioneer families. And at harvest
time great caravans of farm wagons, each heaped with the
largesse of the season, creaked through Freeport, Rockford, and
Elgin (on what is now U.S. 20) bound for Chicago and the
steamer connection with the Eastern market. Two hundred wagons a day, sometimes more, made the State Road one of the
most-traveled highways in the West.

But by mid-century the heyday of the old highways was
over. The trumpeted word was railroads. At first it was no more
than an incredible tale, as in 1828 work was started on the
Baltimore and Ohio—a supposedly fantastic scheme to connect
the Chesapeake with the Midwest. Soon, however, rail lines were
uncoiling throughout the East: in 1831 the Albany to Schenectady wagon road was made obsolete by rails; two years later
traffic on the King's Highway was lessened as portions of a line
running through New Jersey were completed. At the same time
construction was begun on a railroad between Philadelphia,
Wilmington, and Baltimore. By 1840 even the venerable Boston
Post Road was on the decline as New York and New Haven
locomotives puffed into the Bay City.

During the 1850's railroads were on everyone's lips. The
Baltimore and Ohio finally clasped Cincinnati, thereby offering
settlers and merchants far better communication with the interior than the pothole-decorated National Road. Even more important was the line which ran from the coast through Pittsburgh
and Fort Wayne to Chicago.

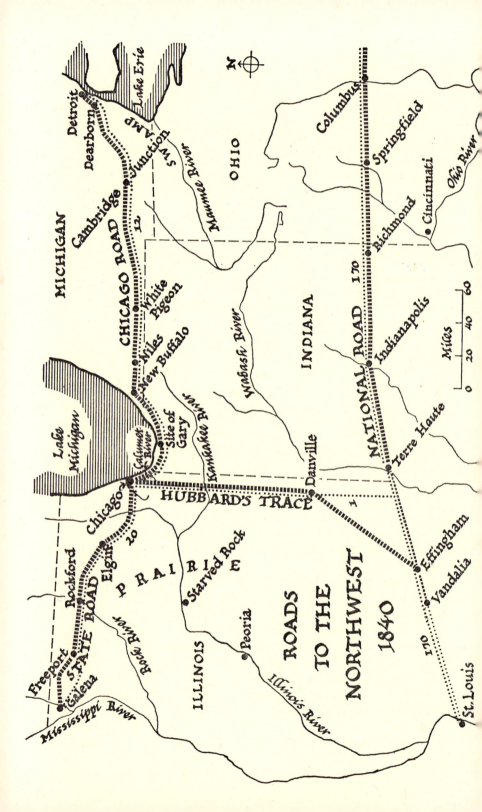

Chicago's strategic position (at the near-southernmost end of the long jab of Lake Michigan which cut off the exploding farmlands of northern Illinois and most of Iowa as well as all of Wisconsin and Minnesota) made it the natural hub at which the rail lines leaping outward from the East should meet those already serving the West.

For the West was not far behind the East in railroading. As early as 1848 the first westward-moving locomotive, resplendent in new plaint, chugged out of Chicago on gleaming rails which would eventually reach Galena and thereby end the glorious wagoning days on the State Road. Soon Illinois Central trains sped southward on lakeside pilings covering the sands over which Charles Hoffman and so many others on the Chicago Road had spurred their steeds. By 1856 the line, with over seven hundred miles of tracks, was considered the railroad titan of the world.

Yes, the steam trains were putting an end to a transportation era. In a single hour an engine could flash over the distance it took a wagon or stagecoach an entire day of the most bone-bruising effort. And one could ride at night on the trains—no longer must he endure the roadside inns with their cramped rooms, sweat-fumed air, hurry-hurry meals, and bug-hosted beds.

Quickly the roads began sporting weeds except where they served as brief connecting links between the omnipotent rail lines. Taverns closed down or became private homes. Milestones were wrenched from their lodgings to be utilized in the masonry of buildings. Eventually only oldsters remembered the bellowing of a coach driver's horn, the bliss of a warm hearth after the climb over Allegheny Mountain or the Cumberland Gap, the good fellowship of strangers-become-friends at a cookout in the Connecticut Valley or beside a tricky ford on the way to Williamsburg. Gone, too, were the swarthy ferrymen whose scows took many a bedraggled pioneer family over the New River or the Susquehanna or the St. Joseph on their way to the precious lands their progeny plow to this very day.

But the roads had accomplished their missions. The King's Highway had helped unite the colonies, thereby giving birth to an American personality as separate from a British colonial. And when the Revolution came, it was this road which enabled Washington to move his armies and supplies to meet and defeat the British sea-based forces. During the Revolution and the harsh years to follow, the Wilderness Road, with its unquenchable stream of men and materiel, was nearly the sole means whereby the beleaguered Kentucky beachhead held out to bring the trans-Appalachian empire into the American fold.

Other roads, too, had played their vital parts. The 1840's were similar to the 1740's in that the future of the continent depended directly on roads. During the 1740's it was the British with the King's Highway and Braddock's and Forbes's roads pitted against the French with their vast network of river highways. During the 1840's it was the North with the National Road and Erie Canal-Great Lakes routes competing for population against the South with the Federal Road and the Atlantic-Gulf shipping routes. Just as the British could never have conquered the French without roads to move troops over the mountains, so without roads it would not have been possible for the North to have gained such a huge population advantage over the South during the crucial decades prior to the Civil War. For had the North been deprived of the National Road and the Erie Canal, Eastern farmers not only would have been forced to remain at home but, ground down by poverty, they would probably have limited their families—whether by abstinence, neglect of the infants, or outright starvation—as was the case in Ireland under similar circumstances. In addition, there never would have been the influx of the three million European immigrants who flocked mainly to the Midwest during the 1850's.

Thus by the time of the Civil War the number of inhabitants of four Midwestern states (Ohio, Indiana, Illinois, and Michigan) was 6,100,000, while that of four New South states settled at the same time (Alabama, Mississippi, Louisiana, and Arkansas) was only 2,900,000—and 1,300,000 of these were Negro slaves. These figures are vital in accounting for the Northern victory in the Civil War, which began in 1861 with the accession to power of Illinoisan Abraham Lincoln.

Although history is a murky colloid in which many diverse elements are inseparably dissolved, one of the more important forces in molding the future are the lines of transportation. For that reason the ancient paths, trails, and highways by which our ancestors won and, later, populated our nation deserve the recognition that has for so long been obscured. Let us remember these old roads. They live yet today in the configuration of our country; and, as the United States has affected international politics, in the configuration of the world.

Truly, they were highways of destiny.

References in Text

1. Cartier, Jacques, *Navigations to Newe Fraunce*, Translated by John Florio, 1580, Ann Arbor: University Microfilms, Inc., 1966, p. 38.

2. Champlain, Samuel de, *Voyages and Explorations, 1604–1616*, Translated by Annie Nettleton Bourne, Ann Arbor: University Microfilms, Inc., 1966, p. 195.

3. *Ibid.*, p. 200.

4. *Ibid.*, p. 212.

5. Kellogg, Louise Phelps, ed., *Early Narratives of the Northwest, 1634–99*, New York: Charles Scribner's Sons, 1917, p. 118.

6. *Ibid.*, p. 220.

7. *Ibid.*, p. 220.

8. *Ibid.*, p. 234.

9. *Ibid.*, p. 236.

10. *Ibid.*, p. 249.

11. Hennepin, Louis, *A Description of Louisiana*, Translated by John Gilmary Shea, Ann Arbor: University Microfilms, Inc., 1966, p. 381.

12. La Salle, Robert, *The Journeys of Rene Robert Cavelier, Sieur de la Salle*, Edited by Isaac Joslin Cox, New York: Barnes, 1905, p. 118.

13. Parkman, Francis, *Discovery of the Great West: La Salle*, Edited by William R. Taylor, Reprint Series, New York: Rinehart & Co., 1956, p. 286.

14. Charlevois, P. F. X. de, *Journal*, Translated by John Gilmary Shea, Ann Arbor: University Microfilms, Inc., 1966, p. 221.

15. Parkman, Francis, *Parkman Reader*, Edited by Samuel Eliot Morison, Boston: Little, Brown & Co., 1955, p. 258.

16. Kellogg, *op. cit.*, p. 75.

17. Hennepin, *op. cit.*, p. 229.

18. *Ibid.*, p. 109.

19. Clark, James I., "Wisconsin: Land of Frenchman, Indians, and the Beaver," Madison, Wisconsin State Historical Society, 1955, p. 10.

20. *Ibid.*, p. 11.

21. Charlevoix, *op. cit.*, p. 304.

22. *Ibid.*, p. 37.

23. Schlarman, J. H., *From Quebec to New Orleans*, Belleville, Ill.: Buechler, 1929, p. 242.

24. Charlevoix, *op. cit.*, p. 247.

25. Hawthorne, Nathaniel, *The Scarlet Letter*, New York: Pocket Books, 1955, p. 194.

26. Hart, Albert Bushnell, ed., *American History Told by Contemporaries*, 5 vols., New York: Macmillan Co., 1929, II, p. 225.

27. Handlin, Oscar, ed., *This Was America: as Recorded by European Travelers*, New York: Harper & Brothers, 1948, p. 123.

28. Adams, John, *Diary and Autobiography. The Adams Papers*, vols. 1–4, Edited by Lyman H. Butterfield and others, New York: Atheneum Publishers, 1964, II, p. 29.

29. Handlin, *op. cit.*, p. 81.

30. *Ibid.*, p. 82.

31. Adams, *op. cit.*, II, p. 103.

32. Franklin, Benjamin, *Autobiography*, New York: P. F. Collier & Son, 1962, p. 27.

33. *Ibid.*, p. 29.

34. Kalm, Peter, *America of 1750: Peter Kalm's Travels in North America*, New York: Dover Publications, 1966, p. 117.

35. Handlin, *op. cit.*, p. 60.

36. *Ibid.*, p. 82.

37. Dickens, Charles, *American Notes*, Greenwich, Conn.: Fawcett Publications, 1961, p. 136.

38. *Ibid.*, p. 156.

39. Mayo, Bernard, ed., *Jefferson Himself*, Boston: Houghton Mifflin Co., 1942, p. 15.

40. Handlin, *op. cit.*, p. 88.

41. Lawson, John, *A New Voyage to Carolina, 1709*, Ann Arbor: University Microfilms, Inc., 1966, p. 131.

42. Schaw, Janet, *Journal of a Lady of Quality, 1774–76*, New Haven: Yale University Press, 1921, p. 284.

43. *Ibid.*, pp. 150–151.
44. Bartram, William, *Travels*, New York: Dover Publications, 1928, p. 373.
45. Marshall, John, *Life of George Washington*, New York: Walton Publishing Co., 1930, I, appendix, p. 9.
46. Angle, Paul M., ed., *A New Continent and a New Nation: Eyewitness Reports of America in the Making*, American Reader, Greenwich, Conn.: Fawcett Publications, 1960, I, p. 116.
47. Craig, Neville B., *History of Pittsburgh*, Pittsburgh: J. H. Mellor, 1851, p. 68.
48. Hulbert, Archer Butler, *The Old Glade Road*, Columbus: F. J. Heer, 1903, p. 97.
49. Parkman, Francis, *Montcalm and Wolfe*, New York: Collier Books, 1966, p. 363.
50. Johnson, William, *The Papers of Sir William Johnson*, Edited by A. P. James, Albany: New York State Press, 1921–51, p. 27.
51. Adams, *op. cit.*, II, p. 150.
52. *Ibid.*, II, p. 150.
53. Burnett, Edmund C., *Letters of Members of the Continental Congress, 1774–1789*, 8 vols., Washington, D.C.: Carnegie Institution of Washington, 1921–36, p. 55.
54. Rankin, Hugh F., ed., *The American Revolution*, New York: G. P. Putnam's Sons, 1965, p. 22.
55. Braeman, John, ed., *The Road to Independence: A Documentary History of the American Revolution*, New York: G. P. Putnam's Sons, 1963, p. 267.
56. Rankin, *op. cit.*, p. 28.
57. *Ibid.*, p. 29.
58. Baker, William S., *Itinerary of General Washington*, Philadelphia: J. B. Lippincott Co., 1892, p. 7.
59. Washington, George, *Washington's Journal of 1754*, Ann Arbor: University Microfilms, Inc., 1966, III, p. 115.
60. *Ibid.*, IV, p. 300.
61. Adams, *op. cit.*, III, p. 417.
62. Scheer, George F. and Rankin, Hugh F., *Rebels and Redcoats*, New York: New American Library, 1959, p. 204.
63. *Ibid.*, p. 241.
64. Scheer, *op. cit.*, p. 241.
65. Anburey, Thomas, *With Burgoyne from Quebec*, Toronto: Macmillan of Canada, 1963, p. 131.

66. Washington, *op. cit.*, p. 36.

67. Angle, *op. cit.*, p. 176.

68. Scheer, *op. cit.*, p. 332.

69. *Ibid.*, p. 474.

70. Washington, *op. cit.*, p. 358.

71. Hatch, Charles E., Jr., "Yorktown and the Siege of 1781," Washington, D.C.: Government Printing Office, 1954, p. 24.

72. Scheer, *op. cit.*, p. 245.

73. Filson, John, *The Discovery, Settlement and Present State of Kentucky: Including Daniel Boone's Own Memoir*, New York: Corinth Books, 1962, p. 51.

74. May, John, *Journal and Letters*, Cincinnati: R. Clarke, 1873, p. 27.

75. *Ibid.*, p. 37.

76. *Ibid.*, p. 56.

77. Spencer, Oliver M., *Indian Captivity*, Ann Arbor: University Microfilms, Inc., 1966, p. 7.

78. *Ibid.*, p. 9.

79. Angle, *op. cit.*, p. 124.

80. Oliver, William, *Eight Months in Illinois*, Ann Arbor: University Microfilms, 1966, p. 111.

81. *Ibid.*, p. 107.

82. Nowlin, William, *The Bark Covered House*, Ann Arbor: University Microfilms, Inc., 1966, p. 18.

83. Smith, Wilson, ed., *Cities of Our Past and Present: A Descriptive Reader*, New York: John Wiley & Sons, 1964, p. 53.

84. Hoffman, Charles Feno, *A Winter in the West*, 2 vols., Ann Arbor: University Microfilms, Inc., 1966, I, p. 290.

In addition to the references cited above and to hundreds of mimeographs, pamphlets, and leaflets from municipal, state, and national historical organizations, the following publications have been used:

Adams, Samuel. *Writings*. Edited by Henry A. Cushing. New York and London: G. P. Putnam's Sons, 1904–08.

Alsberg, Henry, ed. *The American Guide*. New York: Hastings House Publishers, 1949.

Andrews, Charles M. *Colonial Folkways*. New Haven: Yale University Press, 1919.

Bangs, Isaac. *Journal of Lieutenant Isaac Bangs*. New York: Arno Press, 1968.

Banta, R. E. *The Ohio*. New York: Rinehart & Co., 1949.

Billington, Ray A. *Westward Expansion: History of the American Frontier*. New York: Macmillan Co., 1949.

Birkbeck, Morris. *Notes on a Journey to Illinois*. Ann Arbor: University Microfilms, Inc., 1966.

Bolton, Charles K. *The Private Soldier under Washington*. London: G. Newnes, 1902.

Bowen, Catherine Drinker. *John Adams and the American Revolution*. Boston: Little, Brown & Co., 1950.

Brebner, John B. *The Explorers of North America, 1492–1806*. Cleveland: World Publishing Co., 1964.

Bridenbaugh, Carl. *Seat of Empire: The Political Role of Eighteenth-century Williamsburg*. Williamsburg, Va.: Colonial Williamsburg, Inc., 1950.

Bruce, H. Addington. *Daniel Boone and the Wilderness Road*. New York: Macmillan Co., 1910.

Burnaby, Andrew. *Travels through the Middle Settlements in North America in the Years 1759 and 1760*. Ithaca, N.Y.: Cornell University Press, 1960.

Butler, Ruth Lapham. *Doctor Franklin, Postmaster General*. Garden City, N.Y.: Doubleday, Doran & Co., 1928.

Cawley, James and Margaret. *Along the Old York Road*. New Brunswick, N.J.: Rutgers University Press, 1965.

Charlevois, P. F. X. de. *History and General Description of New France*. Translated by John Gilmary Shea. Chicago: Loyola University Press, 1962.

Chitwood, Oliver P. *A History of Colonial America*, 3rd ed. Evanston, Ill.: Harper & Row Publishers, 1960.

Coleman, R. V. *The First Frontier*. New York: Charles Scribner's Sons, 1948.

Cooper, James Fenimore. *The Leatherstocking Saga*. Edited by Allan Nevins. New York: Pantheon Books, 1954.

Cramer, Zadok. *The Navigator*. Ann Arbor: University Microfilms, Inc. 1966.

Crane, Verner W. *The Southern Frontier, 1670–1732*. Ann Arbor: University of Michigan Press, 1929.

Croghan, George. *Journals. Early Western Travels*. Edited by Reuben Gold Thwaites. vol. 1. Cleveland: A. H. Clark, 1904–07.

Cuneo, John R. *Robert Rogers of the Rangers*. New York: Oxford University Press, 1959.

Cunliffe, Marcus. *George Washington*. New York: New American Library, 1960.

Daniels, Jonathan. *The Devil's Backbone: The Story of the Natchez Trace*. New York: McGraw-Hill Book Co., 1962.

DeVoto, Bernard. *The Course of Empire*. Boston: Houghton Mifflin Co., 1952.

Dunbar, Seymour. *A History of Travel in America*. Indianapolis: Bobbs-Merrill Co., 1915.

Earle, Alice Moore. *Stage Coach and Tavern Days*. New York: Macmillan Co., 1900.

Facts and Statistics. Stamford, Conn.: Fairfield Publishers, 1965.

Fleming, Thomas J. *The Story of Bunker Hill*. New York: P. F. Collier & Son, 1960.

Flexner, James Thomas. *Mohawk Baronet: Sir William Johnson of New York*. New York: Harper & Brothers, 1959.

Forbes, John. *Writings*. Edited by A. P. James. Menasha, Wis.: Banta Publishing Co., 1938.

Ford, Worthington Chauncey. *The Writings of George Washington*. New York and London: G. P. Putnam's Sons, 1889–93.

Freeman, Douglas Southall. *George Washington*. 7 vols. New York: Charles Scribner's Sons, 1948–56.

Great Historic Places. New York: American Heritage Publishing Co., 1957.

Halsey, Francis Whiting. *The Old New York Frontier*. New York: Charles Scribner's Sons, 1902.

Hatch, Louis Clinton. *The Administration of the American Revolutionary Army*. New York: Longmans, Green, 1904.

Havinghurst, Walter. *Wilderness for Sale*. New York: Hastings House Publishers, 1956.

Herndon, William H. *Herndon's Life of Lincoln*. rev. ed. Edited by Paul M. Angle. Greenwich, Conn.: Fawcett Publications, 1961.

Hicks, John D. *The Federal Union: A History of the United States to 1865*. 4th ed. Boston: Houghton Mifflin Co., 1964.

Holbrook, Steward H. *The Old Post Road*. New York: McGraw-Hill Book Co., 1962.

Hosmer, James K. *Samuel Adams*. Boston: Houghton Mifflin Co., 1896.

Hulbert, Archer Butler. *The Old National Road.* Columbus: F. J. Heer, 1901.

Hull, William I. *William Penn: A Topical Biography.* London and New York: Oxford University Press, 1937.

Irving, Washington. *The Life and Times of Washington.* New York: G. P. Putnam's Sons, 1876.

James, Alfred P. and Stoltz, Charles M. *Drums in the Forest.* Pittsburgh: Historical Society of Western Pennsylvania, 1958.

————. *Defense in the Wilderness.* Pittsburgh: Historical Society of Western Pennsylvania, 1958.

Kane, Harnett T. *Queen of New Orleans.* New York: William Morrow & Co., 1949.

Keyes, Nelson Beecher. *Ben Franklin: An Affectionate Portrait.* Surrey, Great Britain: The World's Work, 1956.

Kincaid, Robert L. *The Wilderness Road.* Indianapolis: Bobbs-Merrill Co., 1947.

Kogan, Herman and Wendt, Lloyd. Chicago: *A Pictorial History.* New York: E. P. Dutton & Co., 1958.

Langer, William L. *Encyclopedia of World History.* rev. ed. Boston: Houghton Mifflin Co., 1952.

Lathrop, Elise. *Early American Inns and Taverns.* Garden City, N.Y.: Doubleday, Page & Co., 1926.

Mackenzie, John and Marjorie. *Quebec in Your Car.* New York: Rinehart & Co., 1952.

Miller, John C. *Origins of the American Revolution.* Stanford, Calif.: Stanford University Press, 1959.

Montross, Lynn. *The Reluctant Rebels: The Story of the Continental Congress, 1774–1789.* New York: Harper & Brothers, 1950.

Moore, Frank. *Diary of the American Revolution.* New York: Charles T. Evans, 1863.

Morgan, L. H. *Ancient Society.* New York: Henry Holt & Co., 1877.

Munro, William B. *Crusaders of New France.* New Haven: Yale University Press, 1918.

Padover, Saul K. *Jefferson.* New York: New American Library, 1952.

Parrington, Vernon L. *The Colonial Mind, 1620–1800. Main Currents in American Thought,* vol. 1. New York: Harcourt, Brace & World, 1954.

Pease, Theodore C. *The Story of Illinois.* Chicago: University of Chicago Press, 1965.

Peckham, Howard H. *The Colonial Wars, 1689–1762.* Chicago, University of Chicago Press, 1963.

Poole, Ernest. *Giants Gone: The Men Who Made Chicago.* New York: McGraw-Hill Book Co., 1943.

Pooley, William V. *The Settlement of Illinois from 1830 to 1850.* Ann Arbor: University Microfilms, Inc., 1968.

Pound, Arthur. *Johnson of the Mohawks.* New York: Macmillan Co., 1930.

Preston, John Hyde. *Revolution 1776.* New York: Washington Square, 1962.

Quaife, Milo M. *Lake Michigan.* Indianapolis: Bobbs-Merrill Co., 1944.

Radin, Paul. *The Story of the American Indian.* rev. ed. New York: Liveright Publishing Corp., 1944.

Riegel, Robert E., and Athearn, R. G. *America Moves West.* 4th ed. New York: Holt, Rinehart and Winston, 1964.

Rogers, Robert. *Journals of Major Robert Rogers.* New York: Corinth Books, 1961.

Roosevelt, Theodore. *The Winning of the West.* 2 vols. New York and London: G. P. Putnam's Sons, 1920.

Rourke, Constance. *American Humor: A Study of the National Character.* New York: Doubleday & Co., 1953.

Rutledge, Joseph Lister. *Century of Conflict.* New York: Doubleday & Co., 1956.

Saxon, Lyle. *Fabulous New Orleans.* New Orleans: Robert L. Crager & Co., 1950.

Smith, Wilson, ed. *Cities of Our Past and Present: A Descriptive Reader.* New York: John Wiley & Sons, 1964.

Starkey, Marion L. *The Cherokee Nation.* New York: Alfred A. Knopf, 1946.

Stern, Philip Van Doren. *Prologue to Sumter.* Greenwich, Conn.: Fawcett Publications, 1961.

Stewart, Catherine. *New Homes in the West.* Ann Arbor: University Microfilms, Inc., 1966.

Tebbel, John W. *George Washington's America.* New York: E. P. Dutton & Co., 1954.

Thwaites, Reuben Gold, ed. *Early Western Travels, 1748–1846.* 32 vols. Cleveland: A. H. Clark, 1904–07.

Tunis, Edwin. *Colonial Living.* Cleveland: World Publishing Co., 1957.

Vanderbilt, Cornelius, Jr. *The Living Past of America: A Pictorial Treasury of Our Historic Houses.* New York: Crown Publishers, 1955.

Van Doren, Carl. *Benjamin Franklin: A Biography.* New York: Viking Press, 1956.

Van Every, Dale. *Ark of Empire.* New York: New American Library, 1964.

——— *A Company of Heroes.* New York: New American Library, 1963.

——— *The Final Challenge.* New York: New American Library, 1965.

——— *Forth to the Wilderness.* New York: New American Library, 1962.

Volwiler, Albert T. *George Croghan and the Westward Movement, 1741–82.* Cleveland: A. H. Clark, 1926.

Waitley, Douglas. *Portrait of the Midwest.* New York: Abelard-Schuman, 1963.

Weston, George F., Jr. *Boston Ways.* Boston: Beacon Press, 1957.

Wissler, Clark. *Indians of the United States: Four Centuries of Their History and Culture.* Edited by Lucy W. Kluckhohn. New York: Doubleday & Co., 1966.

Wright, Esmond. *Washington and the American Revolution.* New York: P. F. Collier & Son, 1962.

Wrong, George M. *The Rise and Fall of New France.* New York: Macmillan Co., 1928.